A COMMENTARY

ON THE

Book of Revelation

BY

JOHN T. HINDS

GOSPEL ADVOCATE COMPANY
NASHVILLE, TENN.

Complete Set ISBN 0-89225-000-3
This Volume ISBN 0-89225-014-3

PREFACE

Since so many brilliant scholars have written on Revelation, it may seem highly presumptuous to add another commentary to the list. In undertaking the preparation of this book the author was not deluded by the thought that his efforts would prove entirely satisfactory to all his readers. When so many contradictory theories and conflicting views have been presented, one may well approach the task with misgiving.

As Revelation is a part of the divine record, it must have been designed to be of benefit to men, but this can be only in proportion to a knowledge of its contents. Paul's command to study, "handling aright the word of truth," will apply to it just as to other New Testament books. Mistakes, of course, can be made easily in applying prophetic symbols; the same may occur in the study of the plain historical books of the Bible. The possibility of misunderstanding a text is no justification for refusing to study it. If it were, Bible investigation would be at an end.

The author gratefully acknowledges indebtedness to many scholars whose commentaries have been consulted. These, with the numerous quotations from others by them, have furnished a broad field from which to gather suggestive thoughts. Different views about the book as a whole, and conflicting expositions of various texts, have been candidly considered; and any explanation believed correct has been accepted, regardless of its source. Consulting other writers has a twofold value: It opens fields of thought which otherwise might not be seen; and it often prevents radical or dogmatic assertions. Both are highly beneficial in striving to teach the exact truth.

The introduction contains a brief general view of Revelation with the plan of study and rules of interpretation. As preliminary instruction, it should be read first.

With the sincere desire that this volume may prove helpful to its readers, it is prayerfully submitted to those interested in the study of this marvelous piece of divine revelation.

JOHN T. HINDS.

Nashville, Tennessee, January 1, 1937.

CONTENTS

PART THIRD: OPENING OF THE SEALED BOOK
6: 1 to 11: 18

Section One

Section Two

Section Three

Section Four

Section Five

Section Six

Page

Section Seven

PART FOURTH: VISIONS OF THE WOMAN AND HER ENEMIES

11: 19 to 20: 15

Section One

Section Two

Section Three

Section Four — Page

Section Five

PART FIFTH: THE FINAL ABODE OF THE REDEEMED

21: 1 to 22: 21

Section One

PART SIXTH: PRACTICAL WARNINGS, COMMANDS, AND PROMISES

22: 6-21

INTRODUCTION

It is not the purpose to discuss here in detail all matters involved in a relevant introduction, but only enough to enable the reader to understand clearly the nature and design of Revelation and the methods of interpretation used in this commentary.

I. THE AUTHOR, TIME, AND PLACE

The book itself declares that Jesus made known this revelation to "his servant John." (1: 1.) The preponderance of evidence points to the apostle John as the author. He was in the right situation, both as to time and place, to have been the writer. But, supposing some other John wrote the book, it would not change God's purpose in making the revelation.

The time written is affected somewhat by the plan of interpretation adopted. Those who think that most of its symbols were fulfilled by the time Jerusalem was destroyed (A.D. 70) place the time of writing previous to that date. Those who consider the symbols as prophetic pictures of the struggles of the church over a long period accept the year A.D. 95 or 96, in the reign of Domitian, as the most probable time. The most commonly quoted testimony, as well as apparently most decisive, is the statement of Irenaeus that "the Revelation was seen no long time since, but almost in our own generation toward the end of the reign of Domitian." This reign was from A.D. 81-96. Irenaeus was an intimate associate of Polycarp, who died in A.D. 155. He was contemporary with the apostle John for more than fifty years. There is little chance for Polycarp not to have known the true date, or for Irenaeus to have misrepresented his information. The testimony of Irenaeus is of the highest class.

We have direct proof in the book that John received the visions while in exile on the island of Patmos. (1: 9.) The fact that seven churches of Asia were addressed is strong presumptive evidence that John was personally acquainted with the conditions that existed among them. Their nearness to Patmos is also evidence that John was sent into exile from that section. That fact, if true, would be sufficient justification for the tradition that Ephesus had been John's home most of the time since the destruction of Jerusalem. It is not known whether John wrote the book on the island where the visions were received or later.

Those desiring a full discussion on the foregoing questions may consult the Bible (Speaker's) Commentary, Vol. IV, of the New Testament, pp. 405 to 492.

II. NATURE AND DESIGN

The contents of the book and the conditions confronting the churches furnish the information on the nature and design of Revelation. The church was comparatively weak, subject to terrible persecutions from the Roman Empire, and in great danger of heavy apostasies. Warnings against evil and many promises to the faithful definitely indicate that the main purpose of the book is to encourage saints to steadfastness in their struggles against enemies of the truth. Paul had predicted a complete apostasy. (Acts 20: 29, 30; 2 Thess. 2: 3-12.) That another book should be written to describe the rise and fall of such an evil power is really what should be expected. Revelation meets that expectation. The Old Testament has its prophetic books; why should not the New Testament have one?

Revelation contains the same great teaching in a large measure that is found in other New Testament books, but differs from them in two particulars: (1) It points out great epochal changes that would affect the church in the future. (2) It describes these changes in dramatic scenes and highly symbolic language. The latter feature furnishes the chief difficulty in its interpretation, but evidently has some merit, else it would not have been chosen for the purpose. The most plausible explanation seems to lie in the nature of the church's enemies. Under the Jewish system the prophets named Israel's enemies in plain terms, but the Israelites were a temporal kingdom with material means of defense, and had to understand plainly who were their foes. The church being a spiritual kingdom, not to be defended by a carnal sword (John 18: 36), would stand no chance in meeting earthly powers with physical force. If the book had condemned their persecutors by name, it might have created more desperate opposition. Expressed in symbols, wise Christians would be able to know whom to watch, while their enemies, being ignorant of the true facts, would be less exasperated. It may be somewhat like Christ's reasons for speaking in parables during his personal ministry. (Matt. 13: 10-12.)

Symbolism, however, is nothing new in the Scriptures. The Old Testament prophets were much given to the use of such language, as the following passages will show: Isa. 4: 1-13; 11: 6-9; 28: 20; 65: 17-19; Ezek. 37: 1-23. An argument against the use of symbols in Revelation would be an argument against it in the prophetic Jewish Scriptures. Many Old Testament predictions are definitely mentioned by the apostles and about these there can be no room for doubt. Many of the symbols in Revelation have already been fulfilled, but this can only be determined by a careful comparison of the emblems with events that are plain historical facts. That this task is difficult, and there is danger of mistakes, must be conceded; that any understanding of them is impossible does not accord with facts. If that were true, then the writing of the book must be put down as a blunder; for, if none of it can be understood till the final state comes, then it will be too late to do anyone any good. The things to be revealed were to be shown to Christ's servants. This implies ability to understand at least some, or the *showing* was a failure. The book begins and ends with a blessing pronounced upon those who *hear* and *keep* the "things that are written therein." (1: 3, 22: 7.) A thing quite impossible, unless there is some measure of understanding.

III. PLANS OF INTERPRETATION

There are some fairly well-defined plans of interpretation, and a great variety in the applications made in the details by different expositors. No one of them can be followed slavishly as an infallible guide in all views held, however much his suggestions may be worth. The truth will probably be found, if found at all, by carefully testing each human comment by the language of the text and what are known facts of history. Such has been the rule followed in this book.

As given by various commentators, the three most distinct plans may be stated substantially as follows: (1) The *Preterist* system, which applies the visions mainly to the Jewish nation and pagan Rome, with most of them placed before the destruction of Jerusalem. (2) The *Futurist* system, which makes the main part of the symbols to be fulfilled yet. This includes the return of fleshly Israel to Palestine, the rebuilding of the material temple, and the personal reign of Christ upon David's throne here on earth for a thousand years. (3) The *Historical* system, which teaches that the different series of symbols show the future events of the church from soon after John wrote till the final states of men are reached.

Unquestionably some things John wrote have been fulfilled and are now passed, and some are necessarily future; for the Lord has not yet come and we are nearly eighteen hundred years toward the end of time. The author of this commentary has not allowed himself to be bound by any man's system, or to reject any true statement just because its author happened to have an erroneous plan of interpretation. The historical system is that advocated by Mr. Elliott in his four-volume commentary, adopted by Mr. Barnes and others, and is accepted as substantially correct, though there is room for many differences in details.

IV. REASONS FOR THE PLAN USED HERE

Since this commentary has been prepared on the supposition that Revelation was written mainly for the purpose of giving a pictorial history of the church till its ultimate victory, it is appropriate that some reasons shall be given for that view.

1. Regardless of the date when written, the book itself says (1:1) that its purpose is to show the things which "shortly come to pass." This must mean that the fulfillment of the symbols would *begin* soon, not that all would be finished soon. By no fair handling of the text can any other view be taken.

2. There are too many symbols and too much evidence of a succession of events not to require a long period for the fulfillment. This alone is decisive proof against the theory that the major part of the book was fulfilled in the days of the apostles.

3. The statement that the things must "shortly" come to pass is equally decisive against the teaching that practically all the book is yet to be fulfilled.

4. Various reasons sustain the idea that the book was designed to picture the church's struggles and triumphs from the apostolic period till its ultimate victory. The symbols depict the final war, the

judgment, and the eternal city of God as the home of the redeemed.

(1) That the churches in John's day needed the instruction and encouragement that the book contains is evident from the letters to the seven churches. These brief letters clearly imply long-drawn-out opposition both without and within.

(2) Other congregations under equal or more severe persecutions would need the same incentives to make them persevere to the end. Such encouragement is always needed.

(3) Paul foresaw and predicted a great apostasy which he called "the man of sin." That apostasy is now a well-known historical fact; denominationalism is an ever-present proof. That a revelation of things that "must" come to pass, including the coming of the Lord and his victory over that "man of sin" (2 Thess. 2: 8), should not include that archenemy of truth is wholly incredible. Whatever else may be said, the world's greatest religious apostasy would not be overlooked in a book foretelling the enemies of the church. Old Testament prophets made constant reference to the contemporary peoples with whom Israel had to do. In fact, no true history can be written of any people and not mention the nations involved in their existence. Why think that Revelation would give the church's future and say nothing about her apostasies or her chief enemies? The very suggestions kill the idea.

V. RULES OF STUDY ADOPTED

The following rules have been adopted as both fair and necessary in a proper study of Revelation:

1. In the first chapter we have what may be called John's own preface to the book. It is neither fair to the writer nor just to his book to interpret in conflict with his own prefatory explanation. John says he was told to write what he saw, things that are and those which must come to pass. (1: 19.) Any interpretation that ignores the distinctions here made cannot be reliable. In verse 6 he says that Jesus "made us" a kingdom and priests—that is, a kingdom whose subjects are priests. The words *to be* in this verse, in italic letters, have been supplied by the translators. The sense is clearer, if they are omitted. In verse 9 John declares that he was a partaker with them "in the kingdom." If words can be depended

upon to express ideas, the kingdom was in existence when John wrote. Any interpretation that conflicts with that statement rejects his words. Our rule then is this: All passages must be construed in harmony with the writer's own prefatory explanations, which must be final regarding his meaning.

2. The whole tenor of Bible teaching is that man has ability, is free to act, and is personally responsible for his conduct. Revelation's description of the final judgment holds rigidly to these facts. (20: 11-15.) Any theory of the millennium which does not leave man such a free moral agent is of necessity false. Personal responsibility implies ability to do wrong; hence, there can be no age this side of the final judgment when man will be absolutely free from temptation and sin. As the millennium precedes the judgment, it can be no exception to this rule.

3. Any theory in this book, or any other, that places a meaning on figurative language that is contrary to the plain, literal statements of Jesus and his apostles must be false. Figures may beautify the thought, but plain words state the facts. If there is any doubt about the symbol, plain words must rule our decisions.

Note: In reference to texts of Revelation in this commentary the abbreviation "Rev." is omitted. For example (10: 5) means the tenth chapter and fifth verse of Revelation.

A COMMENTARY ON THE BOOK OF REVELATION

PART FIRST

HISTORICAL DESCRIPTION OF THE CHURCH
1: 1 to 3: 22

SECTION ONE

GENERAL INTRODUCTION
1: 1-20

1. PURPOSE STATED AND BLESSING ANNOUNCED
1: 1-3

1 The Revelation of Jesus Christ, which God [1]gave him to show unto his

[1]Or, *gave unto him, to show unto his servants the things &c.*

---

1 **The Revelation of Jesus Christ,**—This expression evidently is a title for the entire book, being comprehensive enough to include all its contents. The Greek word *Apocalypse*—here rendered "Revelation"—properly means the uncovering of anything; an unveiling, so that what is hid may be known. Spiritually it denotes the making known of divine truth that had not before been understood, as the following passages indicate: Rom. 16: 25; Gal. 1: 12; Eph. 3: 3. If it had not been intended that the contents of this book should in some measure be understood, it would not have been called a Revelation. It does not mean a revealing of things concerning Christ, but a revelation which Christ himself made of things involving his church. The book is often referred to by its Greek name—Apocalypse. As its contents clearly show, the revealing is done through words, signs, and symbols, and includes things both present and future at the time John wrote.

which God gave him to show unto his servants,—These words clearly indicate that God is the original source or fountain of truth. Notwithstanding the unexplained unity between God

[2]servants, *even* the things which must shortly come to pass: and he sent and

[2]Gr. *bondservants.*

and Christ (John 17: 20, 21), as mediator between God and man, Jesus recognizes his dependence upon the Father. He said: "My teaching is not mine, but his that sent me." (John 7: 16.) Again he said: "For I spake not from myself; but the Father that sent me, he hath given me a commandment, what I should say, and what I should speak." (John 12: 49.) In John 5: 20 he said the Father "showeth" all things to the Son. Paul shows that a dependence upon the Father still exists by saying that when all things were put under Christ it is evident that God was expected. (1 Cor. 15: 27.) Hence, though at God's right hand, he is represented as receiving from the Father the revelation he was to communicate to man. All Christians are "servants" of God in some sense (1 Pet. 2: 16), and the revealing here promised was intended, doubtless, for all God's children. All would need the encouragement which such a disclosing of events would produce. It would also serve as a protection against being overcome by the disasters that were certain to come upon the church.

even the things which must shortly come to pass:—The words "must shortly come to pass" indicate that the things to be revealed to John in vision would most certainly take place. It does not mean that all the things would "shortly" come to pass, but that they would *begin* to transpire soon after the time John wrote. This must be the correct view since the seals, trumpets, and vials necessarily imply a series of events. To imagine all the things depicted as occurring at exactly the same time is out of the question. The thousand-year period (chapter 20) would prevent any such theory. Since there was to be a succession of events, they began to transpire when the first one commenced. The period covered by the word "shortly" varies according to the nature of the subject in question. A short time could be a few hours, a few days, a few years, or even many years if compared with several centuries.

and he sent and signified it by his angel unto his servant John;—He (Christ) signified the things shortly to come to pass,

signified [3]*it* by his angel unto his servant John; 2 who bare witness of the word of God, and of the testimony of Jesus Christ, *even* of all things that he saw. 3 Blessed is he that readeth, and they that hear the words of the proph-

[3]Or, *them*

sending them to John by his angel. The term "signify" comes from the word "sign" and indicates that the things to be revealed to John would be presented through signs and symbols. This word is used in the same sense by John in the following passages: John 12: 33; 21: 18, 19. It is an appropriate word to express a revelation which was to be made largely through symbols. The symbolic nature of much of the book is evident from even a casual reading of it. The word "angel" means messenger, and this shows that the visions were conveyed to John through the medium of some heavenly messenger. How this was done is a matter that must be left to the secret things known only to divine wisdom. (Deut. 29: 29.) It is a matter of first importance in the study of God's word to stop where Revelation ends. In no part of the sacred record is this more important than in the study of the Apocalypse.

2 **who bare witness of the word of God, and of the testimony of Jesus Christ, even of all things that he saw.**—This language shows that John regarded himself simply as a witness of God's revelation. In general God's word means any declaration or truth coming from him. But here he means that John was giving a true record of the things recorded in this book. This is evident from the explanatory clause "even of all things that he saw." Of course, John was a witness of the things he had seen in the personal ministry of Christ. (John 19: 35; 21: 24.) The "testimony of Jesus Christ," as indicated in verse 1, was the witness that he bore to the word of God; or, that this revelation came through Christ and was delivered by John.

3 **Blessed is he that readeth, and they that hear**—In that early time copies of the sacred writings were scarce and doubtless much truth was imparted through public readings. Many think the language here refers to that custom, because *he* that readeth and *they* that hear imply that one read while many listened. This did not exclude individual and private reading; but, since the other

ecy, and keep the things that are written therein: for the time is at hand.

was probably more common, the blessing was pronounced on both reader and hearers. No special blessing is mentioned, but there are always benefits to come to those who are obedient. Nothing is more conducive to hearty obedience than a faithful hearing of God's word.

the words of the prophecy,—The word "prophecy" here is synonymous with "Revelation" in verse 1 and the "things saw" in verse 2. It is used in its narrow sense of disclosing future events, for the main part of the book is devoted to such matters. John did not say that all who read the book would understand it, for that is not true of any part of the Bible written in literal language. But there would be no point in saying a blessing would come to those who heard it unless some degree of understanding were possible; at least enough to make the study profitable.

and keep the things that are written therein: for the time is at hand.—To keep things written meant that they should not forget what related to the future as a matter of encouragement and warning, and they should obey any duty that the book required. Present-day Christians should maintain the same attitude toward the teachings of this divine volume. It came from God through Christ and was delivered through an inspired apostle. No book of the Bible has stronger claims for its authority. Disobedience is inexcusable when God speaks.

Since the visions presented to John unquestionably cover a long period of time, the expression "at hand" cannot mean that the completion of all the events was near. The thought must be then that the things that were to come to pass would *begin* to transpire in a relatively short time. "At hand" should be understood in the same sense as "shortly," verse 1.

2. ADDRESS TO THE SEVEN CHURCHES
1: 4-8

4 John to the seven churches that are in Asia: Grace to you and peace, from him who is and who was and [4]who is to come; and from the seven

[4]Or, *who cometh*

4 **John to the seven churches that are in Asia**:—As the writer does not call himself an apostle, or use any other descriptive term, it is safe to presume that he was well known to the churches addressed. The fact that he was chosen as the one to write these letters is presumptive proof. To those churches the name John was sufficient identification. The territory here called "Asia" was the Roman province embracing the western part of Asia Minor, of which Ephesus was the capital city. The seven churches addressed were in this territory. There were other churches besides those mentioned, for Colossae and Troas are referred to (Col. 1: 2; Acts 20: 5-7), but there was evidently some divine reason why letters were sent to the seven named. As seven is supposed to be a sacred number indicating perfection, it has been suggested that seven were addressed to signify the perfection of the instruction given; or, that the seven would represent the whole church and the combined instruction be complete and applicable to all congregations for all time. It is unquestionably true that the instruction given the Asiatic churches was for any and all churches in like conditions.

Grace to you and peace, from him who is and who was and who is to come;—Asking for God's favor and peace to rest upon them is the same form of salutation used by Paul in all his epistles. God is here referred to as one who was, who is, and who is to come. That means an everlasting duration, including time past, present, and future. In speaking to Moses God called himself "I AM." (Ex. 3: 14.) The existence of God is, of course, incomprehensible by man, but these expressions include not only his existence, but his unchangeableness. We may therefore depend implicitly upon his power and promises.

and from the seven Spirits that are before his throne;—The most satisfactory explanation of the expression "seven Spirits" is

Spirits that are before his throne; 5 and from Jesus Christ, *who is* the faithful witness, the firstborn of the dead, and the ruler of the kings of the earth. Unto him that loveth us, and [5]loosed us from our sins [6]by his blood; 6 and

[5]Many authorities, some ancient, read *washed.* Heb. 9. 14; comp. ch. 7. 14.
[6]Gr. *in.*

that it means the Holy Spirit. The decisive reason for that is that it is used in the salutation in direct association with God and Christ, and that a blessing is invoked from the three. Though Paul usually leaves the Spirit out of his salutations, he includes it in 2 Cor. 13: 14. It would appear out of place to invoke a blessing from any but a divine being. To ask such benedictions from angels or other creatures would necessarily imply the worshiping of angels, yet we know that angels are required to worship Christ. (Heb. 1: 6.) Worshiping creatures instead of God is clearly wrong. (Rom. 1: 25.) It is true that the Holy Spirit as a person is one (Eph. 4: 4), but symbolically may be referred to as "seven Spirits" to indicate the fullness of his work; the one personality but diverse manifestations of power. (1 Cor. 12: 4.) The word "seven" is used too often in Revelation not to recognize this significance of the term. The Spirit "before his throne" probably represents readiness to carry out God's will just as Christ is presented as a Lamb "in the midst of the throne" ready to open the seals. (5: 5, 6.)

5 **and from Jesus Christ, who is the faithful witness,**—Since this revelation of future events was to be made through Jesus, John here declares that he is "the faithful witness." That means that what he said would be the exact truth and in strict accord with the will of his Father. Of course his testimony on any phase of the plan of salvation was faithfully told, but here John evidently refers to the fact that his witness regarding the future history of the church would be a true portrayal of the facts. Jesus is mentioned after the Spirit here because what follows in this paragraph has direct reference to him, not because the Spirit is in any sense superior to him.

the firstborn of the dead, and the ruler of the kings of the earth.—Paul uses a similar expression in Col. 1: 18, and in 1 Cor. 15: 20 he refers to Jesus after his resurrection as "the firstfruits of

he made us *to be* a kingdom, *to be* priests unto [7]his God and Father; to him

[7]Or, *God and his Father*

them that are asleep." There had been resurrections before Christ (Lazarus and the widow's son), but Jesus was the first to rise to die no more, to become the "firstfruits" and guarantee the resurrection of all at the last day. (John 5: 28, 29; 11: 23, 24.) Paul further states that Jesus was "declared to be the Son of God with power, according to the spirit of holiness, by the resurrection from the dead." (Rom. 1: 4.) He assures us that the promise God made to the fathers and the prediction that he was the begotten Son of God were fulfilled in Christ's resurrection. (Acts 13: 33.)

At the time John wrote Jesus had not only been raised from the dead, but he was the "ruler of the kings of the earth." The word "ruler" means that he was above all kings; occupied a position far more exalted than any earthly ruler. Paul tells us that because of his humility in submitting to death God "exalted him, and gave unto him the name which is above every name." (Phil. 2: 9.) Paul also states plainly when he was given this exalted name and position. It was after his resurrection and ascension to heaven that God made him to sit at his own right hand "far above all rule, and authority, and power, and dominion, and every name that is named." (Eph. 1: 19-21.) This position and power, which had been in existence since Pentecost, could not be less than a reigning King. Whatever interpretations may be placed upon the visions of future events, as we proceed in this book, nothing must set aside this basic truth in John's introductory statements.

Unto him that loveth us, and loosed us from our sins by his blood;—The revised text reads "loveth," present tense, instead of "loved," past tense, in the King James. This is doubtless correct as the love of Jesus did not end with his death. His love not only led him to die for us, but also to provide all else for our salvation here and hereafter. This text has "loosed" from our sins while the King James has "washed." The two Greek words are so nearly

be the glory and the dominion [8]for ever and ever. Amen. 7 Behold, he

[8]Gr. *unto the ages of the ages.* Many ancient authorities omit *of the ages.*

alike that only a slight change would turn either one into the other. This could easily have happened in making copies by hand. It is immaterial which is the true reading since both words state true facts. That Christ "washes"—cleanses—us through the merits of his shed blood is unquestionably true. In fact, that is what occurs, for it is so stated in substance in Rev. 7: 14, a text about which there is no question regarding the translation. But by Christ's blood we are "loosed" from our sins also. The Greek word for "loosed" is in the aorist tense, and expresses a completed past action. Christ had already died, the price had been paid, and the means for securing individual pardon had been provided. That was all past when John wrote this text. The fountain "for sin and for uncleanness" had already been opened "to the house of David" by his descendant, Jesus Christ, making the everlasting atonement in heaven. (Zech. 13: 1; Heb. 10: 12.)

6 **and he made us to be a kingdom, to be priests unto his God and Father;**—The words "to be" are in italics to indicate there is nothing in the original for them. They are unnecessary to the thought here. Christ made his disciples "a kingdom, priests unto his God." The word kingdom describes them collectively; the word priests individually. In 1 Pet. 2: 5 Peter makes the same distinction, calling them *living stones* individually and a *spirit house* collectively. In verse 9 he combines both kings and priests in the name "royal priesthood." Similar language was used in reference to ancient Israel. God said to them: "And ye shall be unto me a kingdom of priests, and a holy nation." (Ex. 19: 6.) In the expression "he made us" John again uses the past tense, showing that they had been made a kingdom and therefore were one at that time. This is doubly certain when we consider the fact that they had also been made priests. That the priesthood of Christ, which justifies calling Christians priests, began on Pentecost does not admit of denial; in fact, it is universally admitted.

cometh with the clouds; and every eye shall see him, and they that pierced him; and all the tribes of the earth shall mourn over him. Even so, Amen.

No one can logically deny the existence of Christ's kingdom without rejecting John's words; their meaning does not admit of doubt.

to him be the glory and the dominion for ever and ever. Amen.—"To him" refers to Christ, as reading verses 5 and 6 will show. In this expression John ascribes both glory and dominion to Christ forever. That means that Christ had both then and will continue to have both until he delivers the kingdom back to the Father after the judgment. (1 Cor. 15: 24-28.)

7 **Behold, he cometh with the clouds; and every eye shall see him, and they that pierced him;**—John had just said that Christ's glory and dominion would be "for ever and ever"; that is, throughout the age. This probably suggested the thought of his return to judgment after which the dominion would be returned to God. He wished to assure the readers that there would be no doubt about Christ's return. This led to his mentioning the fact that he would come "on the clouds," a fact referred to in Matt. 26: 64; Acts 1: 9, 11. That the coming here means his appearance to *judge* is seen in the words "every eye shall see him." That will only be when all the nations are gathered before him as indicated by Matt. 25: 31-46. They that pierced him refer to all those who, directly or indirectly, had anything to do with his crucifixion, and means that even his enemies must face him at the judgment.

and all the tribes of the earth shall mourn over him. Even so, Amen.—All the tribes—peoples—will mourn when he comes because of their sins and the knowledge that their condemnation is a certainty. The redeemed will rejoice, of course, but the lost will bewail their undone condition. In the words "Even so, Amen" the thought probably is that John wished the things to transpire just as they would be revealed, and thus his words would be verified.

8 I am the Alpha and the Omega, saith the Lord God, [9]who is and who was and [4]who is to come, the Almighty.

[9]Or, *he who*

8 **I am the Alpha and the Omega, saith the Lord God, who is and who was and who is to come, the Almighty.**—Alpha and Omega are the first and last letters of the Greek alphabet; hence, mean the first and last, the beginning and the end. (22: 13.) The Revised makes this language refer to God rather than Christ, though elsewhere the same language refers to Christ. (Verses 17, 18.) God is called the Almighty to indicate his power to fulfill his promises and grant the blessing mentioned in verse 3. Being eternal in existence guarantees his promises, however long the fulfillment may be in coming.

3. JOHN'S COMMISSION TO WRITE
1: 9-11

9 I John, your brother and partaker with you in the tribulation and king-

9 **I John, your brother and partaker with you in the tribulation and kingdom and patience which are in Jesus,**—This is the third time that John has named himself in this book. The words "your brother" mean that he belonged to the same divine family as those to whom he was to write—God's house or family in the church. (1 Tim. 3: 15.) By "partaker" he meant that he was sharing in common with them both the joys and sorrows incident to being a member of God's family. Jesus had taught that persecutions and tribulations would come. (Matt. 13: 21.) John's banishment on Patmos was evidence that he was then enduring tribulation. The persecution that sent him there was no doubt felt by the churches in Asia, and the main reason for writing them was to encourage them to faithfulness in spite of their persecutions. And, incidentally, also to encourage the saints of all time to overcome trials. As he was then *in* tribulation, he was also *in* the kingdom. The words "tribulation" and "kingdom" are in the same grammatical relation. If in one, then in both. No doubt about his being in the tribulation; then none about being in the kingdom. This

dom and [10]patience *which are* in Jesus, was in the isle that is called Patmos,
for the word of God and the testimony of Jesus. 10 I was in the Spirit on
the Lord's day, and I heard behind me a great voice, as of a trumpet 11

[10]Or, *stedfastness*

---

again fixes the existence of the kingdom then as beyond question. It was the joy of being in the kingdom that made them endure the tribulation with patience. All these were "in Jesus"—were successful through the means he had provided to meet tribulation. The word kingdom in some passages means the final state or heaven. (Acts 14: 22; Eph. 5: 5; 2 Tim. 4: 18; 2 Pet. 1: 11.) But here John means the present kingdom, for in verse 6 he declared that Christ "made us to be a kingdom."

was in the isle that is called Patmos, for the word of God and the testimony of Jesus.—Patmos is a rocky island in the Aegean Sea not far from the west coast of Asia Minor. It is about ten miles long by five or six wide. The only explanation of his being on that island is that it was "for the word of God and the testimony of Jesus." The commonly accepted view is that he was there in exile because of his fidelity in preaching Christ. It is also supposed that he was banished to this lonely place by Domitian who reigned A.D. 81-96.

10 **I was in the Spirit on the Lord's day, and I heard behind me a great voice, as of a trumpet**—"*Was* in the Spirit" means he came to be in the Spirit; was in a kind of spiritual ecstasy and exalted under the Spirit's influence till he could understand the visions presented and accurately repeat them. The word translated "Lord's" occurs only one other time in the New Testament—1 Cor. 11: 20—where it describes the supper of the Lord. Evidently it refers to something about Jesus. As he arose on the first day of the week, and the Lord's Supper is observed on that day (Acts 20: 7), it is most natural to say John meant the first day of the week by the expression "Lord's day." Several writers in the centuries following the apostolic day say it was the first day of the week. Evidently it was so well understood then that no explanation was needed. The voice he heard is called "a great voice, as of a trumpet." This means that it rang loud and clear like the sounding of

saying, What thou seest, write in a book and send *it* to the seven churches: unto Ephesus, and unto Smyrna, and unto Pergamum, and unto Thyatira, and unto Sardis, and unto Philadelphia, and unto Laodicea. 12 And I turned

---

a trumpet. Such a voice would command instant attention and impress the necessity of obedience to what it said.

11 **saying, What thou seest, write in a book and send it to the seven churches:**—In these words John received his authority and commission to record what he saw. The verb "seest" is present tense, which often means a continuous action. The meaning then would be what you see now and what will continue to be revealed to you. This view is required by the nineteenth verse; the things to be recorded are extended to the future. In the remainder of verse 11 the churches are named. Any necessary description will be given in the comments on the letters sent to them.

4. THE INITIAL VISION
1: 12-18

to see the voice that spake with me. And having turned I saw seven golden [11]candlesticks; 13 and in the midst of the [11]candlesticks one like unto a son

[11]Gr. *lampstands.*

---

12 **And I turned to see the voice that spake with me.**—Turning to see who was speaking was the natural thing to do. The text says to "see the voice." By a common figure of speech the voice is put for the one speaking.

And having turned I saw seven golden candlesticks;—Here the vision proper begins. In the tabernacle and temple there were golden candlesticks. Each had seven prongs with a lamp on each prong. But in this vision there appeared seven distinct lampstands. This is evident from the following verse where Christ is represented as being "in the midst of" them. Neither is there anything said about these candlesticks having more than one lamp. Being made of gold probably represents their great value as well as their enduring qualities. In this book there are a number of things described as golden or made of pure gold. Each will be noted in its proper place.

of man, clothed with a garment down to the foot, and girt about at the breasts with a golden girdle. 14 And his head and his hair were white as white wool, *white* as snow; and his eyes were as a flame of fire; 15 and his

---

13 **and in the midst of the candlesticks one like unto a son of man,**—There is no question but that the one John saw in this vision represented the Lord. The King James Version translates "the" Son of man. Christ often applied this title to himself. (Matt. 8: 20; 9: 6.) A like expression is found in Dan. 7: 13, also referring to Christ. Commentators have disagreed as to whether John saw Jesus himself or the appearance of a human to represent him. Such controversy is useless. Both would lead to the same truth. This part of the vision clearly was intended to represent Christ's relationship to churches. Whether he really appeared or a form of man to represent him affects not the case. The fact that John was looking at a picture favors the Revised Version and the latter view.

clothed with a garment down to the foot, and girt about at the breasts with a golden girdle.—The robe reaching to the feet and the girdle around the breasts are supposed to represent the dignity that belonged to both priesthood and kingship. Girdles were then worn around the body to fasten down the flowing robes, but one richly ornamented with gold placed about the breasts indicates royal dignity. This is what should naturally be expected, as the vision was intended to show Jesus as one having both the power and authority to open the seals—reveal the things that the church should know. As the great Prophet, he would know exactly what was to transpire that should be told; as Priest and King, he would have full authority to make such revelations as were needed to give any commands necessary to the doing of his will.

14 **And his head and his hair were white as white wool, white as snow; and his eyes were as a flame of fire;**—It is perfectly evident that the language here used is not intended as a natural description of the Lord as he lived on the earth; for being in his thirty-fourth year when he ascended he was a young man, and probably in physical appearance not greatly different from others.

feet like unto burnished brass, as if it had been refined in a furnace; and his voice as the voice of many waters. 16 And he had in his right hand seven **stars: and out of his mouth proceeded a sharp two-edged sword: and his**

Neither is it necessary to conclude that the description here correctly represents his glorious appearance in heaven. It seems more probable that the appearance of the one John saw was assumed to impress the apostle with a sense of Christ's majesty and glory. White as a color indicates purity and victory; the expression white as wool and snow means that it was perfectly white. The intention here is not to indicate age, but to show that Jesus was perfectly sinless and fully able to do what was proposed. The eyes appearing as a flame of fire indicates their penetrating power, probably meaning that the Lord was able to look into the future as well as into men's hearts and reveal both the true and false.

15 **and his feet like unto burnished brass, as if it had been refined in a furnace; and his voice as the voice of many waters.**—The feet of the one speaking to John looked like burnished brass that had been fully refined. Perhaps there is no special significance in this more than that it harmonizes with the majestic splendor of Christ as able to do the work proposed. The voice John heard was like the sound of many waters, the roar of the ocean or a great cataract. God himself is referred to in a similar way. "And, behold, the glory of the God of Israel came from the way of the east; and his voice was like the sound of many waters; and the earth shined with his glory." (Ezek. 43: 2.) See also Ezek. 1: 24; Dan. 10: 6. Representing the sound of the voice as the roar of many waters is another sublime way of expressing divine majesty and power.

16 **And he had in his right hand seven stars: and out of his mouth proceeded a sharp two-edged sword:**—In verse 20 these seven stars are said to be the angels of the seven churches. Here we have in this book the first direct explanation of the symbol used, being definitely told what the stars represent. When the book itself explains a symbol, there is an end of controversy on that point whether we understand it or not. Being held in the

countenance was as the sun shineth in his strength. 17 And when I saw him, I fell at his feet as one dead. And he laid his right hand upon me, saying, Fear not; I am the first and the last, 18 and the Living one; and I

---

right hand probably indicates that the angels were to be sustained and protected by the Lord—would receive their support and instruction from him. The appearance of a sword proceeding from his mouth must in some way refer to his words. This is perfectly natural when we note that the word of God is said to be "living, and active, and sharper than any two-edged sword." (Heb. 4: 12.) Isaiah said that Jehovah had made his "mouth like a sharp sword." (Isa. 49: 2.) The words proceeding from the Lord's mouth would not only comfort and instruct the saints, but would also terrify and destroy the ungodly. Through a prophet Jehovah said: "I have slain them by the words of my mouth." (Hos. 6: 5.) Paul said that Jesus at his coming would slay the lawless one "with the breath of his mouth." (2 Thess. 2: 8.) The word "sharp" indicates the penetrating power of Christ's words, while the two-edged nature represents the thoroughness of its work.

and his countenance was as the sun shineth in his strength. —The hair, eyes, mouth, and voice have already been described. This expression is evidently intended as a general description of his appearance; it was as the sun in its full strength and not obscured by any clouds. It was probably like his appearance on the mount of transfiguration. (Matt. 17: 2.) The entire description most appropriately presents the majesty, power, and authority of Jesus to make the revelation intended, and most solemnly to impress John with the necessity of giving heed to what was revealed to him.

17 **And when I saw him, I fell at his feet as one dead. And he laid his right hand upon me, saying, Fear not;**—John was overwhelmed by the divine majesty and the suddenness with which the vision came. Losing consciousness, he fell as one would who was really dead. The overpowering influence of supernatural events was not an uncommon thing. (Dan. 8: 18, 27; 10: 9; Ezek. 1: 28; Acts 26: 13, 14.) John, remembering Jesus as he saw him here on earth, probably did not recognize the being in the

[12]was dead, and behold, I am alive [13]for evermore, and I have the keys of death and of Hades. 19 Write therefore the things which thou sawest, and

[12]Gr. *became.*
[13]Gr. *unto the ages of the ages.*

vision as representing the Lord. The explanation that follows immediately is further proof that he did not at first know who was represented by the vision. Laying his right hand upon John was doubtless for the purpose of raising him up. Compare Dan. 8: 18. The command to "Fear not" was intended to give John assurance to hear what would be revealed to him. Once Jesus gave a similar command to his apostles, saying, "It is I; be not afraid." (Matt. 14: 27.) In the midst of manifestations of divine power man needs assurance from God to calm his fears. Jesus gave it when he was here in person (Luke 9: 34, 35); his words supply the same assurance now (Heb. 6: 18-20).

I am the first and the last, 18 **and the Living one; and I was dead, and behold, I am alive for evermore,**—Alpha and Omega, which mean the first and the last, probably refer to God in verse 8; here the words first and last clearly refer to Christ. They declare his existence from eternity which is also asserted by both John and Paul. (John 1: 1, 2; Col. 1: 16, 17.) If of eternal existence, John could well afford to depend implicitly upon his word and power; hence no reason why he should fear. Referring to Christ as the "Living one" means he was in his very nature the source and fountain of life. Jesus said: "For as the Father hath life in himself, even so gave he to the Son also to have life in himself." (John 5: 26.) Saying that he had been dead, but was now alive effectively identified the one represented in the vision as the Lord. This was evidence that John's faith in the Lord's resurrection had been no delusion. Jesus had died once, but never could die again. This should remove all fear and give perfect assurance that he is able to fulfill all his promises.

and I have the keys of death and of Hades.—Hades is a Greek word and means the "unseen." It refers to the state between death and the resurrection, the place of abode of disembodied spirits of both bad and good. This is evident from the Savior's use of the word in Luke 16: 23. The expression "keys of death and of Hades" is closely related to the preceding statements in reference to Christ once being dead, but now being alive. That Christ's spirit went to Hades while his body was in the tomb is certain from Peter's words in Acts 2: 27. Keys mean authority or power. Since Christ's body was raised and his spirit returned from Hades, he has power to abolish death and bring the waiting spirits from the Hadean world. This he will do when he comes again and the judgment takes place. (Rev. 20: 11-14).

5. COMMISSION REPEATED AND SYMBOLS EXPLAINED
1: 19, 20

the things which are, and the things which shall come to pass hereafter; 20

---

19 **Write therefore the things which thou sawest, and the things which are, and the things which shall come to pass hereafter;**—In verse 11 is the general command to write what he saw; in this verse the command is repeated with more definite instruction about what was to be written. He was to record what he had seen—the initial vision described in verses 12-18. This would show by what power and authority he wrote. The things "which are" would include the state of the seven churches then, which necessitated the instructions and rebukes found in the second and third chapters. Of this fact the contents of these chapters is sufficient proof. The things which were to come to pass "hereafter" must mean the future events from the time that John wrote. They are presented in the symbols found in chapters 4 to 22. The contents of these chapters furnish proof of this fact. That the things recorded in this third division extended into the future is evident because the last two chapters of the book unquestionably describe the final judgment and the heavenly state. Of course the symbols used to portray the future events were given to John in visions that came after he received the command to record them.

20 **the mystery of the seven stars which thou sawest in my right hand, and the seven golden candlesticks.**—The word mystery does not mean something that cannot be understood, but

the mystery of the seven stars which thou sawest [14]in my right hand, and the seven golden [11]candlesticks. The seven stars are the angels of the seven churches: and the seven [11]candlesticks are seven churches.

[14]Gr. *upon.*

something that is secret, hidden, or will not be understood, till its meaning is revealed. To find the hidden thing or make known the secret means that the symbols were to be explained. When the explanation was given the symbols were understood and the mystery known.

The seven stars are the angels of the seven churches: and the seven candlesticks are seven churches.—John was told that the seven candlesticks "are seven churches." This language means that they represent or denote seven churches. Without this explanation the candlesticks would have been an unrevealed mystery, for it is evident that the word is used symbolically. A candlestick is intended to give light. Nothing is more certain than that God's people, individually and as congregations, are to be light bearers. Jesus told his disciples that they were "the light of the world" (Matt. 5: 14); Paul told the Philippians that they were "seen as lights in the world" (Phil 2: 15). Since Jesus is the light of the world (John 8: 12), and is represented in this vision as being in the midst of these seven churches, the light shed abroad by the churches came from him. He alone supplies the true light; faithful congregations reflect it to those about them.

The seven stars are called the "angels of the seven churches." There is much difference of opinion regarding the proper application of the word "angels" in this instance. As a word it means "messenger" and would appropriately apply to any kind of messenger, heavenly or human. In the Old Testament it referred to either priest or prophet. (Mal. 2: 7; Hag. 1: 13.) It also referred to John the Baptist who announced the coming Messiah. (Mal. 3: 1; Matt. 11: 7-10.) In the cases being considered it must refer to beings to whom these short letters were addressed and by whom they would be delivered to the churches, not to heavenly angels. Addressing "the angel" (singular number) of each individual congregation is the reason for such divergence of views among commentators. The angel could not refer to the modern denominational "Bishop," exercising authority over a diocese, for "the angel" of each congregation is addressed. Elders, bishops, and pastors are words referring to the same class and each congregation had a plurality. (Acts 14: 23.) There is no scriptural authority for any elder or bishop having pre-eminence over his fellow elders. Without reference to the various views in detail, the following seems most probable as well as in harmony with known Bible teaching. Seven candlesticks represent the seven congregations; each candlestick (singular) must therefore represent one congregation. But the congregation is made up of a plurality of individuals. In like manner, as the eldership is made up of a plurality of persons, the star—angel—of each congregation may mean the whole eldership, the word being used *collectively* to describe the medium through which the messages would be delivered to the congregation. The position of the elders collectively as teachers and shepherds of the congregation lends much plausibility to this view. It can do no violence to any true scriptural teaching. The value of the seven letters, however, will not be affected by any failure on our part to determine with certainty the proper application of the word "angel" here. No plain facts regarding the apostolic churches must be set aside by any fanciful interpretations.

SECTION TWO

LETTERS TO THE SEVEN CHURCHES

2: 1 to 3: 22

Preliminary Note: The record does not tell why messages were sent to just seven churches, nor why sent to the seven named. Considering the many times the number seven is used in the Bible, the view that it indicates completeness or perfection appears certainly correct. If so, these churches were doubtless selected because they furnished the occasion for just the amount of instruction, exhortation, and warning necessary in completing the divine record. These seven brief messages deal with actual facts that existed at the time John wrote. While primarily intended for the churches named, yet they were, of course, also intended for congregations in all ages; for like conditions would need like treatment. This is also true of all the New Testament letters to churches. It is unnecessary to conclude that these very short letters were sent separately to the respective churches named. It is far more probable that each congregation received all of them along with all the rest of the book, since any one of them might at some future time need the very instruction given to another. Then the symbolical descriptions of things to come, presented in the remainder of the book, would also be needed by all of them. Evidently the entire book was intended for all the seven; if so, then for all congregations for all time.

1. LETTER TO THE CHURCH AT EPHESUS
2: 1-7

1 To the angel of the church in Ephesus write:

---

1 **To the angel of the church in Ephesus write:**—See notes on 1: 20 for the application of the word "angel." At the time John wrote Ephesus was the chief city of Asia Minor. It was noted for magical arts and the temple of the heathen goddess Diana. (Acts 19: 19, 35.) It is generally supposed from tradition that John resided in Asia Minor from about A.D. 70 till his death. If so,

These things saith he that holdeth the seven stars in his right hand, he that walketh in the midst of the seven golden [1]candlesticks: 2 I know thy works, and thy toil and [2]patience, and that thou canst not bear evil men, and

[1]Gr. *lampstands.*
[2]Or, *stedfastness*

Ephesus was doubtless his headquarters. Paul was mainly responsible for the establishment of the congregation there, having labored for them two years and three months at one time which resulted in the gospel being preached in all Asia. (Acts 19: 8-10.) Later Paul wrote them the Ephesian letter. All this shows that the congregation was one of considerable prominence, and probably accounts for the first letter in this chapter being addressed to them.

These things saith he that holdeth the seven stars in his right hand, he that walketh in the midst of the seven golden candlesticks:—Here Jesus repeats two of the descriptive features of the person John saw in the vision. (1 : 13, 16.) These would impress them with the necessity of being obedient to his commands. Holding the stars in his hands would mean that the teachers of the church must depend upon him for the source of their knowledge; walking in the midst of the candlesticks—moving among the churches—indicates that he would not only bless their labors, but punish them for their evil deeds. It also implies that his favor would be necessary to their continued existence. "Walking" among them may imply that he was able to care for all, and would be constantly watching over them. Surely this was an impressive way to introduce the letter.

2 **I know thy works, and thy toil and patience,**—"I know" is the common form of introducing all these letters. It would impress them with the fact that he was able to know the motives of their hearts, and could render just decisions in each case. He would not overlook their faults nor forget their good deeds. This is a peculiar characteristic of Christ. (John 2: 25.) "Works" here mean general conduct rather than simple deeds. The items mentioned to the end of verse 3 are an explanation of what is included in their works. Toil and patience present the positive and negative sides of their commendable works. Toil means excessive labor

didst try them that call themselves apostles, and they are not, and didst find them false; 3 and thou hast [2]patience and didst bear for my name's sake, and

even up to the point of suffering and sadness, shown in their earnest opposition to false teachers. Patience means their steadfast endurance to the right in spite of the influence of such false teaching. Fighting error to the point of suffering and remaining faithful to gospel truth is the compliment here paid this congregation.

and that thou canst not bear evil men, and didst try them that call themselves apostles, and they are not, and didst find them false;—The compliment here is further extended by the statement that they could not endure or tolerate evil men. They had tested certain ones that claimed to be apostles and found them false. John had already given the standard by which such test could be made. Only those who accepted what the apostles said were of God. (1 John 4: 1, 6.) Probably those calling themselves apostles claimed to be directly called as were the true apostles, or that they were successors to them. Either claim was, of course, false. It is no surprise to find such false teachers in the early church, for Paul said he knew that after his departure some among them would speak perverse things "to draw away the disciples after them." (Acts 20: 29, 30.) John had also instructed that those who did not abide in the doctrine should not be received into their houses or given greetings. (2 John 9, 10.) Paul refers to "false apostles" at Corinth as "deceitful workers, fashioning themselves into apostles of Christ," yet being ministers of Satan. (2 Cor. 11: 13-15.) The Ephesian church had insisted on pure teaching, and rejected those who taught falsehood. This deserves unstinted praise.

3 **and thou hast patience and didst bear for my name's sake, and hast not grown weary.**—With steadfastness they had borne up under the burdens of meeting false teachers and against the influence of false doctrines; they had patiently maintained their defense of the truth for the name of Christ. It was their desire to defend his cause that met all opposition to the true gospel without being exhausted or worn out. This language presents a fine balance of Christian conduct. We should not tolerate error in any kind of teaching and should, regardless of any false doctrines, main-

hast not grown weary. 4 But I have *this* against thee, that thou didst leave thy first love. 5 Remember therefore whence thou art fallen, and repent and do the first works; or else I come to thee, and will move thy [3]candlestick

[3]Gr. *lampstand.*

tain our faith in God's word with unfailing steadfastness. Such seems to be the full import of this commendation of the church at Ephesus.

4 **But I have this against thee, that thou didst leave thy first love.**—The warm praise now changes to reproof and warning. Commendations for virtues could not atone for faults or sins. With a casual reading such a strong rebuke immediately following an equally strong commendation seems almost contradictory, yet we know it cannot be. Rather more careful thought will show that the situation was not an unusual one. We have many similar cases in the churches today. The evidence of love to Jesus is obedience to his commands. (1 John 2: 4, 5.) That consists in doing what he says. Hence, the expression "first love" is explained by the expression "first works" in verse 5. While they would not tolerate false teachers and false doctrines, yet their first early enthusiasm for the worship and progress of the church had waned. They were not as untiring in their devotion to the church as they were against false teaching. Multitudes of individual Christians are in that condition all the time. The danger of such a state is that one is likely soon to lose practically all interest in the church. Happy is the Christian who does not allow his early zeal for worship and the spread of truth to burn low. The church at Ephesus had been established many years and their having lost their early spiritual ardor is not surprising when we remember the difficulty of holding a high level in anything.

5 **Remember therefore whence thou art fallen, and repent and do the first works;**—Remember here means to consider; that is, to compare the former burning zeal in the Lord's work with their present apathy and note how much they had lost both in work and satisfaction. Such serious reflections should lead them to repentance, which would be necessary to prevent other losses. Repentance means a change of mind that results in a change of conduct. Honest meditation on their reglect would produce sorrow; that would lead to a decision to change their conduct—be-

out of its place, except thou repent. 6 But this thou hast, that thou hatest the works of the Nicolaitans, which I also hate. 7 He that hath an ear, let

---

come again zealous in good works. Their "first works" do not mean their obedience to the commands by which they became Christians, but to their works in teaching the truth and righteous living.

or else I come to thee, and will move thy candlestick out of its place, except thou repent.—The present tense of "come" here clearly has the force of the future, meaning "I will come." This does not mean a personal coming, but in some kind of judgment that would fall upon the church. Just how or what that would be is not stated. To remove a candlestick would mean to take away the light. But the candlestick, we are told, was the church itself. (1: 20.) Moving the candlestick out of its place, therefore, means that the congregation was to cease to exist. This, however, was conditional; to be prevented only by the fact that the congregation would repent and return to its first love.

6 **But this thou hast, that thou hatest the works of the Nicolaitans, which I also hate.**—Just who and what were these people is conceded by all commentators to be uncertain. They were well known then, of course, else John would have given some description of them. There is uncertainty both as to the meaning and origin of the name and the peculiar works they did. The following probably is as likely to be correct as anything suggested: The word was derived from a leader whose name was Nicholas, and their practices which the Lord hates were gross social sins and idolatry. But whatever their doctrines and deeds were they were severely condemned. The Ephesian church was commended because they hated these abominable practices which God hated. It is useless to speculate on what we have no means of learning, but all good people will hate that which is grossly wicked, whether the practices of the Nicolaitans or other sinners.

7 **He that hath an ear, let him hear what the Spirit saith to the churches.** Those having ears to hear are willing to listen to the message. To such the invitation and exhortation was to give heed to what was said. This shows that God's revelations are spoken to man, not put into his heart through some mysterious spiritual

him hear what the Spirit saith to the churches. To him that overcometh, to him will I give to eat of the tree of life, which is in the [4]Paradise of God.

[4]Or, *garden:* as in Gen. 2. 8.

power. Those who are not willing to hear God's word will never learn his message of life. It also implies man's ability to hear and understand what God says. In chapter 1 Jesus is represented as making the revelation and John is commanded to write it, but here the Spirit is said to be speaking to the churches. Jesus had told the apostles before his death that the Spirit would guide them into all truth (John 14: 26; 16: 13-15) and declare things to come. We know that the Spirit directed John what to write, and was through him speaking to the churches. This shows the method used by the Holy Spirit in delivering his messages to man. He speaks them; man must hear and obey. Those not willing to hear and obey cannot be benefited by the Spirit's work.

To him that overcometh, to him will I give to eat of the tree of life, which is in the Paradise of God.—To overcome translates a Greek word that means to *conquer* in some battle or trial. There is no definite statement regarding the things in which Christians are to gain a victory, the expression being used independently. But the whole passage shows that it means a victory over all kinds of evil that would harm the church or prevent the salvation of the contender. In a general sense it would mean a continued victory over sinful things until one's life is ended. This statement, with an appropriate promise attached, is the way all these short letters are closed. To "eat of the tree of life" is a very expressive figure indicating the spiritual joys to be received in heaven. It is a reference to the "tree of life" in the Garden of Eden. (Gen. 2: 9; 3: 22.) The fruit of that tree was designed to make one live forever; hence, Adam after his sin was forbidden to eat of it. In like manner the things in heaven that sustain eternal life are represented as a "tree of life." In the glorious picture of heaven presented in Rev. 22: 1-5 we again find the same imagery.

Paradise is said to be a Persian word that means a park or pleasure ground; hence, can appropriately be applied to any place especially prepared for enjoyment. For this reason Eden is referred to as "Paradise." The place of the righteous dead in the intermediate state is also a "Paradise." (Luke 23: 43.) Our text calls the final state "Paradise" also. This word, because it means a place of pleasure and may be applied figuratively to any place of pleasure, must be considered in the light of the context each time to learn its proper application. Here the redeemed are viewed as existing upon lifegiving fruit in a garden of delights. An entrancing vision, surely.

2. LETTER TO THE CHURCH AT SMYRNA 2: 8-11

8 And to the angel of the church in Smyrna write:
These things saith the first and the last, who [5]was dead, and lived *again:*
9 I know thy tribulation, and thy poverty (but thou art rich), and the

[5]Gr. *became.*

8 **And to the angel of the church in Smyrna write: These things saith the first and the last, who was dead, and lived again:**—Smyrna was a populous city about forty miles north of Ephesus. Having a fine harbor, it became a great commercial city—was noted both for its educational facilities and the worship of idols. It was the home of Polycarp, who personally knew the apostle John for many years and was martyred after he had served the Lord eighty-six years. It doubtless had a strong Jewish element in its population. This and the idol worshipers and difficulties of living under Roman rule made the stay of Christians there a hard and dangerous existence. They were encouraged by being reminded of Christ "who was dead, and lived again," an attribute of Jesus mentioned to John himself in 1: 18. As their faithfulness to Jesus was likely to result in their martyrdom, it was particularly appropriate to remind them of the fact that the Master himself had once died, but was made alive. It was an assurance that, if they were martyred, they too would be raised from the dead.

9 **I know thy tribulation, and thy poverty (but thou art rich),**—This letter also begins with "I know," meaning that the Lord had a complete knowledge of their condition and needs. This would assure them they could depend implicitly upon his instruction. Tribulation carries the general idea of affliction or distress. In their case, doubtless, all they suffered from the persecu-

[6]blasphemy of them that say they are Jews, and they are not, but are a synagogue of Satan. 10 Fear not the things which thou art about to suffer:

[6]Or, *reviling*

tions of their oppressors was included in the term. The mention of their poverty indicates that they were especially poverty-stricken since that is not said of the other churches addressed. Their poverty may have resulted from oppression and robbery on the part of their enemies. But in spite of it the Smyrna church continued to exist long after all the others were gone. Poverty is usually far less dangerous than great riches. Though poor in material goods, they were "rich in faith" and, as a consequence, were "heirs of the kingdom which he promised to them that love him." (James 2: 5.) This was because they were "rich in good works." (1 Tim. 6: 18.)

and the blasphemy of them that say they are Jews, and they are not, but are a synagogue of Satan.—The Lord also knew the blasphemy of their enemies—the reproaches and bitter revilings which were hurled against them. This was assurance that the Lord would know exactly what reward their enemies deserved, and would see to it that justice would be done in due time. The Christians' religion was probably the occasion for the blasphemies. This particular class of their persecutors were native Jews who were manifesting the same spirit that prompted the betrayers of Christ. They laid much stress upon their claim to be Jews—God's people. The text says they were not Jews. There are two senses in which that would be true. First, as natural Jews they were not following the teachings of Moses, and were not worthy of the name; second, they were not Jews in the spiritual sense. The word in that sense meant Christians (Rom. 2: 28, 29), and they were fighting Christians. They were not then worthy of the name in either sense. The extreme cruelty and wickedness of the Jews in Smyrna is described by Jesus when he calls them a "synagogue of Satan." The synagogue is probably used here in the sense of an assembly or congregation. They claimed to be the congregation of the Lord—God's people—when, in fact, they were in the service of Satan. Their persecution of the saints was under the influence of Satan.

10 **Fear not the things which thou art about to suffer:**—This

behold, the devil is about to cast some of you into prison, that ye may be tried; [7]and ye shall have [8]tribulation ten days. Be thou faithful unto death,

[7]Some ancient authorities read *and may have.*
[8]Gr. *a tribulation of ten days.*

language clearly indicated that there were sufferings about to come to them from which there would be no escape, but they were urged not to be afraid. Confidence in Christ's promises would drive out fear and prepare them for the ordeal.

behold, the devil is about to cast some of you into prison, that ye may be tried; and ye shall have tribulation ten days. —Casting the Christians into prison was not an uncommon thing, especially in the case of the apostles. (Acts 12: 3, 4; 16: 23.) John himself had been banished to Patmos and possibly many others might be put in prison. This prediction of imprisonment was in fact the probable thing to expect at that time. The text says that the devil would cast them into prison. Of course, it was actually done by their enemies and these words show that evil workers are in the service of the devil and operate under his evil influence. This imprisonment would be a test of their fortitude and fidelity to God. The severity of the test would show whether or not they could be driven into apostasy.

The tribulation—including the imprisonment of some—was to last "ten days." This expression has been variously construed by scholars. Some take it to mean ten literal days; some that it refers to prophetic days, meaning a day for a year, or ten years; others that ten days meant frequent, full or complete tribulation, a sense in which the word "ten" seems to be used in Num. 14: 22; Neh. 4: 12; Dan. 1: 20; and others still think that the expression indicates that the tribulation would be brief. Gen. 24: 55; Dan 1: 12, 14 are supposed to give examples of this use. Ten natural days would be too insignificant for such a grave thing. It might have been ten years. If so, there is no way to fix the exact date. Either one of the other views might be true. It seems probable that the statement was made to encourage the brethren not to falter in their fidelity to God. If so, then by "ten days" Jesus meant to say that the tribulation would be comparatively short. This would stimulate them to faithfulness.

and I will give thee the crown of life. 11 He that hath an ear, let him hear what the Spirit saith to the churches. He that overcometh shall not be hurt of the second death.

Be thou faithful unto death, and I will give thee the crown of life.—The singular "thou" is used because it is addressed directly to the "angel" of the church. But, as the letter was to be delivered to the church, everyone was included. They were to continue faithful—meet every rising situation faithfully. "Unto" death does not mean throughout their existence till death (although that was also necessary, Matt. 24: 13), but up to the endurance of death, if necessary; that is, even death should not move them from their steadfastness. The garland of victory, here called "the crown of life," is elsewhere called "the crown of righteousness" (2 Tim. 4: 8), "the crown of glory" (1 Pet. 5: 4), an "incorruptible" crown (1 Cor. 9: 24, 25). Crown is used figuratively for the reward to be received, meaning life as a crown which is given for righteousness.

11 **He that hath an ear, let him hear what the Spirit saith to the churches.**—See notes on verse 7.

He that overcometh shall not be hurt of the second death.—This letter closes just like the one to Ephesus except that a promise of a different blessing is offered. There the promise was to eat of the tree of life; here not to be hurt of the second death. A failure in either case would result in one's being lost. Promising these blessings to one who overcomes implies that those who do not overcome will be lost. Since a Christian may fail to overcome, a Christian may be lost. This is the unmistakable import of the words, and absolute proof that Christians may so apostatize as to be lost finally.

3. LETTER TO THE CHURCH AT PERGAMUM
2: 12-17

12 And to the angel of the church in Pergamum write:
These things saith he that hath the sharp two-edged sword: 13 I know

---

12 **And to the angel of the church in Pergamum write: These things saith he that hath the sharp two-edged sword:**—This church is told that the letter came from the one who had

where thou dwellest, *even* where Satan's throne is; and thou holdest fast my name, and didst not deny my faith, even in the days [9]of Antipas my witness, my faithful one, who was killed among you, where Satan dwelleth. 14 But I have a few things against thee, because thou hast there some that hold the

[9]The Greek text here is somewhat uncertain.

the sharp two-edged sword. In the vision (1: 16) John saw this sword proceed out of Christ's mouth. As the word of God is said to be the "sword of the Spirit" (Eph. 6: 17), and "sharper than any two-edged sword" (Heb. 4: 12), it is evident that the two-edged sword proceeding from Christ's mouth means his words. See note on 1: 16.

13 **I know where thou dwellest, even where Satan's throne is;**—It was, doubtless, encouraging to them to be assured that Jesus knew the unfavorable situation in which they dwelled, the temptations to which they were exposed, and the allurements that tended to draw them away from the truth. The place was so peculiarly filled with wickedness that it was represented as being the very location of Satan's throne. Just what particular form of wickedness led to this designation is not known. It had the ordinary evils that go with a commercial city filled with idolatrous worship. It is said to have been the seat of emperor worship. Evidently Satan incited the people to such atrocious crimes that the place seemed to be his own personal abode. The last expression of the verse, "where Satan dwelleth," has the same meaning as "Satan's throne."

and thou holdest fast my name, and didst not deny my faith, even in the days of Antipas my witness, my faithful one, who was killed among you, where Satan dwelleth.—They had confessed Christ and had not allowed any of their tribulations to make them deny that confession. The name "Christian" which had already been given at Antioch (1 Pet. 4: 16) was held to in spite of all the dangers confronting them. They realized that suffering as Christians they would glorify God in that name. So the apostle Peter had taught in the passage mentioned. That Antipas was a martyr there on account of his faithfulness to Christ is certain from the text, but who he was or the circumstances under which he was killed is not known. His case was probably a local out-

teaching of Balaam, who taught Balak to cast a stumblingblock before the children of Israel, to eat things sacrificed to idols, and to commit fornication. 15 So hast thou also some that hold the teaching of the Nicolaitans in like manner. 16 Repent therefore; or else I come to thee quickly, and I will

---

break of some kind like that when Stephen was killed (Acts 7: 51-60), not a general slaughter of Christians.

14 **But I have a few things against thee, because thou hast there some that hold the teaching of Balaam,**—Like the church at Ephesus the Lord had a general commendation of them, but a few things to condemn. As the Savior condemned evil when he was on earth, so he now condemns the sins that existed in the church at Pergamum. Tolerating only a few serious errors would soon kill the church's influence to do good. The teaching of Balaam is explained in the next clauses.

who taught Balak to cast a stumblingblock before the children of Israel, to eat things sacrificed to idols, and to commit fornication.—Figuratively a "stumblingblock" is something over which one would fall or be led into sin. Balaam taught Balak how to lead the Israelites into sin. Balaam had not been allowed to curse Israel as Balak requested, but later, because of his love for the "hire of wrong-doing" (2 Pet. 2: 15), he taught Balak to lead Israel into sin through fornication and the eating of meats offered to idols. (Num. 31: 16.) The meaning is that there were some in the church at Pergamum that, like Balaam, led people into idolatry and licentiousness through their teaching; that is, taught that such things were not sinful. This was a serious condition.

15 **So hast thou also some that hold the teaching of the Nicolaitans in like manner.**—See note on verse 6. Just what distinction, if any, there was between the teaching of Balaam and the Nicolaitans is not known. They were probably very similar, and some think possibly the same, or at least the same in the two particulars mentioned—fornication and idolatry.

16 **Repent therefore; or else I come to thee quickly, and I will make war against them with the sword of my mouth.**—Repentance—determination of mind—must result in a change of conduct. Two parties were involved in this threat—those guilty of the sins named and the rest of the church that tolerated them. The guilty parties would have to reform, or the rest would have to

make war against them with the sword of my mouth. 17 He that hath an ear, let him hear what the Spirit saith to the churches. To him that overcometh, to him will I give of the hidden manna, and I will give him a white stone, and upon the stone a new name written, which no one knoweth but he that receiveth it.

---

cease fellowshiping them. If the latter occurred, the guilty would still be subject to the punishment indicated. The "sword of my mouth" means that Christ would give the order for the punishment, or he would authorize it to be given. Just how this would be done is not stated, but presumably some natural means at hand would be used or allowed to do the work. It is referred to as making war because the word "sword" had been used.

17 **He that hath an ear, let him hear what the Spirit saith to the churches.**—See note on verse 7.

To him that overcometh, to him will I give of the hidden manna, and I will give him a white stone, and upon the stone a new name written, which no one knoweth but he that receiveth it.—On overcoming and the possibility of being lost finally see note on verse 11. The one who ends this life victoriously will be saved and enjoy the "hidden manna" in heaven. The reference, of course, is to the manna that fell in the wilderness (Ex. 16: 32-34), a memorial portion being put in the ark (Heb. 9: 4). Those refraining from idolatrous meats and remaining pure would be permitted to eat the manna laid up in heaven which is typically represented by the manna in the ark. Leaving off the figurative language, it means that joys in heaven will satisfy our eternal wants as bread satisfies hunger.

There has been much speculation regarding the "white stone" and the "new name"; nothing entirely satisfactory has been suggested. As in voting a white stone indicated justification, it may here be used to indicate that one who overcomes is justified and will be received into the heavenly home. The new name is equally uncertain since no one knows it. It may be in some way the means by which God will receive those who gain the victory. Since it cannot be known by others, it is useless to ask what it is. It is our business to overcome, the white stone and the new name we can leave to God to make plain in his own time.

4. LETTER TO THE CHURCH AT THYATIRA
2: 18-29

18 And to the angel of the church in Thyatira write:
These things saith the Son of God, who hath his eyes like a flame of fire, and his feet are like unto burnished brass: 19 I know thy works, and thy love and faith and ministry and [2]patience, and that thy last works are more than the first. 20 But I have *this* against thee, that thou sufferest [10]the

[10]Many authorities, some ancient, read *thy wife*.

18 **And to the angel of the church in Thyatira write: These things saith the Son of God, who hath his eyes like a flame of fire, and his feet are like unto burnished brass**:—The three cities already mentioned were near the seacoast; Thyatira was some distance inland and about midway between Pergamum and Sardis. Commercially it was noted as the place where dyes were manufactured; in the Bible it is specially known as the home of Lydia whom Paul converted at Philippi. (Acts 16: 13-15.) This church is told plainly that the letter came from the Son of God. The expression about eyes like fire and feet like burnished brass refers to the vision John saw as described in 1: 14, 15. See the notes on those verses.

19 **I know thy works, and thy love and faith and ministry and patience, and that thy last works are more than the first.** —Being the Son of God, Jesus had the authority to give commands (Matt. 28: 18-20), and the right to demand obedience. Knowing their works, both good and bad, assured them that his commands would be strictly just. The general term "works" probably includes the four items following it—love, faith, ministry, and patience; the first two internal, the last external. Love to both God and man is always manifested by obedience and service; faith means not only that they had maintained their confidence in Jesus, but that they had been faithful in his service. In ministry would include religious as well as moral duties. Patience means that they had borne every trial of their faith with fidelity to Christ and the church. The church at Ephesus had fallen from its first love; the brethren at Thyatira had increased in good deeds—the last works being more than the first. A fine compliment indeed!

20 **But I have this against thee, that thou sufferest the woman Jezebel, who calleth herself a prophetess**;—To "suffer"

woman Jezebel, who calleth herself a prophetess; and she teacheth and seduceth my [11]servants to commit fornication, and to eat things sacrificed to idols. 21 And I gave her time that she should repent; and she willeth not to

[11]Gr. *bosdservants.*

the woman Jezebel means that they permitted her teaching without proper condemnation and allowed her to continue in the fellowship of the church. The name "Jezebel" undoubtedly refers to the highly gifted but desperately wicked idolatrous wife of Ahab, king of Israel. Under her influence Ahab was led to allow the introduction of idolatry and to endorse its shameful practices. He also worshiped Baal himself and did more to provoke Jehovah to anger than all the kings before him. (1 Kings 16: 29-33.) Interpreters differ regarding the "Jezebel" in our text. Some think she was a real woman whose wicked influence was so similar to the Jezebel of old that she was called by that name rather than her own. Others think the name refers to a faction or party in the church that taught and practiced as did the real Jezebel. Since the church at Pergamum was rebuked because they had a faction that held the doctrines of Balaam (2: 14), it seems probable that the church at Thyatira had a faction that was described by the name Jezebel. Besides, in this book a woman represents a church; hence, could appropriately represent a party or faction. Claiming to be a prophetess would mean that the faction claimed to teach according to divine authority.

and she teacheth and seduceth my servants to commit fornication, and to eat things sacrificed to idols.—Whether Jezebel means a real person or represents a faction, the lesson would be the same. In imitation of the ancient Jezebel idolatry and licentiousness were taught. Since this was the teaching of Balaam, and probably the Nicolaitans as well, it may be that the person or persons condemned at Thyatira were some of the same false teachers differently described.

21 **And I gave her time that she should repent; and she willeth not to repent of her fornication.**—This may mean that warning had been given in some way that time to continue in such teaching would end unless repentance came or that God had allowed her sufficient time to repent if she would. But since she did not will to repent, then the punishment had to fall upon her.

repent of her fornication. 22 Behold, I cast her into a bed, and them that
commit adultery with her into great tribulation, except they repent of [12]her
works. 23 And I will kill her children with [13]death; and all the churches
shall know that I am he that searcheth the reins and hearts: and I will give

[12]Many ancient authorities read *their*.
[13]Or, *pestilence*. Sept., Ex. 5. 3 &c.

X

22 **Behold, I cast her into a bed, and them that commit adultery with her into great tribulation, except they repent of her works.**—This verse indicates that Jezebel was herself guilty of fornication whether it was natural or spiritual. If the name represents an element or faction in the church, it must be understood spiritually as referring to idolatry as was true of Israel anciently. (Jer. 3: 9.) The word "behold" means that all the churches were to know of her punishment just as they knew of her sins. Verse 23 shows that such punishment would clearly prove that God is able to know human hearts and justly reward for all deeds. Casting "into a bed" means affliction or punishment; no other meaning will do for the expression here. Those led into such sinful practices will have to suffer tribulation and punishment along with their false teachers. These disastrous results can be avoided only by timely repentance.

23 **And I will kill her children with death; and all the churches shall know that I am he that searcheth the reins and hearts: and I will give unto each one of you according to your works.**—"Children" here mean those influenced to practice her false doctrines—her adherents. (Compare John 8: 44; Isa. 57: 3.) By accepting and practicing her teaching they became participants with her as expressed in verse 22. To kill "with death" means thoroughly destroy, as with some kind of pestilence. Such drastic measures serve to make others fear. The design in this case was to demonstrate the infinite knowledge of God as a means of restraining evil. Reins and heart both refer to the inmost part of man's mind, and indicate that nothing, good or bad, can be hidden from God. Rewarding each according to his works is the common teaching of the whole Bible and entirely just. (Matt. 16: 27; 2 Cor. 5: 10; Rev. 20: 13.) This is another reason why sinners should repent.

24 **But to you I say, to the rest that are in Thyatira, as**

unto each one of you according to your works. 24 But to you I say, to the rest that are in Thyatira, as many as have not this teaching, who know not the deep things of Satan, as they are wont to say; I cast upon you none other burden. 25 Nevertheless that which ye have, hold fast till I come. 26 And he that overcometh, and he that keepth my works unto the end, to him

---

many as have not this teaching, who know not the deep things of Satan, as they are wont to say; I cast upon you none other burden.—Those here addressed as the "rest that are in Thyatira" mean those who had not accepted the doctrines and practices of the heretical party. They are described as those who "have not this teaching." This is very strong evidence that Jezebel was not some wicked woman, but rather some corrupt faction. Those commended here did not know or understand the deep or hidden schemes in Satan's wicked designs because they had not been led to participate in them. The expression, "as they are wont to say," may mean that those who opposed the false teaching were in the habit of referring to it as the "deep things of Satan." The false teachers themselves would hardly say that of their own teaching. In Smyrna there was a "synagogue of Satan" (verse 9); in Pergamum Satan's dwelling place (verse 13); here the depths of Satan. All this means that the wickedness in all places may be in some sense attributed to Satan. Jesus promised to put upon them no other burden than such as would naturally result from their allowing such wicked teachers to remain in fellowship, or would come from their efforts in trying to rid the congregations of the pernicious influences of erroneous teachings.

25 **Nevertheless that which ye have, hold fast till I come.**—They had received the gospel and manifested love, faith, service, and patience. All this they should diligently hold; their refusing to participate in the wicked schemes of Satan should continue. "Till" he came did not mean that they were to live till Jesus comes personally, for centuries have passed and he has not yet come. They were to remain faithful until death (Matt. 24: 13), which, so far as they were concerned, would be the same as if he had come in their lifetime.

26 **And he that overcometh, and he that keepeth my works unto the end, to him will I give authority over the nations:**—Here, as in preceding letters, the reward is promised on condi-

will I give authority over the [1]nations: 27 and he shall rule them with a rod
of [2]iron, as the vessels of the potter are broken to shivers; as I also have
received of my Father: 28 and I will give him the morning star. 29 He that

[1]Or, *Gentiles*
[2]Or, *iron; as vessels of the potter are they broken*

tion that they overcome. The one overcoming is explained by the expression, "he that keepeth my works unto the end"; or, the one faithful until his death. For this faithfulness they were to have "authority over the nations." How this is to be exercised is explained in the following expressions.

27 **and he shall rule them with a rod of iron, as the vessels of the potter are broken to shivers; as I also have received of my Father:**—Jesus rules in the absolute sense, being the author of the law; his apostles rule as ambassadors through whom the law has been delivered (2 Cor. 5: 18-20); and all faithful Christians rule in a secondary sense by being an example of the application of his law. (Rom. 5: 17.) By such faithfulness Christtians condemn the world as did Noah in building the ark (Heb. 11: 7); or like Abel, who though dead, "yet speaketh" (Heb. 11: 4). Only in this sense may faithful Christians be said to rule over the nations, This verse with slight variation is a quotation from Psalm 2: 9. Verses 6-8 show clearly that the Psalmist refers to Christ and his rule (after his resurrection) at God's right hand. (Acts 13: 33; Heb. 1: 5.) Since Christians rule in a secondary sense under Christ, they rule during the same period he does—throughout the Christian dispensation. The expression "as I also have received of my Father" means that they received their authority to rule from Christ just as he received his from the Father. Luke 22: 29 proves the former; Psalm 2: 6 proves the latter. With a "rod of iron" indicates a firm, sure, and unbending rule. The Greek word for rule means to "shepherd." Through his words and the examples of those who overcome Jesus will lead the righteous; his law against the wicked will be as inflexible as a rod of iron. It will have its effect with the same certainty that a rod of iron will break a potter's vessel.

28 **and I will give him the morning star.**—Christ is himself called the "morning star" in 22: 16. He probably means that he

Rev 22:16

hath an ear, let him hear what the Spirit saith to the churches.

---

will give himself to those who overcome; that is, to be in fellowship with him in his ruling. The expression is a further development of the thought in the two preceding verses.

29 **He that hath an ear, let him hear what the Spirit saith to the churches.**—See notes on verse 7.

Bob Chewell

5. LETTER TO THE CHURCH IN SARDIS
3: 1-6

1 And to the angel of the church in Sardis write:

These things saith he that hath the seven Spirits of God, and the seven stars: I know thy works, that thou hast a name that thou livest, and thou art

---

1 **And to the angel of the church in Sardis write: These things saith he that hath the seven Spirits of God, and the seven stars:**—Sardis was the capital of Lydia, a province of Asia Minor, and once the home of Croesus who was celebrated for his fabulous wealth. It was situated inland a considerable distance northeast of Ephesus. Though lacking much of its ancient importance as a commercial city, it must have been an important place when the church was planted there. This letter opens with the usual address to the "angel of the church," and a repetition of two characteristics of Christ which John had already learned about. (1: 4, 16.) In 1: 4 he was told that the revelation was to come from the seven Spirits; here Jesus is represented as having the seven Spirits. This is a particularly proper way to present Christ; for the word seven indicates *fullness* and he is said to possess the Spirit without measure. (John 3: 34.) Since Christ promised to send the Spirit (John 15: 26), and the Spirit was to reveal the things of Christ, there was double assurance here that the revelation to this church would be correct. Having the seven stars in his hand means that the angels of the churches were under his authority. See notes on 1: 20.

I know thy works, that thou hast a name that thou livest, and thou art dead.—To have a name to live means that they were nominal Christians—professed to be living the Christian life, but were in fact spiritually dead. A similar expression is used by Paul in 1 Tim. 5: 6. In other words, it may be said that their profes-

Lampstands -> Churches
Candlestick - angels
Stars -

dead. 2 Be thou watchful, and establish the things that remain, which were
ready to die: for I have [3]found no works of thine perfected before my God.
3 Remember therefore how thou hast received and didst hear; and keep *it,*

[3]Many ancient authorities read *not found thy works.*

sion of righteous living was a mere name. This general condemnation must not be understood to apply to all, for a definite exception is made in verse 4 of a "few" who had not defiled their garments.

2 **Be thou watchful, and establish the things that remain, which were ready to die:**—A similar exhortation is given by Paul in Eph. 5: 14. It means that, like a soldier on guard, they should arouse themselves to a faithful performance of the Lord's work. The things that remain probably include some who had not completely lost their love for the Lord, and the various graces and good works that needed to be strengthened and increased. This should be done regardless of how few remain who may be worthy of the name Christian in any sense. Things ready to die mean those that are about to cease to exist. If possible, all Christians should be saved, and all good works increased to the fullest limit.

for I have found no works of thine perfected before my God.—That is, their works had not been made complete, or carried out fully, in the divine estimate of things. "Before my God" indicates that both God and Christ considered their works incomplete. They were self-satisfied, but God was displeased. This is the sad condition with multitudes of churches and individual Christians, who deserve the same rebuke here given those of Sardis.

3 **Remember therefore how thou hast received and didst hear; and keep it, and repent.**—Naturally this exhortation implies that they should remember the things they had heard and received, but the specific thing commanded is that they should recall "how" they had heard and received. This could include the miraculous proof which may have been present when the church was established, a remarkable evidence of the truth of the gospel, but may have reference to the sincerity and enthusiasm with which they accepted the gospel. If so, then, like the church at Ephesus, they had fallen from their first love. Hence, after urging them to keep what they had received at the first, he tells them to repent—that is,

and repent. If therefore thou shalt not watch, I will come as a thief, and
thou shalt not know what hour I will come upon thee. 4 But thou hast a
few names in Sardis that did not defile their garments: and they shall walk
with me in white; for they are worthy. 5 He that overcometh shall thus be

---

they should decide to turn back to their former zeal for the church. This church is not charged with tolerating any wicked doctrines, as in the cases of Ephesus and Thyatira, but rather with slowly dying from loss of interest in what was accepted.

If therefore thou shalt not watch, I will come as a thief, and thou shalt not know what hour I will come upon thee.—The coming of the Lord sometimes means his personal coming at the end of the world (1 Thess. 5: 2; 2 Pet. 3: 10); but here it evidently has the same meaning as in 2: 5, 16, in this book, a sudden judgment sent upon them for their sins. That is clearly the import of the threats made against these churches. The conditional phrase, "If therefore thou shalt not watch," implies that they might not do it and would in that case suffer. This, in principle, shows that Christians may be found unfaithful when the Lord comes at the judgment; hence, the possibility of such being finally lost. This verse is positive proof that no one knows the exact time that the Lord will come, either in providence through punishments or in person at last.

4 **But thou hast a few names in Sardis that did not defile their garments: and they shall walk with me in white; for they are worthy.**—A "few names" means that there were a few members of the church who had not followed the majority off into carelessness and sin, figuratively represented as not soiling their garments. When they obeyed the gospel they were considered as having made their robes white in the blood of the Lamb (7: 14)—that is, they had been purified from sin and made righteous. They had not allowed their lives to be contaminated with evil like soiling a white garment with dirt. To walk with Jesus, the reward offered them, means that they were to be saved. This is clearly implied in the expression "in white." The reason assigned is that such persons are worthy; they have the kind of character which God recognizes as worthy of salvation.

5 **He that overcometh shall thus be arrayed in white gar-**

arrayed in white garments; and I will in no wise blot his name out of the book of life, and I will confess his name before my Father, and before his angels. 6 He that hath an ear, let him hear what the Spirit saith to the churches.

---

ments;—Their being "arrayed in white garments"—saved—is here plainly made to depend upon their overcoming. Unless they might fail to overcome, there would be no point in expressing the condition. Each affirmative proposition necessarily has a corresponding negative one, either expressed or implied. The negative one here is that those who do not overcome will not be arrayed in the white garments. This unquestionably means that such will be lost.

and I will in no wise blot his name out of the book of life, and I will confess his name before my Father, and before his angels.—Here again the promise implies that unless one overcomes his name will be blotted out and his name will not be confessed before the Father. Language could not more definitely indicate the possibility that Christians may be lost. Any other view renders the language not only misleading, but actually false. An implied argument is just as good as a direct statement.

6 **He that hath an ear, let him hear what the Spirit saith to the churches.**—See notes on 1: 7.

6. LETTER TO THE CHURCH IN PHILADELPHIA 3: 7-13

7 And to the angel of the church in Philadelphia write:
These things saith he that is holy, he that is true, he that hath the key of

---

7 **And to the angel of the church in Philadelphia write:**—See notes on 1: 20. Philadelphia was located almost directly on a line between Sardis and Laodicea. In the second century after Christ it came under Roman rule. It is said to have remained a Christian city longer than any of the seven mentioned. It still exists, but with a Turkish name.

These things saith he that is holy, he that is true,—The word "holy" is a designation for both God and Christ; here, of course, it refers to the latter. He is also true; true in himself and in all his words. Such characteristics were a guarantee that all he

David, he that openeth and none shall shut, and that shutteth and none openeth: 8 I know thy works (behold, I have [4]set before thee a door opened, which none can shut), that thou hast a little power, and didst keep my word,

[4]Gr. *given.*

said to them would be the exact truth, the very things upon which they could depend implicitly. As in all the other letters, this was a very appropriate address.

he that hath the key of David, he that openeth and none shall shut, and that shutteth and none openeth:—That Christ had to be David's son is certain from both Old and New Testament teaching. (Isa. 9: 7; Luke 1: 30-33; Matt. 22: 41-45.) Figuratively the word "key" means authority—the right to open and close doors; or, expressed differently, it means the authority to lay down conditions of acceptance or rejection. This authority came to Christ when he, as David's son, began his reign upon David's throne—that is, his authority as a ruling king commenced at that time. This language is borrowed from Isa. 22: 22. The prophet's words primarily referred to Eliakim who executed the king's authority. Spiritually they apply to Christ upon the throne of David because he was David's son. The authority here expressed truly belongs to Christ and has been declared to us by his apostles. (John 20: 22, 23.) The point in the expression being considered is that Christ was said to have the key of David when this letter was written. This settles the matter that he was then upon David's throne. If so, then he is now. The theory that he must come in the future to begin his reign upon David's throne is of necessity false. In addition to his righteousness he, as their ruling king, had authority to address them. Without this, the letter would lose its power as a part of the divine revelation, and could be ignored as a writing of authority.

8 **I know thy works (behold, I have set before thee a door opened, which none can shut), that thou hast a little power, and didst keep my word, and didst not deny my name.**—Here as in the case of the other churches, they are reminded that the Lord knew their works—not only their efforts, but the difficulties under which they labored. The words "thou hast a little power" may mean that the Lord noted their weakness, poverty, and few members. But in spite of such drawbacks they are complimented

and didst not deny my name. 9 Behold, I give of the synagogue of Satan, of them that say they are Jews, and they are not, but do lie; behold, I will make them to come and [5]worship before thy feet, and to know that I have

[5]The Greek word denotes an act of reverence, whether paid to a creature, or to the Creator.

as resisting temptations to the extent that they had kept God's word and had not denied their faith in Christ. For that reason God had opened to them doors of opportunities for greater service. Just what opportunities those open doors brought to them is not stated. We may always expect that duties faithfully performed will lead to chances for doing greater things.

9 **Behold, I give of the synagogue of Satan, of them that say they are Jews, and they are not, but do lie; behold, I will make them to come and worship before thy feet, and to know that I have loved thee.**—The first part of this verse is an incomplete sentence, but the second part begins with the same word and completes the thought. The church was encountering certain opposers who claimed to be Jews, or the true people of God, but were, in fact, a "synagogue of Satan"; hence, not being God's people, their claims were false. The word worship ordinarily means rendering homage; but here it may signify nothing more than that their bitter enemies would be led in some providential way to admit that God loved that church and gave it his blessings. Just how this would be done is not stated. In a broader sense we may understand that the lesson here taught will be applicable to all who oppose the truth. At the judgment, if not before, all enemies of the gospel will be forced to concede that the gospel is true and the church is a divine institution.

10 **Because thou didst keep the word of my patience, I also will keep thee from the hour of trial,**—The conditional nature of God's blessings is here definitely expressed. Because they kept God's word, he would protect them in the time of trial. Keeping God's word means that they obeyed his commands. "The word of my patience" has direct reference to the fact that, in accordance with God's word, they had patiently endured in spite of all kinds of opposition. His promise to keep them in the hour of trial did not mean that they would be unconditionally protected, or that they

loved thee. 10 Because thou didst keep the word of my [6]patience, I also will keep thee from the hour of [7]trial, that *hour* which is to come upon the whole [8]world, to [9]try them that dwell upon the earth. 11 I come quickly: hold fast that which thou hast, that no one take thy crown. 12 He that overcometh, I will make him a pillar in the [10]temple of my God, and he shall go out

[6]Or, *stedfastness*
[7]Or, *temptation*
[8]Gr. *inhabited earth.*
[9]Or, *tempt*
[10]Or, *sanctuary*

would be allowed to escape all trials. It rather means that through his favors and their fidelity they would be able to meet successfully all trials. That is all any Christian should expect or even want.

that hour which is to come upon the whole world, to try them that dwell upon the earth.—The "whole world" may here refer to the Roman Empire or the then inhabited earth. The expression may be used in a free sense to indicate some widespread calamity that would affect the country of which Philadelphia was a part. The particular trial is not named and we have no means of knowing what it was. In principle the same promise would fit the judgment as the great trial for the whole human race. God will keep those who obey his commands. All trials test the genuineness of those who profess to be followers of Christ.

11 **I come quickly: hold fast that which thou hast, that no one take thy crown.**—If the trial referred to meant some calamity that was to befall Asia Minor the time of it may have been near when John wrote; or the expression may indicate the suddenness with which the calamity would come. God's allowing punishment to befall is represented as the Lord coming indirectly; that is, he permits it to happen. Being urged to hold what they had means that they were not to lose their faith, but persist in obedience. Thus they would prevent anything from leading them to lose their crown. The word "crown" here means a token or garland of victory—a reward to those who win. The language implies the possibility of losing it.

12 **He that overcometh, I will make him a pillar in the temple of my God, and he shall go out thence no more:**—The word temple sometimes refers to the church (1 Cor. 3: 16) and sometimes to heaven (Rev. 7: 15). The reference here seems to be to heaven, for the overcomer is to "go out thence no more."

thence no more: and I will write upon him the name of my God, and the name of the city of my God, the new Jerusalem, which cometh down out of heaven from my God, and mine own new name. 13 He that hath an ear, let him hear what the Spirit saith to the churches.

The word pillar carries the idea of something permanent—a fixture—a thing that remains as long as the temple lasts. Leaving off the figurative language, the thought is that one who finally overcomes will be in no danger of being rejected; the one who fails to overcome will be in such danger.

and I will write upon him the name of my God, and the name of the city of my God, the new Jerusalem, which cometh down out of heaven from my God, and mine own new name.—As the name of conspicuous persons might be written on pillars of temples, so the name of God is represented as being written on one who overcomes. Again, omitting figures of speech, it means that the overcomer would be recognized as one of God's redeemed. The name of the city of God would be written upon him —that is, he would be known as one belonging to the city of God. The "new name" referring to Christ was also to be written upon him. This would at least indicate that he was entitled to all that was secured by the name of Christ. In 21: 2 the final state is said to be the "new Jerusalem, coming down out of heaven." If the word temple should be understood as referring to the church, then coming down out of heaven would mean that it originated from heaven, and that faithful members would remain in God's favor. Losing a place in God's temple, with all that means, would result from a failure to overcome. Another proof of the possibility of Christians being lost through disobedience.

13 **He that hath an ear, let him hear what the Spirit saith to the churches.**—See notes on 2: 7.

7. LETTER TO THE CHURCH IN LAODICEA
3: 14-22

14 And to the angel of the church in Laodicea write:

These things saith the Amen, the faithful and true witness, the beginning of the creation of God: 15 I know thy works, that thou art neither cold nor

---

14 **And to the angel of the church in Laodicea write:**—See

notes on 2: 1. Laodicea was located east of Ephesus, near Colosse.

These things saith the Amen, the faithful and true witness, the beginning of the creation of God:—These words refer to Christ. See notes on 1: 5. Since the church at Laodicea was "lukewarm," it was appropriate for Christ to refer to himself as "the faithful and true witness." This thought is also expressed in the one word "Amen." In Col. 1: 16 Christ is referred to as being in the creation with the Father. Hence, it would not be out of place to say that he was the beginner or author of creation. Saying that he was the "beginning of the creation of God" doubtless was intended to impress the Laodiceans with the thought that he had all divine authority to command; hence, obedience was inperatively necessary.

15 **I know thy works, that thou art neither cold nor hot: I would thou wert cold or hot.**—As was said to the other churches, the Laodiceans were told that Christ knew their works. For the church at Philadelphia the Lord had only praise; for the Laodiceans, only censure. In describing their spiritual condition he uses three terms—cold, hot, and lukewarm. He declares that they were neither cold nor hot, and expressed the wish that they were one or the other. The comparison here is based upon water at different degrees of temperature. Either hot or cold, it is palatable; being neither—lukewarm—it is nauseating. So the condition of the Laodiceans spiritually was deeply offensive to God. To be hot means that they should have been fervent in their zeal in God's service. It is easy to understand how that would be better and more pleasing to God than their utter indifference, but just why God would prefer their being cold is not so easily seen; commentators are not agreed on this point, nor exactly on what class is referred to as being in the cold state. Since "cold" and "lukewarm" have about the same significance when used to describe members of the church without zeal for God, it is concluded by some that "cold" refers to those who have made no profession of serving God—the unsaved. But why should one unsaved be preferred to one whose professed Christianity lacks piety, earnestness, and zeal? In short, one who is indifferent, self-satisfied, and heartless? It could not be because it would be finally any better for the individ-

hot: I would thou wert cold or hot. 16 So because thou art lukewarm, and
neither hot nor cold, I will spew thee out of my mouth. 17 Because thou
sayest, I am rich, and have gotten riches, and have need of nothing; and
knowest not that thou art the wretched one and miserable and poor and blind

---

ual, for both characters will be lost. The unsaved man might be more easily aroused to realize this lost condition than the self-satisfied Christian could be aroused from his sleep, because of being deceived in thinking himself safe. A more probable reason, however seems to be that the lukewarm Christian will do the church more harm than the unsaved sinner. Inconsistent and hypocritical members of the church exercise a more deadly influence against the truth, and keep more people from obeying the gospel than outright sinners. This is often made evident by those who justify their refusal to enter the church on the ground that they are "better than some in the church."

16 **So because thou art lukewarm, and neither hot nor cold, I will spew thee out of my mouth.**—This expression, when changed into literal language, means that God will reject such professed Christians. This is plain proof that they are actually no better than those who never entered the church; and, as already suggested, their position renders them more detrimental to it.

17 **Because thou sayest, I am rich, and have gotten riches, and have need of nothing;**—These words seem to assign a reason why they were lukewarm, and also why Christ urged them to reform. "Riches" may refer to material or spiritual things, or to both. Those rich in material goods usually are unduly self-confident; those who are cold and unconcerned in spiritual things consider that they have enough and do not need anything. Both are self-deceived, as the next expression clearly shows.

and knowest not that thou art the wretched one and miserable and poor and blind and naked:—The saddest thing about the lukewarm Christian is that he does not realize his true condition and the fatal results that will finally come to him. If he did, he would not remain lukewarm. He thinks himself in need of nothing when, in fact, he is poor, blind, naked, wretched, and miserable. He is in a wretched and pitiable condition, but wholly unconscious of the fact.

and naked: 18 I counsel thee to buy of me gold refined by fire, that thou mayest become rich; and white garments, that thou mayest clothe thyself, and *that* the shame of thy nakedness be not made manifest; and eyesalve to anoint thine eyes, that thou mayest see. 19 As many as I love, I reprove and chasten: be zealous therefore, and repent. 20 Behold, I stand at the door and knock: if any man hear my voice and open the door, I will come in to him,

---

18 **I counsel thee to buy of me gold refined by fire, that thou mayest become rich; and white garments, that thou mayest clothe thyself, and that the shame of thy nakedness be not made manifest; and eyesalve to anoint thine eyes, that thou mayest see.**—The Lord's counsel here is beautifully impressive. Material things of much value are used to express spiritual lessons. The worth of true Christianity could not be better expressed than by refined gold. White garments are said to be the righteous acts of the saints. (19: 8.) We clothe the body for both protection and decency. Righteousness protects the soul against sin and prevents the shameful inconsistency of professing one thing and practicing something else. Eyesalve would suggest that they carefully consider God's word, applying its teaching to themselves, till they could fully see their pitiable and sinful condition. This would bring them back to a full realization of their true state and bring about a happy reformation.

19 **As many as I love, I reprove and chasten: be zealous therefore, and repent.**—Rebuke and chastening are evidences of genuine love, when they are properly given. Of course, divine perfection would prevent the Lord's giving them improperly. We are told that "whom the Lord loveth he chasteneth," and that too, "for our profit, that we may be partakers of his holiness." (Heb. 12: 6, 10.) For that reason he commanded them to be zealous and repent, and the command comes down to all similar characters now. Repentance leads to a change of conduct; the lukewarm person becomes zealous.

20 **Behold, I stand at the door and knock: if any man hear my voice and open the door, I will come in to him, and will sup with him, and he with me.**—This language is a touching appeal to impress the necessity of heeding the exhortation in the two preceding verses. It is in striking contrast with the severe rebuke for their coldhearted indifference to the Lord's service. The

and will sup with him, and he with me. 21 He that overcometh, I will give to him to sit down with me in my throne, as I also overcame, and sat down

lessons taught by the imagery are too evident to be misunderstood. One knocking at a door for admittance indicates the Lord's appeal to them to give him and his service a place in their hearts. In this he takes the lead. Opening the door or refusing to do so brings out man's ability and the conditional nature of acceptance with God. Perhaps the custom then was to speak as well as knock upon the door. Yielding to the demand of the voice and opening the door shows man's willingness to have the Lord for a divine guest. Association at a meal has always indicated friendship. Lukewarm saints renew their spiritual strength when they invite the Lord to become their guest. Eliminating all figures of speech the thought is, by following the Lord's teaching, we become zealous Christians, which is the lesson of this text.

21 **He that overcometh, I will give to him to sit down with me in my throne, as I also overcame, and sat down with my Father in his throne.**—As a reward for overcoming—completing the work which the Father gave him to do—Jesus was granted the honor of sitting at God's right hand as head of the church, Priest and King. (Eph. 1: 19-23; Heb. 8: 1; John 18: 36; Phil. 2: 7-11.) The word "throne" indicates authority, dominion, and power. He was given this position because he overcame. Sitting with God upon his throne means that the Father gave him the right to rule as king. In like manner those who overcame by doing Christ's commands were to be given authority to rule with him. This faithful Christians do by teaching and practicing his laws by which men are to be governed spiritually. Only in this way can the Lord reign over men. His law has been revealed to the world through the apostles and perpetuated by the teaching and lives of his disciples. He has made no other provision for its dissemination. All faithful Christians, therefore, share with him in ruling through his truth—here called sitting "down with me in my throne." This is the same truth, from a different viewpoint, as is expressed when Christ's disciples are called "the salt of the earth." (Matt. 5: 13.) As Christians are agents through whom men are saved (1 Tim. 4: 16), so they are agents through whom Christ

with my Father in his throne. 22 He that hath an ear, let him hear what the Spirit saith to the churches.

reigns. Hence, they sit with him in his throne—that is, rule with him. It is called the Father's throne because he gave it to Christ; it is Christ's because he, as a descendant of David, sits upon it; it is David's (spiritually speaking) because the Savior had to be of his family—the "throne of his father David" being the only one promised him. (Luke 1: 32.) In like manner the throne in the final state is that "of God and of the Lamb" (Rev. 22: 1), yet the rule is then turned back to the Father (1 Cor. 15: 24-28).

22 **He that hath an ear, let him hear what the Spirit saith to the churches.**—See notes on 2:7.

ADDITIONAL OBSERVATIONS

1. The language of these letters clearly indicates the individual and personal responsibility of man to God. Each congregation received its praise or rebuke, or both just as its own case required. Even the distinct classes in each congregation were pointed out and held to account for their peculiar sins. The principles that "God is no respecter of persons" (Acts 10: 34), and that "each one of us shall give account of himself to God" (Rom. 14: 12), are verified in these letters in a most unmistakable manner.

2. Each letter closes with one or more promises on the condition that the individual "overcome." This logically implies that these rewards would be lost, if one failed to overcome. This also implies individual ability either to fail or to overcome. The exhortation would be without meaning, if this were not true. The sum of all the rewards mentioned to these churches shows how much one may lose by disobedience. They include so much that no one can be saved who loses them. This will be amply clear, if all of them are written together. In these conditional promises we have the strongest possible argument that Christians may be finally lost; or, that the doctrine, "Once in grace, always in grace," is not true.

3. In order that the full force of this argument on the possibility of apostasy may appear, the rewards that may be lost by failing to overcome are listed here. They are as follows:

(1) Privilege to "eat of the tree of life, which is in the Paradise of God." (2: 7.)

(2) To receive a "crown of life" and not be "hurt of the second death." (2: 10, 11.)

(3) To receive the "hidden manna," "white stone," and "new name." (2: 17.)

(4) To receive authority to rule the nations. (2: 26, 27.)

(5) To be "arrayed in white garments," not have name blotted "out of the book of life," and be confessed before God and angels. (3: 5.)

(6) To be made a "pillar in the temple of my God" and have the names of God and Christ written upon him. (3: 12.)

(7) To be allowed to sit with Christ in his throne. (3: 21.)

As all these may be lost, how much more would one have to lose to be eternally lost? The answer is, nothing.

PART SECOND

PREPARATORY VISIONS
4: 1 to 5: 14

SECTION ONE

GOD SEEN IN HEAVEN
4: 1-11

1. THE APPEARANCE OF GOD UPON HIS THRONE
4: 1-3

1 After these things I saw, and behold, a door opened in heaven, and the first voice that I heard, *a voice* as of a trumpet speaking with me, one saying, Come up hither, and I will show thee the things which must [1]come to

[1]Or, *come to pass. After these things straightway &c.*

---

1 **After these things I saw, and behold, a door opened in heaven,**—"After these things" means after the things mentioned in the preceding chapters—the initial vision and the reception of seven letters. The words "I saw, and behold" introduce a new vision that was opening to John, which is fully described in the two chapters of this part of the book. The brief vision of 1: 10-19 represents Christ as standing by John; in this the scene is transferred to heaven and John is permitted to view it through the door opened for that purpose. This is similar to the words of Ezekiel, "The heavens were opened, and I saw visions of God." (Ezek. 1: 1.) Just how John was enabled to see things in heaven is not explained, but we know it was by the exercise of miraculous power in some way.

and the first voice that I heard, a voice as of a trumpet speaking with me, one saying, Come up hither, and I will show thee the things which must come to pass hereafter.—Some commentators understand that the "first voice that I heard" refers to the same voice mentioned in 1: 10 that spake to John first. Others think it means that the first sound or speaking that he heard was a voice saying, "Come up hither." The latter seems the more natural view. The essential point, however, is what the voice said. The promise to show what "must come to pass here-

pass hereafter. 2 Straightway I was in the Spirit: and behold, there was a throne set in heaven, and one sitting upon the throne; 3 and he that sat *was* to look upon like a jasper stone and a sardius: and *there was* a rainbow

after" is unmistakable proof that the things to be shown in the visions to follow would be events that would take place after the time the voice was speaking them. No other meaning for these words is possible. Some scholars join the word "hereafter" with the next verse, the meaning, as they view it, being that after the voice said "Come up hither" he was straightway in the Spirit. This would not change the meaning of verse 1; for things which "must come to pass" refer to things in the future.

2 **Straightway I was in the Spirit: and behold, there was a throne set in heaven, and one sitting upon the throne;**—Seeing the open door in heaven and hearing the voice, mentioned in verse 1, implies some degree of spiritual exaltation for John, but being "in the Spirit," as expressed here, probably means that he was given such measure of spiritual enduement that he could fully see and describe the visions that passed before him. This is clear from the command to come up hither and he would be shown certain things that must come to pass. He was so deeply absorbed that the things before his mind appeared as if material objects. Such miraculous experiences are inexplicable to man; they are accepted as true by faith. Heaven is represented as a great room into which John looked through the open door. He saw a throne upon which a glorious being was sitting. Though not named, the description unquestionably refers to God.

3 **and he that sat was to look upon like a jasper stone and a sardius: and there was a rainbow round about the throne, like an emerald to look upon.**—It is worthy of note that no personal description of God is attempted here or elsewhere by divine writers. No suggestion is given that might lead to images or idolatrous practices. The stones mentioned and the rainbow that circled about the throne were doubtless meant to show the divine majesty and royalty of God as the supreme Ruler of the universe. From such a description no one could make an image, yet the glorious splendor of God in heaven could be presented most impressively. Speculating as to what is signified by the stones mentioned is probably time wasted. The entire scene presents the indescriba-

ble majesty of God; nothing more was necessary in showing his position and power.

2. THOSE ABOUT THE THRONE DESCRIBED
4: 4-8a

round about the throne, like an emerald to look upon. 4 And round about the throne *were* four and twenty thrones: and upon the thrones *I saw* four and twenty elders sitting, arrayed in white garments; and on their heads crowns

---

4 **And round about the throne were four and twenty thrones: and upon the thrones I saw four and twenty elders sitting, arrayed in white garments; and on their heads crowns of gold.**—The visions of this section (chapters 4 and 5) are evidently intended to represent the authority and power of God; his authority to determine the destiny of all classes of beings and his power to execute his decrees. Hence, the general setting is that of a kingdom—the exercise of royal power and its consequential glory and praise. God sitting upon his throne is represented as being surrounded by twenty-four elders sitting upon thrones. These, though inferior to God, are clearly presented as ruling in some secondary sense, for they have crowns of gold on their heads. The essential and most important lesson here, doubtless, is that all intelligent creatures are required to worship and serve Jehovah. Commentators have disagreed much as to why they were called "elders" and why the number twenty-four. It should be remembered that heavenly things can only be described understandingly through something earthly. The term "elders" represents a leading class in both Jewish and Christian systems and, therefore, is an appropriate word to describe those who exercise a secondary rule under God's authority. The number twelve probably indicates completeness, and double that number may be used to emphasize that idea. Some think the number was suggested by the twelve patriarchs of the old covenant and the twelve apostles in the new. If they only describe a class of purely angelic beings, and have no typical significance at all, it shows that all creatures of that class worship God. If all heavenly beings worship God, then all human beings should do so. This sustains the leading purpose of the vision. Clothed in white robes indicates purity and shows their worthiness to sit in positions of secondary authority.

of gold. 5 And out of the throne proceed lightnings and voices and thunders. And *there were* seven lamps of fire burning before the throne, which are the seven Spirits of God; 6 and before the throne, as it were a [2]sea of glass like unto crystal; and in the midst [3]of the throne, and round about the throne,

[2]Or, *glassy sea*
[3]Or, *before* See ch. 7. 17; comp. 5. 6.

5 **And out of the throne proceed lightnings and voices and thunders.**—These awe-inspiring sounds which John heard were, doubtless, intended to indicate the majesty and power of God. Proceeding from the throne would show that whatever they represented was to come from God's power. It is almost the same description that Moses gave as literally occurring at Mount Sinai (Ex. 19: 16) when God spake directly to the people, giving commands and prohibitions. This shows God's power to bless or punish according to his promises. As the display of power at Mount Sinai warned the people to hear and give heed to what was to be spoken, so this display of the same powers in the vision warned John, and through him all others, to give heed to the things about to begin to be revealed. It was a divine assurance that the things to be revealed to John would surely come to pass.

And there were seven lamps of fire burning before the throne, which are the seven Spirits of God;—Seven lamps burning show that the scene was perfectly and continuously illuminated. John himself says that these lamps are "the seven Spirits of God." This is final as to what they mean in this verse. On the expression "seven Spirits" see notes on 1: 4, where it is argued that the Holy Spirit is meant. It indicates that the Holy Spirit would make a complete and accurate revelation to John of all the things to come to pass just as he had made a correct revelation in things contained in other scripture.

6 **and before the throne, as it were a sea of glass like unto crystal;**—To John there appeared spreading out before the throne a sea smooth and clear as ice or crystal. It is useless to spend time speculating as to what this sea symbolizes; it might be only a part of the heavenly vision with no special significance. Still it will do no harm to mention two facts, true in themselves, that may be involved in the language: (1) The broad expanse may suggest the world-wide extent to which God's rule can go. (2) The calm-

four living creatures full of eyes before and behind. 7 And the first creature

ness and smoothness of a glassy sea may indicate the peace of those who are pure worshipers of God in his kingdom. This would be in contrast with the raging and turbulent sea that symbolizes the upheavals in sinful nations.

and in the midst of the throne, and round about the throne, four living creatures full of eyes before and behind.—Commentators are agreed that the word "beast," found in the King James Version of this verse, is an indefensible translation. It is a different Greek word from that correctly translated "beast" in 13: 1, 11. "Living creatures" is broad enough in meaning to include all creatures having life, but here the expression is applied to the four described in the next verse. What these four creatures represent is a question answered in a variety of ways by scholars. The most plausible explanation is based upon information furnished by the prophets Ezekiel and Isaiah. In his first chapter Ezekiel describes "visions of God" which he saw by the river Chebar in the land of the Chaldeans. These visions are so similar to what John saw that either may be used in explanation of the other. Ezekiel also saw "four living creatures," but his description of them varies some from that of John. Seeing in the visions some things that did not appear to John does not change the fact that he was viewing God surrounded by heavenly attendants. In his tenth chapter Ezekiel describes another vision and says, "This is the living creature that I saw by the river Chebar." (Verse 15.) Mentioning the faces which he saw he said, "They were the faces which I saw by the river Chebar." (Verse 22.) Referring to the creature again (verse 20) he said, "And I knew that they were cherubim." In Gen. 3: 24 we learn that cherubim guarded the approach to the tree of life, and in Ex. 25: 18 that two cherubim made of gold were placed upon the mercy seat in the tabernacle. Since those John saw were living creatures, not a gold image, the cherubim must refer to some kind of heavenly beings that continually wait upon and worship God. An understanding of their nature, of course, is impossible. In Isa. 6: 1-4 the prophet gives a similar vision of the "Lord sitting upon a throne" and above him *seraphim.* This word means "fiery ones," and probably indicates a

was like a lion, and the second creature like a calf, and the third creature
had a face as of a man, and the fourth creature *was* like a flying eagle. 8
And the four living creatures, having each one of them six wings, are full of
eyes round about and within: and they have no rest day and night, saying,

---

bright and glorious appearance on those about God's throne. The sum of the matter seems to be that the creatures John saw were heavenly beings who are continually about God's throne.

In the midst of the throne and round about the throne is supposed to mean that one stood on each of the four sides of the throne. "Full of eyes before and behind" probably means their ability to see in all directions or comprehend all God's glory and be ready to give proper adoration.

7 **And the first creature was like a lion, and the second creature like a calf, and the third creature had a face as of a man, and the fourth creature was like a flying eagle.**—The living creatures that Ezekiel saw (1: 6, 10) appeared to have four faces each; those John saw appeared with one face each. But the faces of a lion, ox, man, and eagle are mentioned by both. These faces represent four classes of created life—man, wild animals, tame animals, and birds. This is strictly a vision of what John saw in heaven about God's throne, but doubtless was intended to show that all classes of God's creatures must render proper honor to him as creator. It may also imply that all God's creatures must share properly in whatever punishments that may be inflicted against evil.

8 **And the four living creatures, having each one of them six wings, are full of eyes round about and within:**—Full of eyes is repeated here from verse 6. See note there. Wings naturally indicate the swiftness of movement, and probably show the readiness and speed with which they serve God.

3. THE HEAVENLY WORSHIP DESCRIBED
4: 8b-11

Holy, holy, holy, *is* the Lord God, the Almighty, who was and who is and
[4]who is to come.
9 And when the living creatures shall give glory and honor and thanks to

[4]Or, *who cometh*

8b **and they have no rest day and night, saying, Holy, holy,**

him that sitteth on the throne, to him that liveth [5]for ever and ever, 10 the four and twenty elders shall fall down before him that sitteth on the throne, and shall worship him that liveth [5]for ever and ever, and shall cast their crowns before the throne, saying,

[5]Gr. *unto the ages of the ages.*

holy, is the Lord God, the Almighty, who was and who is and who is to come.—Already these creatures have been described as being "full of eyes"; here they are said to be sleepless, having no rest day or night. Their praise and worship of God goes on unceasingly. The thrice used word *holy* in their song of praise indicates perfect sacredness of God as a supreme and faultless Being to be worshiped by all intelligent creatures. The fact that these creatures spake their praise of God shows they were intelligent beings, not animals, though three of them appeared to have faces of animals. Compare the note on verse 7. Being called the "Almighty" shows that God has abundant power to bring to pass all the future events that were to be revealed to John. On the expression who was, is, and is to come, see the note on 1 : 4. Past, present, and future indicate the everlasting or unending existence of God. This shows that, however long he might be in bringing to pass the things to be revealed to John, his words would be verified, for neither his existence nor power could cease.

9 **And when the living creatures shall give glory and honor and thanks to him that sitteth on the throne, to him that liveth for ever and ever,**—Since verse 8 shows that the living creatures give glory to God continually, the expression "when" they shall give glory must mean they repeated their praises again and again. God is so perfect in being and acts that the heavenly intelligences were continually repeating their thanksgiving because of his glory—ascribing to him all honor. "Liveth for ever and ever" is an explanation of what is meant by "who was and who is and who is to come."

10 **the four and twenty elders shall fall down before him that sitteth on the throne, and shall worship him that liveth for ever and ever, and shall cast their crowns before the throne,**—Whatever caused the living creatures to give glory and honor to God also caused the twenty-four elders to fall before him and do the same. The elders wearing crowns show that in some

11 Worthy art thou, our Lord and our God, to receive the glory and the honor and the power: for thou didst create all things, and because of thy will they were, and were created.

sense they were rulers. Casting their crowns before God evidently indicates that they recognized that all their success came from God, and that their garlands of victory were as nothing in comparison with worshiping God. John's seeing them cast their crowns down most impressively shows that fact.

saying, 11 **Worthy art thou, our Lord and our God, to receive the glory and the honor and the power: for thou didst create all things, and because of thy will they were, and were created.**—This song of praise is practically the same as that of the living creatures, adding the word "power" and declaring God to be the Creator of all things. The power indicates that he has strength to do all he has promised, and being Creator he has the right to do as his infinite wisdom and justice may direct. Even if the living creatures and elders do not represent anything on earth, two important facts are apparent: (1) The vision shows that all heavenly intelligences render strict obedience to God. This implies that all responsible human beings on earth should obey him. (2) The display in the vision of God's power, majesty, and eternal existence proves that he will bring to pass the things which he revealed to John in the following visions. These are the essential lessons in the visions of this section.

SECTION TWO

VISION OF THE SEALED BOOK
5: 1-14

1. THE LAMB WORTHY TO OPEN THE BOOK
5: 1-7

1 And I saw [6]in the right hand of him that sat on the throne a book

[6]Gr. *on*.

1 **And I saw in the right hand of him that sat on the throne a book written within and on the back, close sealed with seven seals.**—As the vision of chapter 4 shows God's power as Creator to bring to pass the things to be revealed, so the vision of chapter 5 shows Christ's power as Redeemer to reveal what things would come to pass. What John saw was God sitting upon the throne with a book in or lying upon his right hand. This changed view was for the purpose of giving proper praise to Christ as the only one able to make the revelation. This was in harmony with the statement already made. (See 1: 1.) This book was not printed as ours are today, for there were no such books then, but it was a manuscript rolled as a scroll. (Jer. 36: 2; Heb. 10: 7.) "Written within and on the back" probably means that it was written on both sides. "Close sealed" means that the edge of the roll was fastened down with a seal. Being rolled together and sealed indicates that the contents writen could not be known till the seals were broken. Since the seals were opened in succession, and a vision appeared at the opening of each seal, the natural conclusion is that the roll was made up of sheets and when a seal was broken that sheet was unrolled and its writing seen. The book contained symbolic visions of what was to come to pass; hence, revealed the destiny of the church and its enemies from that time till the end of the world. There is nothing said about the writing being read by the Lord when the seals were opened; in fact, it may have been only the symbols that were written. This may account for the fact that when a seal was opened there appeared before John the vision—living picture—not the reading of words. What John did was to put in words a description of the picture which he saw. Occasionally he tells what some feature of a vision means, but

written within and on the back, close sealed with seven seals. 2 And I saw a strong angel proclaiming with a great voice, Who is worthy to open the book, and to loose the seals thereof? 3 And no one in the heaven, or on the earth, or under the earth, was able to open the book, or to look thereon. 4 And I wept much, because no one was found worthy to open the book, or to

---

aside from that the visions are left without explanation. How their meaning may be determined will be discussed later. Seven sheets rolled together and sealed with seven seals probably indicate that the book contains a full revelation of the future history of the church.

2 **And I saw a strong angel proclaiming with a great voice, Who is worthy to open the book, and to loose the seals thereof?**—The angel appeared as strong to harmonize with the fact that he proclaimed with a "great voice," as indicating perhaps that his question was to be heard by all intelligent creatures. This would put in bold relief the one who alone was worthy to open the seals. This means one whose rank and authority was such that God would grant him the privilege of revealing the future.

3 **And no one in the heaven, or on the earth, or under the earth, was able to open the book, or to look thereon.**—The angel's question was a challenge to all creation. No one possessed either the ability or the moral worthiness to disclose the future hidden things. This inability belonged to all realms; none of the angelic hosts in heaven, none of the nations of men on earth and none of the righteous dead in the intermediate state was able. This means that no creature in all God's universe could perform this solemn task.

4 **And I wept much, because no one was found worthy to open the book, or to look thereon:**—To open the book meant to break the seals and to look thereon meant to see and describe the symbols that were written in it. When no one came forward to open the book, John was so affected that he wept much. Apparently the promise made in 4: 1 that he was to be shown things "which must come to pass hereafter" would fail. Being in exile and deeply concerned about the future of the churches, he was moved to tears because no one was ready to make the coveted

look thereon: 5 and one of the elders saith unto me, Weep not; behold, the Lion that is of the tribe of Judah, the Root of David, hath overcome to open the book and the seven seals thereof. 6 And I saw [7]in the midst of the

[7]Or, *between the throne with the four creatures, and the elders*

disclosures. His sorrow and distress are no surprise, when we consider his love and sacrifices for the churches. Men and women yet claim to reveal the secrets written in the book of the future by some mysterious power or by communicating with the dead, but this vision is proof that the future belongs to God. All the revelations he wants us to have are now recorded in the Bible.

5 **and one of the elders saith unto me, Weep not; behold, the Lion that is of the tribe of Judah, the Root of David, hath overcome to open the book and the seven seals thereof.**—Regarding the elders, see notes on 4:4. The text gives no reason why one of the elders rather than some other heavenly being spoke this message to John. This instructing the apostle by one of the elders shows that they were a class of heavenly worshipers. Christ's overcoming Satan and death is the reason for his exaltation to God's right hand (Phil. 2: 7-11), and for "angels and authorities and powers being made subject unto him" (1 Pet. 3: 22). The elders here mentioned being in heaven would know of his exaltation and power; hence, could appropriately speak the comforting words to John. That this language refers to Christ is unquestionable, and the descriptions used show in a vivid way his worthiness to open the book. Jesus was of the tribe of Judah (Heb. 7: 14), and calling him a Lion is probably in reference to Gen. 49: 9. The lion, as king of the forests, was a fitting symbol of Christ endowed with royal authority—a ruler exercising over angels in heaven, men on earth, and the spirits of the departed in Hades. The Root of David means a descendant of David—one whose lineage gave him the right to exercise this royal authority. Being endowed with this authority because of his victory, he was the only one worthy and able to show John the future struggles and triumphs of the church.

6 **And I saw in the midst of the throne and of the four living creatures, and in the midst of the elders, a Lamb standing, as though it had been slain, having seven horns, and seven**

throne and of the four living creatures, and in the midst of the elders, a Lamb standing, as though it had been slain, having seven horns, and seven eyes, which are the [1]seven Spirits of God, sent forth into all the earth. 7

[1]Some ancient authorities omit *seven*.

---

eyes, which are the seven Spirits of God, sent forth into all the earth.—Here a change is made in the scene—a Lamb appears in the midst of the group composed of God, the living creatures, the twenty-four elders, and the strong angel. The Lamb was standing, which indicated it was alive, though it bore marks of having been slain. Since John had probably heard John the Baptist declare Jesus to be the "Lamb of God" (John 1: 36), and had witnessed his crucifixion, he knew, of course, that what he saw in heaven was a symbol of Christ. The lamb was a type of innocence and sacrifice; Jesus was both manifested in highest form.

The further description of the Lamb shows Jesus to be the proper one to open the book. He had "seven horns, and seven eyes." It is generally understood that the number "seven" signifies perfection. John explains that the seven eyes represent the "seven Spirits of God, sent forth into all the earth." The "seven Spirits" probably refers to the Holy Spirit. See notes on 1: 4. As the eyes see all natural objects that come within the range of vision, they are appropriate symbols to represent the Holy Spirit's power to see and know what facts should be revealed. The disclosures therefore to be made would be perfect. The use of the word "horn" in the Bible indicates that it is a symbol of power, as the following passages show: Deut. 33: 17; 1 Kings 22: 1; Jer. 48: 25; Zech. 1: 18; Luke 1: 69. Seven horns mean perfect power to do what was necessary. In this part of the vision John was shown that whatsoever things that would appear in the symbols to follow were sure to come to pass; for there would be sufficient power to accomplish what was predicted. This must have been great encouragement to the then suffering congregations to be faithful to God in spite of any trial.

7 **And he came, and he taketh it out of the right hand of him that sat on the throne.**—The one here called "a Lamb" is represented as taking the book out of the hand of the one who sat upon the throne. This means that Christ received the authority of the Father to open the book—make the revelations it contained.

And he came, and he [2]taketh *it* out of the right hand of him that sat on the

[2]Gr. *hath taken.*

But scholars have asked this puzzling question: Did John see the form of a lamb? If so, how could a real lamb be represented as taking a book out of the hand of the one on the throne? Some answer by supposing that the vision may have been changed just at this point from the image of a lamb to that of a man. The text does not so indicate. Others suggest that the word "Lamb" may be used figuratively, as in John 1: 29, to describe the characteristics of Christ, but the real appearance was of some heavenly being in the form of man. When we speak of the "Lamb of God" now, we never visualize a real lamb, but only transfer the lamb characteristics to Christ. Then we should remember that human beings are probably unable to understand fully heavenly representations. The essential point here made is that Christ only was able to make the revelations of future events.

2. THE HEAVENLY WORSHIP
5: 8-14

throne. 8 And when he had taken the book, the four living creatures and the four and twenty elders fell down before the Lamb, having each one a harp, and golden bowls full of incense, which are the prayers of the saints.

8 **And when he had taken the book, the four living creatures and the four and twenty elders fell down before the Lamb,**—In 4: 8-11 the living creatures and elders are represented as worshiping God upon his throne; in this verse they are seen worshiping Christ by bowing before the being called the Lamb. Since he was able to break the seals and open the book of the future, naturally he was worthy of receiving their adoration. The manner in which their worship was rendered is described in the following expressions.

having each one a harp, and golden bowls full of incense, which are the prayers of the saints.—Whatever the different features of this vision may signify, we should not forget that John was seeing things in heaven, not on earth. There is no question about the language indicating that the four living creatures and twenty-four elders all fell down to worship the Lamb. The words also seem to mean that each of the twenty-eight had a harp and a bowl of incense; certainly the twenty-four elders did. The text clearly indicates the individual worship of each for each is represented as having a harp. To understand a material harp in a purely spiritual realm, played by spirit beings, is, of course, incongruous. It will be necessary to find what they, as symbols, represent if any application is made to things on earth, just as is necessary in other features of the vision. If all is to be taken as strictly literal and applied to the church, then each Christian would have to use a harp individually in worshiping. This would require as many harps as individuals in the congregation, which is quite enough to show the absurdity of any such interpretation.

John declares that the incense represents the "prayers of the saints." Just as incense arose when the priests offered it in the tabernacle and temple, so the prayers of those in the church ascend to God. This symbolic sense of the word "incense" is in harmony with the following texts: Lev. 16: 12, 13; Psalm 141: 2; Acts 10: 4. When John explains the application to be made of this word as being figurative, why conclude that "harp" is to be taken literally. The natural and reasonable application of the word here is that it represents praise. Since Paul tells us to make melody "with your heart to the Lord" (Eph. 5: 19), we know that the human heart is represented as the spiritual instrument that should vibrate (make the melody) in harmony with the sentiments of the song we sing. Each saint has one of these spiritual "harps" which can be used in perfect unison with all other singers. From any viewpoint the passage absolutely excludes the mechanical instrument.

9 **And they sing a new song, saying, Worthy art thou to take the book, and to open the seals thereof: for thou wast slain, and didst purchase unto God with thy blood men of every tribe, and tongue, and people, and nation,**—This part of their song of praise states that Christ's worthiness to open the seals of the book is shown by the fact that he shed his blood as the price sufficient to purchase men of every class and nation. In Acts 20: 28 he is represented as purchasing the church. In this passage the church is looked upon as a body; in our text it is viewed as being

Worthy art thou to take the book, and to open the seals thereof: for thou wast slain, and didst purchase unto God with thy blood *men* of every tribe, and tongue, and people, and nation, 10 and madest them *to be* unto our God a kingdom and priests; and they reign upon the earth.

---

composed of individuals. This and similar passages furnish the unquestioned proof that Gentiles are included in the purchase price paid. Incidentally it also shows that men are saved by entering the church; for none can be saved without Christ's blood, and none can be saved by it, if responsible for conduct, outside of the institution purchased by the blood. If saved out of the church, then saved without his blood.

10 **and madest them to be unto our God a kingdom and priests; and they reign upon the earth.**—In verses 9 and 10 here the heavenly host repeats in very similar words the same thoughts which John uttered in 1: 5, 6. "Didst purchase" and "madest" are coordinated terms in the same grammatical construction. They express a completed past act, which must of necessity be true regarding his purchase of the church with his blood. Then the church purchased with his blood he made a kingdom. As certainly as the church existed at the time John was writing, just that certain had it been made a kingdom. The kingdom was in existence; hence, the premillennial theory that Christ must come in person to establish a kingdom is of necessity false. The saved in the church had also been made priests. Since the church is described as a tabernacle or temple, those who render service in it are called priests. That relationship was in existence then. (1 Pet. 2: 5.) This is not denied. Since establishing the Christian priesthood and the purchase of the church are conceded as past events, there can be no reason assigned for denying that the kingdom had been established.

The King James Version says "shall reign," but the Revised says "they reign" which is present tense. The distinction is not especially important, for if they were then reigning, they would still reign. But as they were then a kingdom the present tense is evidently the correct expression, especially since the present tense often means continued or repeated action. The reign "upon the earth" is perfectly natural, for the church (kingdom) is upon the earth. Just as the priesthood must be spiritual, so the reign must

11 And I saw, and I heard a voice of many angels round about the throne
and the living creatures and the elders; and the number of them was ten
thousand times ten thousand, and thousands of thousands; 12 saying with a
great voice,

Worthy is the Lamb that hath been slain to receive the power, and riches, and wisdom, and might, and honor, and glory, and blessing.

13 And every created thing which is in the heaven, and on the earth, and

---

be. The saints on earth, but under Christ, reign through the teaching and living of Christ's law; they exercise a leading, directing and restraining influence.

11 **And I saw, and I heard a voice of many angels round about the throne and the living creatures and the elders; and the number of them was ten thousand times ten thousand, and thousands of thousands;**—Surrounding the company that was worshiping the Lamb, John saw a host of angels of too many thousands to be numbered.

12 **saying with a great voice, Worthy is the Lamb that hath been slain to receive the power, and riches, and wisdom, and might, and honor, and glory, and blessing.**—The myriads of angels join with the group about the throne in ascribing praise to Christ. Like the preceding song, they base his worthiness upon the fact that he was slain. Being worthy to receive all these things showed he was not only the one to open the seals but to reign. That he had the honors here mentioned at that time is unquestionably a fact. Their words probably mean that he was worthy to possess them as he then did, because he had been made worthy by his death to receive them.

13 **And every created thing which is in the heaven, and on the earth, and under the earth, and on the sea, and all things that are in them, heard I saying,**—By a figure of personification even animals and inanimate nature are represented as praising God. (Psalm 148: 7-10.) Hearing voices from created things in every realm showed John that all creation in its proper manner must honor God and Christ. Adding this song to the two previous ones of the heavenly beings made the praise universal.

Unto him that sitteth on the throne, and unto the Lamb, be the blessing, and the honor, and the glory, and the dominion, for ever and ever.—The same thought is expressed here as in the preceding verse, except that God is also praised.

under the earth, and on the sea, and all things that are in them, heard I saying,

Unto him that sitteth on the throne, and unto the Lamb, *be* the blessing, and the honor, and the glory, and the dominion, [3]for ever and ever.

14 And the four living creatures said, Amen. And the elders fell down and [4]worshipped.

[3]Gr. *unto the ages of the ages.*
[4]See marginal note on ch. 3. 9.

---

14 **And the four living creatures said, Amen. And the elders fell down and worshipped.**—When the hymn of praise closed the four living creatures pronounced the Amen, and the twenty-four elders bowing in worship gave their assent. All of these ascribing to Christ authority and power was a most solemn and impressive way of showing him to be able to break the seals and reveal the future. This feature John introduces in the next chapter.

PART THIRD

OPENING OF THE SEALED BOOK
6: 1 to 11: 18

SECTION ONE

BREAKING OF FIRST FOUR SEALS
6: 1-8

PRELIMINARY NOTES

1. Since 1: 1 declares the book to be a revelation of things which "must shortly come to pass," there can be no doubt that it was intended to disclose events that were to happen in the future from the time John saw the visions. But we have already learned that the first five chapters contain words and visions that prepare for the opening of the real revelation. This begins with the sixth chapter. This part of the book should be approached with extreme caution for two reasons: (1) Because the many and conflicting views presented by commentators indicate how easily mistakes can be made for it is certain all of them cannot be correct. (2) John describes the visions in sublime and symbolic language. He names neither places, nor persons, nor periods in definite and plain terms. He leaves the reader to make the application, if such be possible. That these pictures in heaven are intended to represent things that would happen on earth must be true to make the book of any value to "his servants" for whom it was written; otherwise it would impart no useful information. The difficulty is in deciding the time, place, and persons that fit in the picture that John describes.

2. No history or prophecy regarding God's people has been written without references to contemporary peoples with whom they come in contact. This is abundantly evident from the Old Testament books, and the historical books of the New Testament. It is wholly incredible that the prophecies of Revelation, though presented in the form of moving pictures, should not include their enemies at whose hands they were destined to suffer so much. No interpretation has any chance of being correct that fails to include that fact. We know that the church was established within the Roman Empire and that no political power ever influenced it more

effectively. Papal Rome—the great apostasy—was the most inveterate religious enemy the church ever had. Pagan Rome lasted for nearly five hundred years after the church was established, and papal Rome's iron rule continued more than twelve hundred years. That the opening of these seals should not include some or many of the church's struggles against these two enemy powers is seemingly impossible. What other powers could have been so well included? At the present time we stand more than eighteen hundred years this side of John's visions. History lays before us the events of these past centuries. Whether we are able certainly to locate the exact ones that the seals represent or not, we feel sure that some of them must describe things now in the past. That all the momentous events in these centuries that produced such terrible effects on the church should be passed over by all the pictures in Revelation is too utterly improbable to be accepted. Since pagan and papal Rome affected the church more than any other powers that have existed, a true explanation of the symbols of revelation must include them. The persecutions, the great apostasy, and the reformation must be a part of the imagery.

3. Great care should be observed in applying symbolic or figurative texts of scripture. False interpretations easily come from two sources: First, giving a literal meaning when the word or expression is plainly figurative. Examples: calling Christ a Lion or a Lamb, or representing animals as having a change of nature. (Isa. 11: 6-9.) Second, trying to make every word in a text figurative. When Jesus is said to be the Lamb of God that "taketh away the sin of the world" (John 1: 29), the word "Lamb" clearly is figurative, but the word "sin" is literal. Since words used figuratively and literally may be in the same scripture, we may misrepresent the text by failing to make the proper distinction.

The following are clear examples: In Psalm 80: 8 we read: "Thou broughtest a vine out of Egypt: thou didst drive out the nations, and plantedst it." Here *vine* is clearly figurative, but *Egypt* and *nations* are both literal. Verse 11 says: "It sent out its branches unto the sea, and its shoots unto the River." *Branches* and *shoots* are figurative, but *sea* and *River* are literal. The former refers to the Mediterranean Sea and the latter to the Euphrates river. In Jer. 3: 6 the word "harlot" is figurative; "high mountain" and "green tree" are literal. Words used literally in a picture or symbol, when applied to the thing they represent, may have a natural or a spiritual meaning according to the nature of the case.

In Isa. 2: 2-4 we have some figurative expressions and some plain ones that are to be taken in their natural sense. "The mountain" of Jehovah is figurative; "the word of Jehovah from Jerusalem" is literal. The words "servants" and "son" (Matt. 21: 34-37) have the same meaning in both the parable and the application; the same is true with the word "avenge" (Luke 18: 3, 5, 7).

1. THE FIRST SEAL OPENED
6: 1, 2

1 And I saw when the Lamb opened one of the seven seals, and I heard
one of the four living creatures saying as with a voice of thunder, Come[5]. 2
And I saw, and behold, a white horse, and he that sat thereon had a bow;

[5]Some ancient authorities add *and see.*

---

1 **And I saw when the Lamb opened one of the seven seals, and I heard one of the four living creatures saying as with a voice of thunder, Come.**—We should not forget that the scene John had been looking upon was in heaven. (4: 1.) The Lamb ready to open the seal represents Christ, and the opening means that some symbolic pictures were to be disclosed to John so he could give a written description of them. What John saw here was the first picture that appeared as soon as the seal was broken. One of the living creatures said "Come." Some apply this to the horse and his rider mentioned in verse 2, meaning that they were summoned to appear before John. But it seems more natural to apply the word to John. No use to speculate how he could "Come" when he was on earth and the vision in heaven. He had been seeing the previous visions from earth. Perhaps nothing more was intended than a command to give earnest consideration to what he saw. If he were in some miraculous way mentally transported to heaven, the general truth would not be affected. The verse needs no further comment.

2 **And I saw, and behold, a white horse, and he that sat**

and there was given unto him a crown: and he came forth conquering, and to conquer.

---

thereon had a bow; and there was given unto him a crown: and he came forth conquering, and to conquer.—Here we enter the field where speculation runs riot, and where a multitude of contradictory views are presented with equal confidence of correctness. Any new expositor may well begin his task with a fear of not being able to stand where so many have already fallen. These notes are written in harmony with the natural assumption that the seals represent things that were to transpire after John wrote. Since he was to be shown things which must "shortly come to pass," the conclusion that seems evident is that the first seal disclosed things that were to begin about the end of the first century. It is doubtless unnecessary to insist upon exact dates. Historically considered, periods of time often come in gradually and close the same way. If the leading events fall in a given period, we are probably correct in saying that is the time meant, though many details are not certainly known.

This vision represents some kind of victorious work; the language allows no other application. One class of commentators thinks it refers to Christ and the successful spread of his gospel in the first centuries of the Christian era; another class applies it to the Roman Empire in a successful period beginning about the time of John's writing. The history of the church for many centuries is so closely interwoven with that of Rome—pagan or papal—that any large view of one must necessarily include the other; hence, this vision would involve a period of Roman prosperity and church success, however applied. The general facts of both Rome and the church might be presented from either viewpoint. Moreover, it may be true that these composite symbols are intended to represent both Rome and the church during certain periods because of their interlocking influence upon each other. If so, the main point is to find the important thing that happened to each in the period meant. However, for reasons to be given, the view entertained here is, that the vision refers primarily to Rome, though greatly affecting the church.

The four words—white, horse, bow, and crown—all have some

special significance or they would not have been mentioned by John in describing what he saw. Words are not always used in the same sense in every passage, but when the language or context fixes their meanings that must be accepted as final, regardless of the meanings in other texts. While the horse was used for other purposes, yet the scriptures clearly show he was used in war. The most magnificent representation of this is in Job 39: 19-25. The same fact is found in Prov. 21: 31; Zech. 10: 3. The expression "conquering, and to conquer" shows that this vision pertains to war and determines the use made of the horse. The white color represents either purity or victory. (6: 11; 7: 15.) Roman generals who were victors are said to have entered the city in chariots drawn by white horses. The entire setting of this verse implies victory; hence, the word "white" must indicate triumph—successful war. The bow anciently was used as an implement of war or for hunting. (Gen. 27: 3; 48: 22; Isa. 7: 24.) The entire setting of this vision shows that it indicates war here. The crown is not the royal diadem which indicates authority to reign, but the garland or chaplet (Greek *stephanos*) of victory bestowed upon those who triumph. Other passages where this word is used in the same sense are these: 1 Cor. 9: 25; 2 Tim. 2: 5; 4: 8; Rev. 2: 10. It was then a crown of honor to represent the victory gained. The text does not say when the rider wore the crown, but only that it was given to him. If worn before he went forth to conquer, it was to indicate by anticipation that he *would* be victorious. This, however, is a minor matter.

The following considerations are offered for accepting the view that this vision primarily refers to Rome instead of the church, though the church is involved because affected by acts of the empire:

1. In the first four visions horses appear. If the rider on the white horse refers to Christ, and the victories to the spreading of the gospel by the church, then the three following should also refer to the church with Christ riding the horse. The descriptions of them, however, will not harmonize with that view. Besides the rider of the fourth horse is said to be "Death."

2. Those who think Christ is represented by the rider of the white horse refer to Rev. 19: 11-15 as meaning the same thing.

There is no doubt about this passage referring to Christ, but the following will show that the passages are different: (1) The crowns in 19: 11 are diadems, crowns of ruling authority; in 6: 2 it is the crown of reward for victory. (2) In 19: 15 the horseman smites with "a sharp sword"; and 6: 2 he carries a "bow." (3) If a horse may signify war and the color white represents triumph, it could as well picture such warfare in the Roman Empire as warfare carried on by the church. (4) The passage in 19 is connected with the final overthrow of the church's enemies; the one in 6 is the first of future events to begin soon after John wrote. (5) It is not reasonable that Christ should, in the same symbol, be represented as a Lamb breaking the seals and also as the rider on the white horse. However considered, there is no reason for saying the rider *must* represent Christ. As the symbol undoubtedly signifies triumphant war, any successful war period, whether carnal or spiritual, would meet the demands of the language. The proper application must, therefore, depend on historical facts.

Since 6: 2 *may* refer to the Roman Empire, it is appropriate to ask if there was a period soon after John wrote which corresponds with the vision revealed in opening this seal. The description is given in a single verse of thirty-two English words. Evidently only the general features and outstanding events of the period are presented in this symbol. At the very outset in trying to find the things signified by these visions we should be reminded that they are composite pictures which John saw in heaven, but with the purpose of indicating things that would happen to the church and contemporary peoples.

Beginning in the reign of Nero (A.D. 64), the church suffered several (some say ten) persecutions before the close of the third century. Since the vision clearly indicates aggressive and successful warfare, the persecutions are presumptive proof that it applies to Rome; for during the time of such intense persecutions the church must have grown mainly through fortitude in sufferings and martyrdom rather than open fighting for the truth. A few Christians comparatively had little chance against the powerful empire, its barbarian subjects, and the unbelieving Jews, all of whom were their enemies. Certainly not a very suitable situation to be represented by a conquering soldier. There was a second great persecution under Domitian, in which the apostle John was banished to Patmos. Domitian's death (A.D. 96) is considered a division point in Roman history. The period following (96-180) is described by historians as one of prosperity and military triumph for the Roman Empire. Gibbon in his *Decline and Fall of the Roman Empire* (Vol. 1, chap. 1) calls it a "happy period" when five good emperors ruled—Nerva, Trajan, Hadrian, and the two Antonines.

Probably the man upon the white horse may refer only to the Roman emperors throughout the period, not to any one alone. Nerva was doubtless the best one of the five good emperors, but he ruled only two years. The symbol probably began to be fulfilled in the reign of Trajan, during which time there was another persecution against the church in Bithynia. But Trajan was especially noted for his extension of the empire by conquering other kingdoms. Gibbon (Vol. 1, p. 4) says the Caesars had done little to extend the country's borders during the first century of the Christian era. But he compares the military exploits of Trajan with Alexander the Great and says his success was "rapid and specious," and that "every day the astonished senate received intelligence of new names and new nations that acknowledge his sway." (Vol. 1, p. 7.) Beginning with Trajan's successes, we surely have a period that harmonizes with John's vision, and one that seems to have more in its favor than any other that has been suggested.

Regarding this period Gibbon further speaks: "In the second century of the Christian era, the empire of Rome comprehended the fairest part of the earth, and the most civilized portion of mankind." (Vol. 1, p. 1.) Again: "If a man were called to fix the period in the history of the world, during which the condition of the human race was most happy and prosperous, he would, without hesitation, name that which elapsed from the death of Domitian to the accession of Commodus. The vast extent of the Roman Empire was governed by absolute power, under the guidance of virtue and wisdom." (Vol. 1, p. 95.) Such is Gibbon's description of the success of Roman arms and the internal peace of the empire during the period named. Paraphrasing a suggestion in Barnes' commentary, it may be said: If the angel of the Lord had designed to give a symbol that would be a perfect picture of that period of

Roman prosperity, no better one could have been chosen; likewise, if Gibbon had purposely tried to show that the period of Roman history fulfilled the demands of the symbol, he could not have made a better comment on the text.

Elliott (Vol. 1, pp. 139-146) has given an argument in full detail to show that the "bow" held by the rider is proof that the symbol should be applied to that prosperous period of the Roman Empire. This argument has been adopted or referred to by others. It carries a strong degree of probability, and if true, is a very decisive factor in solving the problem.

That the "bow" was a war implement is certain from many texts in the Old Testament, but the argument is based upon the fact that the sword and javelin were Roman emblems. The bow in the symbol would then introduce some singular feature. The five good emperors—Nerva, Trajan, Hadrian, and the Antonines—succeeded to the throne by the law of adoption, not by blood lineage. Historical proof (given by Elliott) seems to show that Nerva's ancestry came from the island of Crete, and that the Cretans were noted as bowmen; so much so that the bow was a national emblem. If so, the rider going forth with a bow instead of a sword could well represent the military successes of the five good emperors, chief and most successful of whom was Trajan as already noted; for Nerva, the originator of that line of rulers, was of Cretan origin.

It is worthy of mention again that, though the symbol primarily refers to Rome's great military achievements in that period, the events affected the church with far-reaching consequences.

2. THE SECOND SEAL OPENED
6: 3, 4

3 And when he opened the second seal, I heard the second living creature
saying, Come[5]. 4 And another *horse* came forth, a red horse: and to him

---

3 **And when he opened the second seal, I heard the second living creature saying, Come.**—The language here is substantially the same as that used to describe the opening of the first seal. See notes on verse 1.

4 **And another horse came forth, a red horse: and to him**

that sat thereon it was given to take [6]peace from the earth, and that they should slay one another: and there was given unto him a great sword.

[6]Some ancient authorities read *the peace of the earth.*

that sat thereon it was given to take peace from the earth,—Concerning the significance of the term *horse* see the notes on verse 2. The language of this seal indicates the same general idea as the first—it represents a period of war, though in some respects it is different in its results. If we were correct in the conclusion that the first symbol referred primarily to the Roman Empire, then this one should be applied in the same way. The reasoning on this point given under the first seal will apply here equally as well. The reader is referred to that. The word *red* would naturally suggest carnage—excessive bloodshed and disastrous war. This is confirmed by the expression "slay one another," found in the following verse. It is further confirmed by the words that the rider of the red horse was "to take peace from the earth." While the first seal indicated warfare, it was a successful period for the empire. Trajan's victories had extended Rome's borders and brought many weaker nations in subjection to its authority. It was a time of great prosperity and internal peace. The margin says "the peace" which implies that the peace they had was to be destroyed in the time indicated by the second seal. This conclusion is further sustained by the statement that peace was to be taken "from the earth." Since the symbol had to do with matters that would affect the church, and the church was scattered throughout the Roman Empire, the term "earth" meant that part of the world subject to Rome.

and that they should slay one another: and there was given unto him a great sword.—This symbol represents internal strife; the fighting was to be among themselves. They were to kill each other. In this particular the warfare of this seal was very different from that of the first. To the rider here was given a great sword. This is the full and final proof that this seal refers to warfare. The rider of the white horse in Rev. 19: 15 also had a sword, but it proceeded "out of his mouth," and could not therefore mean a literal sword, but his words. In the symbol of the second seal the great sword was "given unto him." This furnishes another reason why the rider in these seals does not refer to Christ.

It is again suggested that the rider of the horse need not refer to any special emperor, but rather to the ruling power, whoever the ruler might be, for a period of time when the general facts stated may have found their counterpart in Roman history. If the preceding reasoning is correct, it would have to come after the time covered by the reigns of the "five good emperors." The two symbols are too clearly different to refer to the same period of time. Historians describe this period as one of almost continuous civil warfare. Sismondi's *Fall of the Roman Empire,* Vol. 1, p. 36, says:

"With Commodus commenced the third and most calamitous period. It lasted ninety-two years, from 192 and 284. During that period thirty-two emperors and twenty-seven pretenders alternately hurled each other from the throne by *incessant civil warfare. Ninety-two years of almost incessant civil warfare* taught the world on what a frail foundation the virtue of the Antonines had placed the felicity of the empire."

In the *Decline and Fall of the Roman Empire,* Vol. I, chapters IV to XII, Gibbon gives the history of this period in much detail. He shows that of these more than thirty emperors all were murdered except a very few. He also says there were nineteen pretenders in the reign of Gallienus who ruled from A.D. 260 to 268. Regarding this part of the period Gibbon says:

"Such were the barbarians, and such the tyrants, who, under the reigns of Valerian and Gallienus, dismembered the province, and reduced the empire to the lowest pitch of disgrace and ruin, from whence it seemed impossible that it should ever emerge." (Vol. I, p. 326.)

No effort is here made to apply the symbol to the reign of any one emperor, such being unnecessary, but the general facts of that period, as history presents them, are such as fit the demands of the case. Certainly the rulers slew one another with the sword, and the peace and prosperity of the Roman Empire during the preceding century were taken away. This is all that is necessary to show that this symbol could refer to this period of Rome's civil warfare.

3. THE THIRD SEAL OPENED
6: 5, 6

5 And when he opened the third seal, I heard the third living creature saying, Come[5]. And I saw, and behold, a black horse; and he that sat there-

---

5 **And when he opened the third seal, I heard the third living creature saying, Come.**—See the notes on verse 1.

And I saw, and behold, a black horse; and he that sat thereon had a balance in his hand.—The significance of the horse has already been explained under the first seal. The difference is that here the horse is black. It should be noted that neither bow nor sword was given the rider, but instead he carried a pair of balances in his hand. The description of the first two visions clearly indicates that both refer to active fighting—aggressive warfare. The first pictures successful warfare for the Roman Empire; the second disastrous. The absence of any expression in the third vision to indicate fighting shows that this symbol should have a different interpretation. This will be evident as we examine the meanings of the various expressions found in it. A surface glance at the terms used suggests that it represents some terrible results that follow in the wake of continued and devastating battles—that is, distress and sufferings because of great scarcity. Death, another horrible result of war, as presented in the fourth vision is attributed to four causes, one of which is famine. The third seal, therefore, is picturing the scarcity of the necessities of life and the difficulty of getting them by reason of high prices.

As an emblem the black color represents deep distress manifested in mourning. Jeremiah said: "Judah mourneth and the gates thereof languish, they sit in black upon the ground; and the cry of Jerusalem is gone up." (Jer. 14: 2.) Compare Ezek. 32: 7. The cause of mourning might be deep distress on account of famine, pestilence, death, oppression, or invasion of the country. The particular thing that causes the mourning in any case will have to be learned from its description in the text.

Balances and scales are symbols of justice and exactness. (Prov. 11: 1; Job 31: 6.) Things may be weighed because of their intrinsic value or their scarcity. According to the view taken in this commentary there would result from the many devastating

on had a balance in his hand. 6 And I heard as it were a voice in the midst of the four living creatures saying, [7]A measure of wheat for a [8]shilling, and three measures of barley for a [8]shilling; and the oil and the wine hurt thou not.

[7]Or, *A choenix* (i.e. about a quart) *of wheat for a shilling*—implying great scarcity. Comp. Ezek. 4. 16 f.; 5. 16.
[8]See marginal note on Mt. 18. 28.

wars and internal strife such scarcity of food supplies as would have to be carefully preserved and dispensed with rigid exactness. The rider carrying a balance indicated that the Roman government would cause that state of things to exist. This could have meant that such laws could have been enacted by the government for the common safety of the citizens or the exactness with which the taxes were collected, or both. We should not forget that any distress that came to the empire would directly affect the church, for it was for many centuries within, and subject to, the Roman power. Hence, the picturing of this future fact was intended evidently to warn the churches then about what awaited them when great happenings would take place in countries where they lived—within the bounds of the Roman Empire. Lev. 26: 24-26 and Ezek. 4: 16 both show that bread sold by weight, which indicates scarcity. Doubtless the same was true of other commodities.

6 **And I heard as it were a voice in the midst of the four living creatures saying, A measure of wheat for a shilling, and three measures of barley for a shilling; and the oil and the wine hurt thou not.**—John heard a voice that seemed to come from the midst of the four living creatures. It is not stated who spake, but it seemed directed to the rider of the horse. This indicated that his mission in going forth was to produce such a situation that wheat and barley would sell at enormous prices. This does not indicate famine conditions where there is nothing to sell, but great scarcity when extreme and exacting methods have to be used to protect the supply. The word "measure" is equal to about one quart. The Greek term for shilling had the value of sixteen and two-thirds cents. This made a bushel of wheat worth more than five dollars. The purchasing power of money then was probably much more than ours, so the price of wheat in the value of our money would, doubtless, be two or three times that much. These prices show that great scarcity of food products, which is doubtless all that was intended by the expressions.

Expositors are hopelessly disagreed about the meaning of "the oil and the wine hurt thou not." It is useless to attempt to state the various views. It is evident, however, that the proper application will harmonize with what has just been said about the wheat and barley. Since the whole symbol indicates the devastating results of warfare and the scarcity of common necessities, the instruction pertains to the extreme care in protecting them. Oil and wine then being necessary articles of food, great care was to be observed not to damage that source of support. Though this command seems directed to the rider, who represented the ruling power of the empire, it may have been general instruction to be carried out by all the people.

Perhaps the fulfillment of the symbol need not be limited to the reign of any one particular emperor, since such conditions would follow after internal warfare and oppression at any time. But the rule of Caracalla (A.D. 211-217), both in nature and time, would probably come within the limits required. He is referred to in history as one of the most "blood-thirsty tyrants," giving the empire a reign of terror. Gibbon calls him the "common enemy of mankind," and says: "The most wealthy families were ruined by partial fines and confiscations, and the great body of his subjects oppressed by ingenious and aggravated taxes." (*Decline and Fall*, Vol. I, p. 160). Regarding the same Gibbon says further: "In the course of this history, we shall be too often summoned to explain the land tax, the capitation, and the heavy contributions of corn, wine, oil, and meat, which were exacted from the provinces for the use of the court, the army, and the capital." (*Ibid.*, p. 195.) In such conditions the church in all the Roman provinces would suffer with other subjects of the empire. This condition would naturally interfere with the preaching of the gospel.

4. THE FOURTH SEAL OPENED
6: 7, 8

7 And when he opened the fourth seal, I heard the voice of the fourth living creature saying, Come[5]. 8 And I saw, and behold, a pale horse: and he that sat upon him, his name was Death; and Hades followed with him.

---

7 **And when he opened the fourth seal, I heard the voice of the fourth living creature saying, Come.**—See notes on verse 1.

And there was given unto them authority over the fourth part of the earth, to kill with sword, and with famine, and with [9]death, and by the wild beasts of the earth.

[9]Or, *pestilence* Comp. ch. 2. 23 marg.

8 **And I saw, and behold, a pale horse: and he that sat upon him, his name was Death;**—Here, as in the other three seals, the horse appears, indicating that the idea of war is still in the symbols. But the imagery is changed. The rider is no longer in the form of a person, carrying some implements, but Death, personified, is said to be seated on the horse. Death represented as a tyrant reigning is a figure of speech found in other books of the Bible. (Rom. 5: 14; 6: 9; 1 Cor. 15: 55.) The emblem shows Death as a soldier gaining great victories over all efforts at resistance that man might make. The term "pale" applied to the horse probably was intended to represent the color of a body in death. All this would show the power of death over men, and the effect it would have on the empire, and on the church because it was at that time under the Roman dominion.

and Hades followed with him.—Hades literally means the "unseen" and applies to the place of the dead. The idea seems to be that so many would die that even the place of the dead would appear to be before John in the emblem. Or that Hades would follow to take those who had been killed.

And there was given unto them authority over the fourth part of the earth, to kill with sword, and with famine, and with death, and by the wild beasts of the earth.—Authority was given "unto them"—that is, to Death and Hades. This means that Death would have a broad sway—many would die—and they would pass to the intermediate state. Commentators interpret the "fourth part" as meaning a considerable or great number, or in all quarters of the Roman Empire, or that it was not to be universal. The first seems the more likely, for definite numbers are often used for an indefinite amount, and it is not at all probable that exactly one-fourth part would be affected. The "earth," doubtless, meant the territory governed by the Romans.

The remainder of the verse tells the means by which Death, ruling as an emperor, would reach so many. To "kill with sword" would include those who would die in murders and assassinations as well as wars. Others would die in famines. This is different from the third seal where the symbol showed only a scarcity of food. Another statement is that they would be killed "with death." Since Death, personified, is represented as riding the horse, the word "death" here probably has a different meaning. To kill with death is at least an awkward expression. The margin says *pestilence.* The meaning is that plagues of various kinds would destroy many. It is immaterial whether the expression "wild beasts" be understood literally or as referring to the insatiable, bloodthirsty tyrants that would murder without mercy. In sections infested with wild beasts, they would become more dangerous when the country had been despoiled by war and famines. The point is that great numbers would be killed through the various means mentioned.

As suggested regarding the third seal, it is doubtless unnecessary to limit the application of this vision to the reign of any one emperor. From A.D. 192 to 284 has already been alluded to as a period of internal strife in the Roman Empire. As the third vision seems to fit the time of Caracalla, A.D. 211-217, so this vision will harmonize with the period of Gallienus, A.D. 260-268, as a time in which events most strikingly fit the requirements of the symbol. Gibbon declares that the empire at that time was attacked on every side by the "blind fury of foreign invaders, and the wild ambition of domestic usurpers." He also says: "But the whole period was one uninterrupted series of confusion and calamity." *(Decline and Fall,* Vol. I, p. 299.) One more quotation from Gibbon will suffice. He said: "But a long and general famine was a calamity of a more serious kind. It was the inevitable consequence of rapine and oppression which extirpated the produce of the present, and the hope of the future harvests. . . . Other causes must, however, have contributed to the furious plague, which, from the year two hundred and fifty to the year two hundred and sixty-five, raged without interruption to every province, every city, and almost every family, of the Roman Empire. During some time five thousand persons died daily in Rome; and many towns, that had escaped the hands of the barbarians, were entirely depopulated." *(Ibid.,* p. 329.) If inspiration had intended to describe that period, no symbol, it seems, could have been better suited to the purpose than that revealed by the fourth seal. The probability is that it was at least included in what the symbol was intended to represent.

If the reigns of Caracalla and Gallienus are not the periods to fulfill the third and fourth symbols, it must be that some other periods in that general age of the world did; the lessons would be the same even if the exact periods and events are not definitely located. These two are suggested as possessing a high degree of probability. As already mentioned regarding the third seal, the fourth indicates results that follow devastating warfare, and the language would fit any such period of time. But the seals' place in the record shows the probability of their closely following the second seal—the time of internal strife in the Roman Empire. If that is true, the suggestion made in this paragraph is doubtless correct.

SECTION TWO

OPENING OF THE FIFTH AND SIXTH SEALS
6:9-17

1. THE FIFTH SEAL OPENED
6:9-11

9 And when he opened the fifth seal, I saw underneath the altar the souls of them that had been slain for the word of God, and for the testimony

---

Preliminary Note: The central idea of the first four visions was war. The first was victorious and the second disastrous for the Roman Empire. The third and fourth picture various calamities that came as a result of internal strife and enemy invasion. But all these refer primarily to the Romans. Since the church was mainly in Roman provinces, it was affected by whatever befell the empire. While the Christians suffered in some measure, along with others, the calamities that came to provinces, yet during these two centuries the government was so much concerned with political and economic conditions that the church enjoyed religious liberty more than would otherwise have been possible. Naturally this resulted in a marvelous growth of Christianity. The persecutions they endured doubtless strengthened their faith and courage. So the first four seals bear strongly, but indirectly, upon the spread of the church. Following a Savior who had been crucified made them willing to suffer for the truth.

With the fifth seal the scene changes and the horses and riders disappear. The experience of the church now is the primary thing, and the fifth vision presents the martyred saints. But, as the Roman Empire is the persecutor, no exposition can be correct that does not include it. The history of the persecuted involves that of the persecutor.

9 **And when he opened the fifth seal, I saw underneath the altar the souls of them that had been slain for the word of God, and for the testimony which they held:**—We should continually remember that John saw these visions in heaven, and that we are not to confuse them with the things they represent.

John did not see saints in the body, but their "souls"; for they had already been slain. Their souls were in the Hadean state, but

which they held: 10 and they cried with a great voice, saying, How long, O Master, the holy and true, dost thou not judge and avenge our blood on them that dwell on the earth? 11 And there was given them to each one a white robe; and it was said unto them, that they should rest yet for a little time, until their fellow-servants also and their brethren, who should be killed even as they were, should [1]have fulfilled *their course.*

[1]Some ancient authorities read *be fulfilled* in number. 2 Esdr. 4. 36.

the picture John saw was in heaven. In the temple service the animal sacrifices were made at the brazen altar in the court. (Lev. 4: 7.) As they had been slain because of their faithfulness to God's word, it was appropriate that they appear under the altar as if they had been sacrificed and blood poured at its base. As they suffered martyrdom because they held to the testimony concerning Christ, it was consistent that they ask that their blood be avenged. The altar which represented that suffering was an appropriate place for their cry to be made.

10 **and they cried with a great voice, saying, How long, O Master, the holy and true, dost thou not judge and avenge our blood on them that dwell on the earth?**—These words show that the soul or spirit of man does exist in a conscious state after it leaves the body. Their referring to those that "dwell on the earth" shows that they were in the spirit abode—Hades. Those souls knew that vengeance belongeth unto God (Heb. 10: 30), and that only just and righteous punishment would be administered. This is evident from the fact that they called the Master "holy and true." They were, therefore, not crying for revenge upon their persecutors, but rather that justice be done, and their lives vindicated. Their cry was not so much an asking for God's vengeance to be meted out as to know how long they must wait; for they did not doubt that it would be done.

11 **And there was given them to each one a white robe; and it was said unto them, that they should rest yet for a little time, until their fellow-servants also and their brethren, who should be killed even as they were, should have fulfilled their course.**—White robes were given them as an emblem of their innocence, purity, and victory over sin. This is the significance of white robes in other places in this book. (3: 4; 7: 9, 13.) They had sealed their testimony with their blood and were entitled to such an emblem of victory. Giving to each a robe, which John

saw in the picture in heaven, was to signify that the martyrs in the Hadean world were approved and in a state of joy. (See Luke 16: 20-23.) To "judge and avenge" means that the martyrs in some way were to be approved and vindicated. How that would be done is not stated here. It might have meant the truth preached by the martyrs would so prevail that the Roman Empire would accept or endorse it. If so, this vindication occurred in the reign of Constantine about A.D. 325. With this view of the seal, the martyrs seen in it would probably refer to those who suffered before the reign of Diocletian, which began about A.D. 303, and their fellow servants and brethren who were yet to suffer would mean those who suffered in his reign. But if those John saw represented those who were to be slain during his reign, then the fellow servants would have to mean a class of martyrs that later suffered under papal Rome—the "man of sin." With this view the time of vindicating the martyrs would have to be when their murderers will be punished at the judgment. This would require that the expression "a little time" would have to be understood as God sees time, not as we do. According to the former view they were to rest—patiently wait—a little time for their vindication to take place; according to the latter they were to remain in the rest of Hades till all martyrs for the truth had been slain, and at the judgment they would enter upon the full measure of their reward. All things considered, the first view seems more probable. In either case the persecution in the reign of Diocletian fits the main point in the vision.

Historians and commentators generally agree that in the last few years of Diocletian's reign occurred one of the bitterest persecutions known in the history of the church. At first he was disposed to show kindness to the Christians; but, later under the influence of others, he began in A.D. 303 a series of edicts that subjected multitudes to the most inhuman kinds of torture and death. The passage from Gibbon which is usually quoted to prove this is the following:

"The resentment, or the fears, of Diocletian at length transported him beyond the bounds of moderation, which he had hitherto preserved, and he declared, in a series of cruel edicts, his intention of abolishing the Christian name. By the first of these edicts, the governors of the provinces were directed to apprehend all persons of the ecclesiastical order; and the prisons, destined for the vilest criminals, were soon filled with a multitude of bishops, presbyters, deacons, readers, and exorcists. By a second edict, the magistrates were commanded to employ every method of severity, which might reclaim them from their odious superstition, and oblige them to return to the established worship of the gods. This rigorous order was extended by a subsequent edict, to the whole body of Christians, who were exposed to a violent and general persecution." (*Decline and Fall,* Vol. II, p. 69.)

What John saw in the vision, this skeptical historian shows to have actually transpired in this reign. No other occasion known fits the symbol better. The glorious promises here made to those who had been faithful "unto death" were as strong incentives as could be offered for fidelity to Christ, even though it cost martyrdom. It also shows that the death of the body does not end the soul's existence; consciousness between death and the resurrection must be a fact. Such passages are a deathblow to the "soul-sleeping" doctrine of materialism.

2. THE SIXTH SEAL OPENED
6: 12-17

12 And I saw when he opened the sixth seal, and there was a great earthquake; and the sun became black as sackcloth of hair, and the whole

---

12 **And I saw when he opened the sixth seal, and there was a great earthquake;**—When this seal was opened John saw in the picture in heaven the appearance of a great commotion in which the material elements of the universe seemed to be rocking and falling from their natural places. He also saw the effect that such commotion had on the people of the earth. All this, it must be remembered, was in the symbolic vision, and should not be confused with what it represented. An earthquake naturally would represent some great disturbance, the nature of which must be learned by a careful study of scripture texts.

and the sun became black as sackcloth of hair, and the whole moon became as blood; 13 **and the stars of the heaven fell unto the earth, as a fig tree casteth her unripe figs when**

moon became as blood; 13 and the stars of the heaven fell unto the earth, as
a fig tree casteth her unripe figs when she is shaken of a great wind. 14
And the heaven was removed as a scroll when it is rolled up; and every
mountain and island were moved out of their places. 15 And the kings of
the earth, and the princes, and the [2]chief captains, and the rich, and the

---

she is shaken of a great wind.—The only excuse for taking this language literally is the view of some expositors that the seal refers to the coming of the Lord and the end of the world. But this position will not do, for it is followed by a period in which a multitude of the redeemed will be sealed, and the opening of the seventh seal under which the seven trumpets are to be sounded. Since in all the preceding seals the language is mainly symbolical, the presumption is that it is so in this seal. A figurative use of the words sun, moon, and stars is clearly evident in such texts as the following: Joel 2: 10; Isa. 13: 9, 10; Jer. 4: 24.

14 **And the heaven was removed as a scroll when it is rolled up; and every mountain and island were moved out of their places.**—This too is what John saw in the picture, and therefore is to be applied figuratively just as the words sun, moon, and stars. Rolled up "as a scroll" is unquestionably symbolic language and indicates the removal of the heaven. Though John saw what appeared as the literal heaven rolled up, that must represent the removal of something else. A great earthquake refers to some terrible agitation. Sun, moon, and stars refer to prominent persons. (Gen. 37: 9.) The prophet referred to Jesus as the "sun of righteousness." (Mal. 4: 2.) The sun becoming black, the moon like blood, and the stars falling mean that prominent persons through commotions and bloodshed would lose their places and cease to function in their usual manner. Such fall would be comparable to the untimely dropping of unripe figs when the tree is violently shaken. Mountains refer to governments. The kingdom of Christ was prophetically described as the "mountain of Jehovah's house." (Isa. 2: 2.) Mountains and islands being moved out of their places must, therefore, refer to radical changes in forms of governments. No small changes would be represented by such a breaking up of the material universe.

15 **And the kings of the earth, and the princes, and the chief captains, and the rich, and the strong, and every bondman and**

strong, and every bondman and freeman, hid themselves in the caves and in the rocks of the mountains; 16 and they say to the mountains, and to the rocks, Fall on us, and hide us from the face of him that sitteth on the throne, and from the wrath of the Lamb: 17 for the great day of their wrath is come; and who is able to stand?

[2]Or, *military tribunes* Gr. *chiliarchs.*

freeman, hid themselves in the caves and in the rocks of the mountains;—John is still describing the picture in heaven. This is another scene that passed before his eyes, which evidently was intended to show the effect that such a commotion would have on men. A literal darkening of the sun, moon turning red, the heavens disappearing and mountains moving would so agitate all classes of men that they would cry for help and seek places of shelter if possible. This would be the natural effect of such material disturbances on the mind of men. It symbolically represents the consternation and commotions that political and national upheavals would have upon the people in the affected kingdoms. Since the picture shows how the mind will be affected by any calamitous disturbance, material or spiritual, the language itself here does not say which it is. In nature the consternation would be the same regardless of what produced it; the cry for escape from serious consequences would also be the same. The language shows that all classes—high and low—would be equally distressed. The classes mentioned are representative; it means that the disturbance would be so great that none would escape from the terror. As a radical change in government would disturb them, they would be trying to avoid persecution and death. This is further brought out in the next verse.

16 **and they say to the mountains, and to the rocks, Fall on us, and hide us from the face of him that sitteth on the throne, and from the wrath of the Lamb:** 17 **for the great day of their wrath is come; and who is able to stand?**—This is the language of terror on the part of those in danger of some impending calamity. The particular thing feared must be determined by the general teaching of the text or context. Hos. 10: 8 has the same thought when Israel was threatened with punishment. Substantially the same language is used by Jesus in Luke 23: 30, referring to the destruction of Jerusalem. It is simply a poetical

way of expressing the cry of distress. When the calamity came, they would consider it a day of wrath coming from God and Christ. Or, they would acknowledge that their being overcome was because God's permission or power was with their enemies. Their conclusion would be that, if divine favor was against them, no one would be able to stand. This is true regardless of when or what particular wrath of God may be in view here.

Since the seventh seal, under which there are seven trumpets, must intervene between this seal and the end of time, the language of this text cannot refer to Christ's coming and the end of the world. It must, therefore, mean some special day (period) of wrath. If the fifth seal found its striking fulfillment in the persecution in the reign of Diocletian, the position here taken, then we would expect the sixth to be fulfilled later when some great change would take place in the Roman Empire—such changes as would affect both the empire and the church. The well-known relationship of the church to pagan Rome during those centuries is ample proof of this view. We insist that no exposition of Revelation can be correct which ignores the vital influence each had on the other, as the plain facts of history show. The fact that those who cried for the rocks to fall upon them wanted to be hid from the face of God shows them to be sinners, not God's people. The great changes indicated by the commotion in the material universe must have occurred among the church's enemies within the Roman Empire. In such a governmental change all false religions, particularly the national form of them, would suffer defeat; rulers and those in authority would lose their powers, and general weeping among them would be common.

The changes that transpired in the reign of Constantine, who was emperor from A.D. 307 to 337, will harmonize with the things pictured in this seal. In 308 the empire was divided among six emperors. By A.D. 313 they were reduced to two—Constantine and Licinius. The latter, who was a champion of Paganism, was defeated in A.D. 323 and Constantine became the sole emperor of the Roman world. Since Constantine was favorable to Christianity, the struggle was really a war between Christianity and Paganism. The defeat of the latter caused great mourning and distress among the enemies of Christianity. In the Edict of Milan, A.D.

313, privilege was granted for each man to worship as he saw fit, and none were to be prevented from practicing or embracing Christianity. In A.D. 321 he decreed that Sunday, the day the Christians observed as a day of worship, should be a day of rest in towns from business and labor. This was a concession to Christianity. In A.D. 325 he convened the first general counsel of the church over which he presided. In A.D. 326 he began the building of Constantinople to which he removed the capital of the Roman Empire. (Encyc. Brit., 14th ed., pp. 297-9.) He is supposed to have entered the church himself before he died. Gibbon refers to him as the patron of the church who "seated Christianity on the throne of the Roman world." (*Decline and Fall,* Vol. II, p. 273.) He also says: "War and commerce had spread the knowledge of the gospel beyond the confines of the Roman provinces; and the barbarians, who had disdained an humble and proscribed sect, soon learned to esteem a religion which had been so lately embraced by the greatest monarch, and the most civilized nation, of the globe." (*Ibid.,* p. 275.) Surely all this was a political and spiritual earthquake that shook pagan nations to their foundations, and brought mourning to their rulers, but honor and glory to the church. Whatever might be said in favor of other times, certainly none could more fittingly fulfill the scenes depicted in this seal.

Unless the correct application of the sixth seal is understood, the remainder of the book will be in hopeless confusion; there will be no place for the sealing of the saints mentioned in the seventh chapter and the seventh seal, under which the seven trumpets are to sound. The last trumpet brings the end of time. (11: 15-18; 1 Cor. 15: 52.) The man of sin, Babylon, and the scarlet-robed woman—emblems of the apostate church—are all to be destroyed when the Lord comes. (2 Thess. 2: 8; Rev. 19: 19-21; 18: 21-24.) The sixth seal mentions nothing about this great event. The changes in the material universe at the end of time will be literal. (2 Pet. 3: 10.) All the scriptural facts demand that the changes indicated by the sixth seal are to be understood as symbols and applied to the events mentioned in the preceding notes.

The prophet Isaiah used the following language concerning the destruction of ancient Babylon: "For the stars of heaven and the constellations thereof shall not give their light; the sun shall be darkened in its going forth, and the moon shall not cause its light to shine. . . . Therefore I will make the heavens to tremble, and the earth shall be shaken out of its place, in the wrath of Jehovah of hosts, and in the day of his fierce anger." (Isa. 13: 10-13.) Clearly this is symbolic language, and plain proof that the emblems of the sixth seal may be applied to the overthrow of the pagan Roman Empire rather than to changes in the material elements mentioned.

SECTION THREE

A SYMBOLIC INTERLUDE SHOWING GOSPEL SUCCESS
7: 1-17

1. THE VISION DESCRIBED
7: 1-3

1 After this I saw four angels standing at the four corners of the earth, holding the four winds of the earth, that no wind should blow on the earth, or on the sea, or upon any tree. 2 And I saw another angel ascend from the sunrising, having the seal of the living God: and he cried with a great voice

---

1 **After this I saw four angels standing at the four corners of the earth,**—"After this" means that after viewing the scenes revealed by the sixth seal he saw the two visions described in this chapter. They form an interlude between the sixth and seventh seals and show what results came to the church during the period of prosperity following the sixth seal. Angels mean messengers of some kind sent to carry out a purpose. Four standing at the four corners of the earth indicate that their work was to affect the whole earth, which in this case was limited to the inhabited part.

holding the four winds of the earth, that no wind should blow on the earth, or on the sea, or upon any tree.—The language here clearly means a destructive wind, such as causes unripe fruit to fall (6: 13), or breaks and scatters things (1 Kings 19: 11; Jer. 49: 36). Such winds lash the sea into billows and break limbs and uproot trees. This is the picture John saw, but it represents something else. It indicates that four destructive powers would be restrained for some time for a certain work to be accomplished, after which they would be released and come like a fierce wind.

2 **And I saw another angel ascend from the sunrising, having the seal of the living God:**—While John was viewing the four angels who held the winds back he saw another angel who was a messenger sent to tell the four angels what not to do. This angel ascended from the sunrising (the east) which was the direction to Palestine from Patmos where John was. As Palestine was the homeland of the Savior, the language perhaps means that it

to the four angels to whom it was given to hurt the earth and the sea, 3
saying, Hurt not the earth, neither the sea, nor the trees, till we shall have

was a divine providence which held the destructive powers in check. Seals are placed upon things for the purpose of identification or showing genuineness. Figuratively the name of God would be stamped upon them; plainly expressed they would be approved of God because of their obedience to him. Here we have an instance of words used both literally and figuratively in the one expression. "Seal" is clearly in a figurative sense; "living God" is just as clearly in a literal sense.

and he cried with a great voice to the four angels to whom it was given to hurt the earth and the sea,—As the four angels represent some divine agency that could control the damaging powers, it was given to them to hurt the earth and sea by permitting these powers to come. The angels, therefore, were said to be able to hurt the earth because they could restrain these powers or turn them loose.

3 **saying, Hurt not the earth, neither the sea, nor the trees, till we shall have sealed the servants of our God on their foreheads.**—The destructive powers represented by the four winds are to be restrained till the servants of God would be sealed—that is, till they would become servants of God by believing and obeying his word. Having the seal placed upon their foreheads indicated that the gospel truth would be received into the mind. If servants of God mean all in the future from the sixth seal, then the sealing will not be finished till the Lord comes; but if the destructive powers to be turned loose after the sealing refers to the events under the seventh seal, then the sealing occurred during the time between these seals. The latter seems the probable view for two reasons: (1) It harmonizes better with the number said to be sealed. (2) Placing the number sealed in the record between the two seals would indicate that when the destructive powers mentioned under the seventh seal had been turned loose, the sealing meant would be over. This is implied in the word "till" in verse 3. Of course, this does not mean that nobody would be saved after the events of the seventh seal began, but only that the period between these seals would be one of peace for the church when great numbers would become Christians without serious opposition.

2. NUMBER SEALED FROM THE TRIBES OF ISRAEL
7: 4-8

sealed the [3]servants of our God on their foreheads. 4 And I heard the number of them that were sealed, a hundred and forty and four thousand, sealed out of every tribe of the children of Israel:
5 Of the tribe of Judah *were* sealed twelve thousand;
Of the tribe of Reuben twelve thousand;
Of the tribe of Gad twelve thousand;
6 Of the tribe of Asher twelve thousand;
Of the tribe of Naphtali twelve thousand;
Of the tribe of Manasseh twelve thousand;

[3]Gr. *bondservants.*

4 **And I heard the number of them that were sealed, a hundred and forty and four thousand, sealed out of every tribe of the children of Israel:**—John heard the number sealed, but it is not stated who did the speaking. The word "every" is used in the sense of "all"—the 144,000 being the sum total sealed from the twelve tribes. Israel and Jew are both used spiritually to mean Christians. (Rom. 2: 28, 29; Gal. 6: 16.) But here the term evidently refers to those who were to be sealed (saved) from fleshly Israel. Mention is made of the tribes and the number given and named. Besides, they are put in contrast with a great unnumbered multitude from "every nation," who must be the Gentiles. Evidently the 144,000 is a definite for an indefinite number, for it is not a reasonable supposition that there would be exactly 12,000 from each tribe, or that amount would be all that would be saved. It means that a large number of Abraham's descendants would be saved in the period of prosperity for the church that followed the sixth seal, but not all that would be saved from the Jews throughout the Christian dispensation.

5-8 **Of the tribe of Judah were sealed twelve thousand;**—See the text above for the other tribes. Judah was not the firstborn son of Jacob, but may be mentioned here first because of his being the ancestor of Christ. The tribes are not always mentioned in the same order in the Old Testament. Joseph's descendants were divided into two tribes—Ephraim and Manasseh; hence, with Levi, the priestly tribe, there were thirteen in all. Dan is omitted from this list, supposedly because the tribe became idolatrous. Joseph is given in place of Ephraim. But since there is no regularity in the

7 Of the tribe of Simeon twelve thousand;
Of the tribe of Levi twelve thousand;
Of the tribe of Issachar twelve thousand;
8 Of the tribe of Zebulun twelve thousand;
Of the tribe of Joseph twelve thousand;
Of the tribe of Benjamin *were* sealed twelve thousand.

---

order in which the tribes are mentioned, it was only necessary to mention twelve, the original number of Jacob's sons, to indicate the whole nation of Israel.

3. A GREAT MULTITUDE SEALED
7: 9, 10

9 After these things I saw, and behold, a great multitude, which no man
could number, out of every nation and of *all* tribes and peoples and tongues,
standing before the throne and before the Lamb, arrayed in white robes, and
palms in their hands; 10 and they cry with a great voice, saying,
Salvation unto our God who sitteth on the throne, and unto the Lamb.

---

9 **After these things I saw, and behold, a great multitude, which no man could number, out of every nation and of all tribes and peoples and tongues,**—All these scenes appeared before John as he looked into heaven. They are "moving pictures" that represent something else. "After these things" means that after hearing the number sealed from the Israelites he saw this great multitude. Since they were out of every nation and all peoples, they must have been those sealed from the Gentile nations.

standing before the throne and before the Lamb, arrayed in white robes, and palms in their hands;—The scenes are still in heaven. The visions were opened in chapters 4 and 5 with God seated upon the throne and Christ as Lamb standing beside him. The setting for the visions has remained in heaven. John saw the multitude of the saved standing there. That indicates that their obedience was acceptable to God. The white robes represent their righteousness. (19: 8.) The palms were an emblem of victory. This symbolic picture shows that those saved during the period here in view will be accepted at the judgment. Of course, the same will be true of those saved in all other ages or periods.

10 **and they cry with a great voice, saying, Salvation unto our God who sitteth on the throne, and unto the Lamb.**—John heard those he saw before God and Christ ascribing praise by at-

tributing their salvation to God. That is what the redeemed will do when heaven is reached.

4. ANGELS JOIN IN PRAISE
7: 11, 12

11 And all the angels were standing round about the throne, and *about* the elders and the four living creatures; and they fell before the throne on their faces, and worshipped God, 12 saying,

Amen: [4]Blessing, and glory, and wisdom, and thanksgiving, and honor, and power, and might, *be* unto our God [5]for ever and ever. Amen.

[4]Gr. *The blessing, and the glory &c.*
[5]Gr. *unto the ages of the ages.*

11 **And all the angels were standing round about the throne, and about the elders and the four living creatures;**—In 5: 11 we learn that there were many angels round about the throne. As the place of the visions has not been changed, doubtless they are the angels referred to in this paragraph. The elders and living creatures are also mentioned in both texts.

and they fell before the throne on their faces and worshipped God, 12 **saying,**—Jesus said, "there is joy in the presence of the angels of God over one sinner that repenteth." (Luke 15: 10.) In the words of this paragraph we have, in a symbolic picture, a demonstration of their rejoicing with the saved, which indicates the final joy when all the redeemed shall get home.

Amen: Blessing, and glory, and wisdom, and thanksgiving, and honor, and power, and might, be unto our God for ever and ever. Amen.—The "Amen" affirms that the things to be said are most certainly true. Being repeated at the end of the sentence adds emphasis to the assertion. God has glory, wisdom, power, and might and deserves to be thanked for his wonderful blessings; in short, all things good can be ascribed to God as their source, both by angels and men.

5. THE MEANS OF SALVATION EXPLAINED
7: 13-17

13 And one of the elders answered, saying unto me, These that are arrayed

[6]Gr. *have said.*

13 **And one of the elders answered, saying unto me, These**

in the white robes, who are they, and whence came they? 14 And I [6]say unto him, My lord, thou knowest. And he said to me, These are they that come out of the great tribulation, and they washed their robes, and made them white in the blood of the Lamb. 15 Therefore are they before the throne of God; and they serve him day and night in his [1]temple: and he that

[1]Or, *sanctuary*

---

that are arrayed in the white robes, who are they, and whence came they?—The text says one of the elders "answered," which probably means that he was explaining an inquiry that was in John's mind, but not expressed. The elder did not ask the question to be answered by John, but to give the occasion for explaining why the white-robed multitude were in God's presence. Telling how they happened to be before God in the symbolic picture would show how they would finally be in his presence in heaven. That would settle the questions, Who will be saved? and how will they be saved?

14 **And I say unto him, My lord, thou knowest. And he said to me, These are they that come out of the great tribulation, and they washed their robes, and made them white in the blood of the Lamb.**—John recognized the fact that the elder did not ask the question to be answered, and so he said "thou knowest." Two things are expressed as the reasons why they were in God's presence—faithfulness in tribulation and having their robes washed in Christ's blood. The logical order is here reversed; being washed in the blood of the Lamb comes first and then meeting tribulation in following him. "Washing" is clearly used figuratively, for washing in the blood of Christ does not occur, if it means his literal blood and literal washing. This is only a figurative expression that means one's sins are forgiven through Christ's blood. The word "washing" is used figuratively and the word "blood" is used literally. Another proof that symbolic expressions or sentences may contain words used in both meanings. "Great tribulation" shows that only those will be saved who are faithful "unto death" (2: 10) in spite of all difficulties and persecutions. Paul expressed the same thought in Acts 14: 22.

15 **Therefore are they before the throne of God; and they serve him day and night in his temple: and he that sitteth on the throne shall spread his tabernacle over them.**—For the

sitteth on the throne shall spread his tabernacle over them. 16 They shall hunger no more, neither thirst any more; neither shall the sun strike upon them, nor any heat: 17 for the Lamb that is in the midst [2]of the throne shall be their shepherd, and shall guide them unto fountains of waters of life: and God shall wipe away every tear from their eyes.

[2]Or, *before* See ch. 4. 6; comp. 5. 6.

two reasons given in the preceding verse they are before the throne in the vision John was viewing. That, however, was a guarantee of God's approval, and the assurance that they would serve him day and night (continually) in his temple. Since the Jews served God in the temple, and Christians serve him in the church (called the temple of God, 1 Cor. 3: 16), it is perfectly appropriate that the saved in heaven finally should be said to serve him continuously in his temple. God's spreading his tabernacle over them implies that he would approve of their service by dwelling among them. Their appearance in the symbolic picture was proof that they would dwell in that eternal temple.

16 **They shall hunger no more, neither thirst any more; neither shall the sun strike upon them, nor any heat:**—This pictures the final blessings for the faithful, and is the same as expressed in 21: 3-5. The troubles, pain, worry, and burdens incident to living in the flesh here will all be gone when the redeemed dwell with God.

17 **for the Lamb that is in the midst of the throne shall be their shepherd, and shall guide them unto fountains of waters of life: and God shall wipe away every tear from their eyes.**—The Lamb that stood before the throne in the vision, and was able to break the seals and reveal the future, would, like a shepherd guides his sheep, bring them to fountains of joy. Omitting the figurative language, it means that through his redemptive work they would enjoy all the blessings of heaven. God's wiping away every tear means that he will enable us to forget all the sadness that wrings our hearts in this sin-troubled world. What a joyous anticipation!

No one who properly appreciates the blessings of sins forgiven, to say nothing about the inexpressible happiness that awaits in heaven, will fail in trying to meet the obligations which the Christian life imposes. The terms upon which pardon is secured are too plain and easy to obey to allow any excuse for disobedience. Tribulations, naturally, are not pleasant experiences, but the reward of eternal life is too important to be lost. Great favors do not come without cost. Christians should be the last to complain or try to justify neglect.

Additional Note: The purpose of the visions in this chapter must have been for the encouragement of the seven churches to whom the letters were sent. The hope of such glorious rewards would stimulate them in the struggles against persecutions, suffering, and death that had been pictured in the seals. In the same way such promises should encourage all saints to meet faithfully any trials they are called to face. So used, the lessons in Revelation are of great value to Christians in all ages.

SECTION FOUR

SOUNDING OF FIRST FOUR TRUMPETS

8: 1-12

1. THE SEVENTH SEAL OPENED

8: 1, 2

1 And when he opened the seventh seal, there followed a silence in heaven about the space of half an hour. 2 And I saw the seven angels that stand before God; and there were given unto them seven trumpets.

---

1 **And when he opened the seventh seal, there followed a silence in heaven about the space of half an hour.**—When the preceding seals were opened there was an immediate disclosing of the things they contained, but in this there is a brief silence before the scenes begin to appear. Commentators offer various explanations of what is represented by the half-hour silence, but the text gives no hint why such delay occurred before the things of the seal were made known. Often there is a brief, impressive calm before the storm in material elements. So this short silence in heaven between breaking the seal and appearance of its visions may have been intended only to emphasize the storms that would break loose when the four restraining angels no longer held back the destructive winds mentioned in 7: 1-3.

2 **And I saw the seven angels that stand before God; and there were given unto them seven trumpets.**—All the events revealed by the sounding of the seven trumpets come under the seventh seal, else there would be no disclosures at all by that seal. The acts of worship described in verses 3-5 are only preliminary to the sounding of the trumpets, as verse 6 indicates. This demands the view that events of the seventh seal did not end till the sounding of the seventh trumpet; or, that the seventh seal extends to the end of the world. All we know about these angels is that they were some that stood "before God." Probably the only reason for seven is the fact that there were seven trumpets to be sounded. If more than one was needed, then naturally there would be seven. It is not stated by whom the trumpets were given to the angels, but, as they "stand before God," it would be a reasonable presumption to say that God gave them. It was by his authority, of course, that they were to sound them.

2. A PRELIMINARY VISION
8: 3-6

3 And another angel came and stood [3]over the altar, having a golden censer; and there was given unto him much incense, that he should [4]add it unto the prayers of all the saints upon the golden altar which was before the

[3]Or, *at*
[4]Gr. *give.*

3 **And another angel came and stood over the altar, having a golden censer;**—The verses of this paragraph present a vision of worship after the manner of the Jewish tabernacle service, which is declared to be a figure of the "true tabernacle." (Heb. 8: 2; 9: 1-11.) Therefore this was an appropriate way to represent a worship scene, and would be understood by all because they were familiar with that method of worship. Christians who knew the typical nature of Jewish worship would not be surprised when John described this pictorial scene in heaven. There was the brazen altar of sacrifice in the outer court, and the golden altar of incense in the holy place of the tabernacle over against (in front of) the mercy seat in the most holy place. Incense was offered in the holy place at the golden altar, but the fire was obtained from the brazen altar. (Lev. 16: 12, 13.)

and there was given unto him much incense, that he should add it unto the prayers of all the saints upon the golden altar which was before the throne.—All along in the visions John saw God upon the throne in heaven. The golden altar which he saw in this vision was before the throne; hence, no doubt that the vision was in heaven. (See also 4: 1.) In 5: 6 the golden bowls of incense were said to be "the prayers of the saints," probably meaning that incense typically represented prayer. In the text above is a similar worship scene, but it is said the angel should "add it" unto the prayers of all saints. Perhaps the idea is that incense was symbolically represented as bearing their prayers up to God. The thought in both passages is substantially the same. While the priests were inside the temple burning incense, the people were outside praying. (Luke 1: 9, 10.) Hence, appropriately the incense was represented as prayer or as bearing the prayers up to God.

throne. 4 And the smoke of the incense, [5]with the prayers of the saints, went up before God out of the angel's hand. 5 And the angel [6]taketh the censer; and he filled it with the fire of the altar, and cast it [7]upon the earth: and there followed thunders, and voices, and lightnings, and an earthquake.

[5]Or, *for*
[6]Gr. *hath taken.*
[7]Or, *into*

4 **And the smoke of the incense, with the prayers of the saints, went up before God out of the angel's hand.**—Here it is said that the incense went up "with" the prayers of the saints, but the margin says "for" the prayers. This will harmonize better with the words in 5: 8, and shows that incense is an emblem of prayer. In the seventh chapter we have the sealing of the servants of God, after which the four angels were to let loose the destructive winds which would hurt the earth. These referred to the terrible disasters that would occur when the first four trumpets would sound. This vision of the saints' prayers ascending to God evidently means that they were pleading for mercy and help to sustain them in such fearful times as were about to come upon them. At least the vision was designed to encourage the saints to perseverance in prayer as a means of preserving their faith. The evident general purpose of all these visions was not only to warn the saints of dangers that had to be met, but also to prepare them for successfully meeting any difficulties that might come to them.

5 **And the angel taketh the censer; and he filled it with the fire of the altar, and cast it upon the earth:**—Here the censer, but no incense, was filled with fire from the brazen altar and the angel cast it upon the earth. "Much incense"—many prayers—had been offered to God, but in spite of all of them the destructive powers represented by the four winds had to come. This is here symbolized by casting the coals of fire upon the earth.

and there followed thunders, and voices, and lightnings, and an earthquake.—Casting down the coals of fire indicated fearful judgments that were to fall upon the earth, which, as viewed in these symbols, was limited to that part controlled by the Roman Empire at that time. The disturbances in the material elements here mentioned mean that these judgments in the form of commotions, destruction, and bloodshed were doing their deadly work. They are symbols which are more fully described in the visions of

6 And the seven angels that had the seven trumpets prepared themselves to sound.

---

the first four trumpets in the following verses. They are not to be taken literally, but there is no reason why the word "prayers" here should not be thus understood. Again we have evidence that literal expressions may be used as a part of a description which, in the main, is symbolical.

6 **And the seven angels that had the seven trumpets prepared themselves to sound.**—Trumpets were used to give warning or announce some events. (Josh. 6: 16; Joel 2: 1, 15; 1 Cor. 15: 52.) The silence of verse 1 had ended, the coals of fire had been thrown upon the earth and the angels prepared to sound. As each trumpet was sounded there appeared before John the vision of dreadful disasters. What do these pictures represent? Who were primarily affected by them? Here again the expositor stands on treacherous ground, and should move with special care and caution. Having already accepted the view that Revelation portrays the history of the church from the time John saw the visions, including also the nations with which it came in contact, we are forced to say that these trumpet visions referred to the church and the Roman Empire.

Constantine placed imperial approval upon the church—Rome and Christianity were allied. During the reign of Theodosius, A.D. 381-395, Christianity triumphed and Paganism was destroyed. Gibbon says: "The zeal of the emperors was excited to vindicate their own honor, and that of the Deity: and the temples of the Roman world were subverted, about sixty years after the conversion of Constantine." (*Decline and Fall,* Vol. III, p. 131.) It was between the endorsement of Christianity by Constantine and the destruction of Paganism that the sealing of the servants of God was in progress, as mentioned in chapter seven. After the destruction of Paganism in the Roman Empire, the next important period in her history ended with the fall of the empire itself in A.D. 476. The view of several commentators is that the visions that appear at the sounding of the first four trumpets refer to the destructive powers which accomplished that end. This not only seems the most plausible, but harmonizes best with the general principle of interpretation that both the church and Rome must be included in any view that is correct. Therefore the four outstanding powers that came against the Roman Empire after the death of Theodosius, A.D. 396, must be the ones signified by the four symbolic trumpets.

3. SOUNDING OF THE FIRST TRUMPET
8: 7

7 And the first sounded, and there followed hail and fire, mingled with blood, and they were cast [7]upon the earth: and the third part of the earth was burnt up, and the third part of the trees was burnt up, and all green grass was burnt up.

---

7 **And the first sounded, and there followed hail and fire, mingled with blood, and they were cast upon the earth:**—This was what John saw and heard in the vision; finding what it symbolizes is another matter. Hail and fire are evidently used to indicate punishment or destructive forces, fire probably meaning lightning when joined with hail. Referring to the plagues in Egypt (Ex. 9: 23), the Psalmist said: "He gave over their cattle also to the hail, and their flocks to hot thunderbolts." (Psalm 78: 48.) See also Psalm 105: 32. Any devastating, withering, or destroying power that came against Rome would fulfill the signification of these words. John saw the hail and fire mingled with blood, which doubtless means that the two elements would produce bloodshed, the whole scene representing destructive warfare, bringing dreadful punishment and loss of life to the empire. This is indicated by these combined elements being cast upon the earth which meant the Roman world. (Luke 2: 1.)

and the third part of the earth was burnt up, and the third part of the trees was burnt up, and all green grass was burnt up.—On this language two important questions present themselves: (1) What is meant by "the third part"? (2) Are any of these words to be taken literally? Confessedly both are difficult questions. A failure satisfactorily to answer them, however, will not affect our duty to God, nor make it necessary to change the general plan of interpreting this book. The visions must apply to the Roman Empire in the period indicated, even if we cannot certainly find the exact thing signified by every term used. We have already found that passages of general symbolic significance may contain both figurative and literal expressions. A splendid example, already mentioned, is Psalm 80: 8-11. The words "vine," "plantedst," "root," and "boughs" are all figurative. But "Egypt," "nations," "sea" (Mediterranean), and "river" (Euphrates) are all very literal. In Jer. 3: 6 the harlotry of backsliding Israel is figurative, but "high mountains" and "green trees" where their idol altars were placed are literal. Hence, the words "trees" and "grass" in this vision can be applied either figuratively or literally according to what the facts may require.

Commentators vary greatly in their views of what is signified by the expression "third part." Only two applications of it seem worthy of consideration. One is that it signifies an indefinite but "large amount"; the other, that the word "earth" means the Roman Empire, and the third part means practically one-third of the empire. In either case it is not necessary to say it means exactly one-third. The expression "third part," however, is used literally as signifying a part of the whole. It seems a natural view to say that the expression means one-third of the Roman Empire, and that as each of the four trumpets is sounded, one-third of some particular part of the empire was affected by the destructive power indicated in the vision.

As already shown the four destructive powers to be let loose at the sounding of the first four trumpets must come between A.D. 396 and the end of the Roman Empire, A.D. 476. Of the expositors consulted, three (Elliott, Barnes, and Johnson) hold the view that the Gothic invasion, under Alaric, in the first part of the fifth century is signified by the first trumpet vision. This application of the language seems to have all the probabilities in its favor and is therefore accepted as correct. The leading features of Alaric's invasions may be gathered from chapters 30 and 31 of Gibbon's *Decline and Fall of the Roman Empire*. They are as follows: In 403 Alaric was defeated by a Roman general and retired from Italy. In 408 he laid siege to Rome the first time when, according to Gibbon, "that unfortunate city gradually experienced the distress of scarcity, and at length the horrid calamities of famine" and "many thousands of the inhabitants of Rome expired in their houses, or in the streets, for want of sustenance." The miseries of famine were aggravated by pestilential disease. This siege was raised by the payment of an enormous and humiliating ransom. In 409 Alaric again attacked the city by capturing the source of supplies, by which he forced the acceptance of his demand for a new emperor. In 410 by his third and final siege the city was taken, buildings plundered and burned, both men and women inhumanly tortured and murdered till the streets were filled with dead bodies. After six days the Gothic army evacuated the city, and a few days later Alaric, their leader, was dead.

Surely such destruction of life and property would be fittingly represented by the symbols of hail, fire, and blood. The word "trees" is sometimes used symbolically to represent men. (2 Kings 19: 21-23; Dan. 4: 20-22.) Grass also may represent people. (Isa. 40: 7.) Probably trees, because of their height, indicate rulers, leaders, and those of prominence, while grass would mean the common people. As rulers, military leaders, and the people suffered, the vision fits the facts, if trees and grass are understood symbolically. A "third part" of the trees would signify that not all the rulers were relieved of their position; all the people, however, felt the effect of the siege.

If trees and grass are to be taken literally, the symbol still finds fulfillment; for the invasion of such a devastating army produces just that kind of results. An invading force that could overrun a country which had subdued and civilized a large part of mankind, sack its capital city which had stood for more than eleven hundred years, and carry away its richest treasures was undoubtedly strong enough to leave the country as if swept by devastating fires. The Gothic blow staggered the Roman Empire, but did not end it. In 1412 Adolphus, Alaric's brother-in-law and successor, concluded a treaty of peace with Rome. He says that at first he aspired "to obliterate the name of Rome" and gain immortal fame as "the founder of a new empire"; but deciding that the Goths were incapable of sustaining a well-constituted government, he determined to "restore and maintain the prosperity of the Roman Empire." (*Decline and Fall,* Vol. III, p. 295.)

4. SOUNDING OF THE SECOND TRUMPET
8: 8, 9

8 And the second angel sounded, and as it were a great mountain burning with fire was cast into the sea: and the third part of the sea became blood; 9 and there died the third part of the creatures which were in the sea, *even* they that had life; and the third part of the ships was destroyed.

---

8 **And the second angel sounded, and as it were a great mountain burning with fire was cast into the sea: and the third part of the sea became blood;**—The sounding of the second trumpet was the signal for the second vision to appear, indicating a second power that would contribute to the downfall of pagan Rome. The words "as it were" show that it was not a real mountain, but appeared as one to John. It was burning with fire—probably volcanic—and when cast into the sea gave it the appearance of blood. Here it may be observed, as under the first trumpet, the "third part" of the sea may mean a large part, not exactly one-third. Since the picture could not represent the casting of a real mountain into the sea, the word must be used symbolically. In that sense it means "kingdom." (Isa. 2: 2, 3; Jer. 51: 24, 25; Dan. 2: 35.) If "sea" and "water" mean the same thing, then in a figurative sense sea means "peoples." (17: 15; Jer. 47: 1, 2.)

9 **and there died the third part of the creatures which were in the sea, even they that had life; and the third part of the ships was destroyed.**—If a literal burning mountain were cast into the sea, the natural result would be that fish and other sea animals would be killed and ships would be destroyed. While John saw all this in a vision, it must signify something else. The things represented, however, must be suggested by the things seen in the picture. The whole scene is one of carnage, bloodshed, and destruction. The burning of ships would indicate the destruction of maritime commerce and national protection. With the destruction of ships would go the lives of those who manned them. Placing this destruction on the sea instead of land, as in the first trumpet, shows that the attack on Rome would come from the sea; that is, the struggle would be in the waters near that part of the empire. The "third part" means not all would be destroyed, but a large part would.

In harmony with the line of interpretation of the expositors already mentioned, it is very probable that the vision of the second trumpet was fulfilled in the invasion of the Vandals under Genseric. If the explanation of the first trumpet is correct, this scourge of the empire came at the proper time. Something must be its fulfillment and nothing else seems more appropriate. Concerning Genseric, Gibbon says that in "the destruction of the Roman Empire" his name "has deserved an equal rank with the names of Alaric and Attila." (*Decline and Fall,* Vol. III, p. 370.) In A.D. 429 he began his conquest in Africa, which ended in A.D. 439 when Carthage was taken. This whole province was lost to the empire. Speaking of Genseric's ambition Gibbon says "he cast his eyes towards the sea; he resolved to create a naval power," which resolve he carried into effect, and the "fleets that issued from the ports of Carthage claimed the empire of the Mediterranean." In due time he cast anchor at the mouth of the Tiber, advanced from the port of Ostia to the gates of the city of Rome. The results, in part, are thus described by Gibbon: "But Rome and its inhabitants were delivered to the licentiousness of the Vandals and Moors, whose blind passions revenged the injuries of Carthage. The pillage lasted fourteen days and nights; and all that yet remained of public or private wealth, or sacred or profane treasure, was diligently transported to the vessels of Genseric." This occurred in A.D. 455, and three years later the Roman emperor had prepared a navy of "three hundred large galleys, with an adequate proportion of transports and smaller vessels." By a surprise attack by the Vandals the Romans were defeated, "many of their ships were sunk, or taken or burnt; and the preparations of three years were destroyed in a single day." (*Decline and Fall,* Vol. III, p. 482.)

The significant thing here is that the attack upon the western part of the empire was from the sea. A fact that does suitably correspond with the vision John saw.

5. SOUNDING OF THE THIRD TRUMPET
8: 10, 11

10 And the third angel sounded, and there fell from heaven a great star, burning as a torch, and it fell upon the third part of the rivers, and upon the

---

10 **And the third angel sounded, and there fell from heaven**

fountains of the waters; 11 and the name of the star is called Wormwood: and the third part of the waters became wormwood; and many men died of the waters, because they were made bitter.

---

a great star, burning as a torch, and it fell upon the third part of the rivers, and upon the fountains of the waters;—Surely there must be some significance in the change of place where the events occurred. Under the first trumpet it was on the earth, under the second on the sea, and this on the rivers and fountains of waters. This difference could not be a matter of chance. The thing John saw in the vision was a great burning star falling upon the third part of rivers and fountains. It is generally understood, and correctly, that the star refers to a ruler, prince, or person of rank. (1: 20; Num. 24: 17.) Whoever is here represented by this star, he was to bring a destructive power against the Roman Empire. One-third of the rivers and fountains in the western part of that empire were to become bitter and cause many to die. Coming like a flaming meteor would indicate the suddenness with which his work would begin or be accomplished. Since earth, sea, and rivers were three different parts or places in the empire, there is no special reason why they should not be used in their natural sense, for we have already seen that symbolic scenes may have in them both figurative and literal language. Even if these words should be applied symbolically to the people rather than the literal places, it would still be true that these places were the theaters where these events were to occur. They had to occur somewhere.

11 and the name of the star is called Wormwood: and the third part of the waters became wormwood; and many men died of the waters, because they were made bitter.—We should not forget that the "third part" does not have to mean that exact amount, but may stand for a considerable part of the population that might suffer from an invasion coming by way of the rivers. The term "wormwood" is defined by the text itself as meaning "bitter," and indicates an extreme kind of suffering. The meteoric leader would become as destructive in his work as the wormwood would be deadly to those who drank it.

If the two preceding trumpets have been correctly interpreted, then the third trumpet should find its fulfillment in the attacks made against Rome by Attila, whose career extended from A.D.

433 to A.D. 453. The history shows that Genseric and Attila were contemporary part of the time. Genseric, however, began about five years earlier than Attila; hence, takes the lead in point of time, although Attila's invasion of Italy came about three years before the sack of the city by Genseric in A.D. 455.

Gibbon says that "in the the reign of Attila, the Huns again became the terror of the world," and that Attila "alternately insulted and invaded the East and the West, and urged the rapid downfall of the Roman Empire." The facts here gleaned from Gibbon are found in the *Decline and Fall of the Empire,* chapters 34 and 35. Attila was marvelously successful in gaining ascendancy over neighboring peoples and is said to have been able to bring into the field an army of some five to seven hundred thousand soldiers. As a military leader he was a star of the first magnitude. Gibbon further says that Attila considered himself the recipient of "celestial favor" and "asserted his divine and indefensible claim to the dominion of the earth." Quite an appropriate view to harmonize with a burning star falling "from heaven." The last few years his operations were upon the river—frontiers leading to Italy; conflagrations and enormous bloodshed followed in his path. In the spring of 452 he is said to have set forth to conquer Italy. Before reaching Rome the emperor and senate sent a commission to meet him to obtain a treaty of peace. The deliverance of Italy was purchased at an immense ransom, and Attila departed, recrossed the Danube, and soon died. Thus ended the career of one who was considered the "scourge of God." If his work was not what was intended by the third trumpet vision, nothing else seems more probable. It is certain, at least, that something was intended. No harm can be done to the text or the plan of salvation by pointing out the similarity between his work and the vision.

6. SOUNDING OF THE FOURTH TRUMPET
8: 12

12 And the fourth angel sounded, and the third part of the sun was smitten, and the third part of the moon, and the third part of the stars; that the

---

12 **And the fourth angel sounded, and the third part of the sun was smitten, and the third part of the moon, and the third**

third part of them should be darkened, and the day should not shine for the third part of it, and the night in like manner.

part of the stars;—John here sees one-third of the sun, moon, and stars smitten. Naturally this would represent some dire calamities that would affect the people in a certain part of the Roman Empire. Some understand the heavenly bodies to represent rulers, princes, and others in authority as being hurled from their positions. Possibly such events are involved in the calamities indicated, but they are not necessarily the fulfillment of the vision. Darkening of these luminaries may only indicate the gloom that disasters would bring regardless of the nature of them.

that the third part of them should be darkened, and the day should not shine for the third part of it, and the night in like manner.—The light was not completely blotted out; or, if so, only for a time. This implies that either some dim light continued to shine or the light would come back. Here, as suggested before, the third part may indicate only a considerable period of time or part of the time mentioned. An exact one-third is hardly probable. If the three preceding interpretations are correct, the fourth trumpet vision found fulfillment in some devastating power that came against the Roman Empire, the same western division affected by the preceding powers. According to historians the Western Empire ended in A.D. 476. In the last half of the century the most of the Western Empire was controlled by barbarians and the emperors at Rome were only such in name. The rule was exercised by a patrician, the officer of highest military rank. In 476 the soldiers under Odoacer mutinied and ousted Augustulus, the young emperor, from the throne, and offered submission to Zeno, emperor at Constantinople. The former glory of both emperor and senate was gone, and Odoacer by authority of the Eastern emperor ruled Italy as patrician for fourteen years. (*Decline and Fall,* Vol. III, p. 512.) So ended the Western Empire; the rulers lost their power, yet enough was left to show the light had not been completely extinguished; or, if so, it would be restored by another and different kind of ruler in the city of Rome.

It should never be forgotten that in all the calamities that befell pagan Rome there was an indirect effect upon the church. The overthrow of pagan rulers naturally gave religious teachers more influence, with the consequent result that the Bible was gradually taken from the people, and spiritual darkness began to spread. This in time led to the inauguration of a new spiritual ruler in the imperial city who, with the title of Pope, claims to be the universal father of the church.

SECTION FIVE

SOUNDING OF THE FIFTH AND SIXTH TRUMPETS 8: 13 to 9: 21

1. THE WOE TRUMPETS ANNOUNCED 8: 13

13 And I saw, and I heard [8]an eagle, flying in mid heaven, saying with a great voice, Woe, woe, woe, for them that dwell on the earth, by reason of the other voices of the trumpet of the three angels, who are yet to sound.

[8]Gr. *one eagle.*

---

13 **And I saw, and I heard an eagle, flying in mid heaven, saying with a great voice,**—The King James Version has "angel" instead of "eagle." This is a question of textual criticism which it is unnecessary to give here. The true facts may be derived from either one. Angels have been the usual agents through whom announcements have been made in the visions; but an eagle in the symbol may be the appropriate emblem to proclaim the coming woes. Its cry may have been especially significant for the purpose. The word "woe" sets the last three trumpets off in a separate class from the four preceding.

Woe, woe, woe, for them that dwell on the earth, by reason of the other voices of the trumpet of the three angels, who are yet to sound.—Doubtless the "earth" as John understood it was the Roman Empire. The woes promised then would affect those who dwelt in some part of that empire. Of course all classes, saints and sinners, would be affected more or less. The general results can be seen, though we may not always be able to find definitely what particular thing may be designated by every feature of the vision. Of course the preceding trumpets signified "woes" too, but these three indicated some that were distinctly different.

2. THE SOUNDING OF THE FIFTH TRUMPET 9: 1-12

1 And the fifth angel sounded, and I saw a star from heaven fallen unto the earth: and there was given to him the key of the pit of the abyss. 2 And

---

1 **And the fifth angel sounded, and I saw a star from heaven fallen unto the earth: and there was given to him the key of**

he opened the pit of the abyss; and there went up a smoke out of the pit, as the smoke of a great furnace; and the sun and the air were darkened by reason of the smoke of the pit. 3 And out of the smoke came forth locusts upon the earth; and power was given them, as the scorpions of the earth

---

the pit of the abyss.—The language of 8: 13 shows an evident division between the first four trumpets and the last three. How long a period intervened between the fourth and fifth is not indicated in the text. Only historical facts can give any light on that. We have already found that a star indicates a person of rank or distinction. The star had already fallen (had been cast down) when John saw it. "From heaven" would indicate that the person represented probably claimed divine honors. The pronoun "him" shows that a person is meant. The "abyss" means the abode of Satan and evil spirits. (20: 1-3.) The "key" given him indicates his power to turn loose the multitude of evil workers described in the following verses.

2 **And he opened the pit of the abyss; and there went up a smoke out of the pit, as the smoke of a great furnace; and the sun and the air were darkened by reason of the smoke of the pit.**—There poured out of the open pit smoke as if coming from a furnace. Such a smoke would darken the sun in the section where it spread. This emblem indicated some evil influence coming directly or indirectly from Satan. Probably referred to false teaching which would darken the minds of men.

3 **And out of the smoke came forth locusts upon the earth; and power was given them, as the scorpions of the earth have power.**—There is nothing in verses 1 and 2 to indicate either time or place for the fulfillment of the vision. The word "locusts" is the first significant term. John saw them upon the earth; hence, they must represent a host of men bent on some evil work. The description of the locusts (verses 7-11) will not allow them to be understood literally. In the eighth plague of Egypt the locusts came from the east—that is, from Arabia. (Ex. 10: 12-15.) This, doubtless, indicates that the hosts they represent would come from that part of the world, and would strike its blow against the Eastern Empire, the capital of which was Constantinople. If so, the fallen star was Mahomet, and the vision was fulfilled in the rise and spread of Mahometanism. This is the view of several expos-

have power. 4 And it was said unto them that they should not hurt the grass of the earth, neither any green thing, neither any tree, but only such men as have not the seal of God on their foreheads. 5 And it was given them that they should not kill them, but that they should be tormented five months: and their torment was as the torment of a scorpion, when it striketh

---

itors, and is accepted here as the view that best accords with all the facts. Since the Roman Empire was divided into Western and Eastern, the fall of the Western in 476 left the Eastern standing. Against this the Mahometans came in the first part of the seventh century. The history, then, if the facts fit the vision, will justify the application to them. The sting of the scorpion is extremely painful, indicating the terrible damage and distress to be accomplished by the powers they represent.

4 **And it was said unto them that they should not hurt the grass of the earth, neither any green thing, neither any tree, but only such men as have not the seal of God on their foreheads.**—Real locusts would destroy grass, vegetation, and leaves. Those John saw were forbidden to damage vegetation; hence, they were symbolical of something else. Regarding the invasion of Syria (A.D. 632), Abubeker, the successor of Mahomet, said: "Destroy no palm trees, nor burn any fields of corn. Cut down no fruit trees." (*Decline and Fall,* Vol. 5, p. 189.) This is another significant item in helping to identify the Mahometan scourge as the fulfillment of this emblem. Hurting men on earth is a feature that must be taken literally, as there is no other apparent way to understand it. Another proof that in symbolical passages some things may be understood literally. Seal on forehead indicates a convert—one who receives a doctrine in the mind. The command not to hurt such shows that the vision refers to a religious conflict. The text does not say who gave the command to hurt only those not sealed. If from Satan, then it could mean those who would not accept Mahomet as a prophet of God, which he claimed to be. His converts would be considered as having God's seal on their foreheads. It seems improbable that the leader of such a host would have respected the true people of God.

5 **And it was given them that they should not kill them, but that they should be tormented five months: and their torment was as the torment of a scorpion, when it striketh a man.**—

a man. 6 And in those days men shall seek death, and shall in no wise find it; and they shall desire to die, and death fleeth from them. 7 And the [1]shapes of the locusts were like unto horses prepared for war; and upon their heads as it were crowns like unto gold, and their faces were as men's

[1]Gr. *likenesses.*

This does not mean that no individuals would be killed; wars of invasion do not usually result that way. But the purpose was not to kill, but to convert men to the so-called prophet. Killing would have defeated that purpose with those destroyed. They were to be tormented with ills comparable to the stings of scorpions. This was clearly the nature of the Mahometan scourge. It is not credible that such a torment as here described would last only five literal months—150 days. Hence, the prophetic day, according to Ezek. 4: 6, is probably meant. That means a day stands for a year, and the torment would last 150 years. Expositors are not agreed on the date when this period of time began, but this is an immaterial point since we know that about this time (seventh century) the followers of Mahomet started out to make the world submit to the Koran.

6 **And in those days men shall seek death, and shall in no wise find it; and they shall desire to die, and death fleeth from them.**—This language indicates that the torment was to be so terrible that men would desire death as a release, but would not find it.

7 **And the shapes of the locusts were like unto horses prepared for war; and upon their heads as it were crowns like unto gold, and their faces were as men's faces.**—This is how the locusts appeared to John—what he saw in the vision. Horses prepared for war would indicate warfare, and probably cavalry in the main. Such seems to have been the Mahometan method of war. The words "as it were" show that what they wore on their heads were neither crowns nor gold, but only what looked like crowns made of gold. If the Mahometans are represented by this symbol, their yellow turbans would fill the demand for this part of the picture. Faces like men must be in contrast with the faces of women. The essential difference is that men's faces grow beards. As the Arabians wore beards, this feature of the symbol would also fit them.

faces. 8 And they had hair as the hair of women, and their teeth were as *the teeth* of lions. 9 And they had breastplates, as it were breastplates of iron; and the sound of their wings was as the sound of chariots, of many horses rushing to war. 10 And they have tails like unto scorpions, and

---

8 **And they had hair as the hair of women, and their teeth were as the teeth of lions.**—The women wore long hair. (1 Cor. 11: 15.) As a fulfillment of this some refer to the Arabian poem, "Antar," from which Elliott (Vol. I, p. 438) quotes as follows: "He adjusted himself properly, twirled his whiskers, and *folded up his hair under his turban,* drawing it from off his shoulders."

Teeth like those of lions indicate the fierceness with which they would prosecute their operations. That the Arabians were fierce and unmerciful in forcing submission to Mahometan teaching is perfectly evident from their history. This characteristic is manifested in their actions more than any other feature of the Mahometan soldier. It would be nothing against this interpretation if some feature in the symbol found no likeness in the thing represented; for in all figurative language only similarity is necessary to justify the comparison, not likeness in everything. This is true of parables, metaphors, or other figures. Hence, it could be true in these symbols as well.

9 **And they had breastplates, as it were breastplates of iron; and the sound of their wings was as the sound of chariots, of many horses rushing to war.**—The locusts had breastplates that looked like iron. This would indicate the strong protection they would have against their enemies. Mahomet said to his soldiers: "God hath given you coats of mail to defend you in your wars." The sound of the wings of the locusts seemed to John as the onrushing of war chariots. Doubtless this was a fair representation of the way that the Arabian cavalry made their charges. To say the least, there are too many similarities between the locusts and the Arabian soldiers to deny that they may be the ones indicated by the symbol.

10 **And they have tails like unto scorpions, and stings; and in their tails is their power to hurt men five months.**—See notes on verse 3. As the sting of the scorpion's tail would be intensely painful, so the torment inflicted by the Mahometan army would be fearful torture. On the five months see notes on verse 5.

stings; and in their tails is their power to hurt men five months. 11 They have over them as king the angel of the abyss: his name in Hebrew is Abaddon, and in the Greek *tongue* he hath the name [2]Apollyon.

12 The first Woe is past: behold, there come yet two Woes hereafter.

[2]That is, *Destroyer.*

It does not mean that this false religious system would last only 150 years, but that the torment would continue that long. The history of the Mahometan scourge harmonizes with that fact.

11 **They have over them as king the angel of the abyss: his name in Hebrew is Abaddon, and in the Greek tongue he hath the name Apollyon.**—The king over the locusts is said to have been the angel (messenger) of the abyss. If the application to the Mahometan scourge is correct, the king or leader was first Mahomet and then his successors, the Caliphs. But the real leader was Satan himself who inspires and influences men in all evil. These Hebrew and Greek words both mean *destroyer,* a term which accurately describes the work of Satan. On the word "abyss" see notes on verse 1.

12 **The first Woe is past: behold, there come yet two Woes hereafter.**—This verse simply announces the interval between the first and second woes, but gives no hint as to the time limit—the beginning or ending of either.

ADDITIONAL OBSERVATIONS

Some further facts should be observed here, if the symbol is correctly applied to the Mahometan uprising. Note the following:

1. As collected from various sources these items give the general history of the movement. Mahomet was born about A.D. 570, and in due time became one of the most effective false teachers known to the world. He began his preaching privately in A.D. 609, and his public work in 612. In 632 the Saracens left Arabia to begin their work in forcing the world to accept the Koran; in 634 the city of Damascus was taken; Jerusalem fell to them in 637, and Alexandria in Egypt in 640. Elliott (Vol. I, p. 449) says that in ten years, 634 to 644, the Caliph had reduced 36,000 cities or castles to obedience, destroying 4,000 churches, and built 1,400 mosques for the worship of Mahomet. Twice, 675 and 716, they

besieged Constantinople, but were repulsed each time; in 762 their capital was moved from Damascus to Bagdad on the Tigris River, and was called "the city of peace." From this time, says Gibbon (Vol. V, p. 300), "War was no longer the passion of the Saracens."

A.D. 609, 612, and 632 are all suggested dates to begin the 150-year period. If 612, the time that Mahomet began public preaching, be taken, the period ended with the founding of Bagdad, when war ceased as their passion. This is as probable as any, and fits this feature of the symbol.

2. If it be contended that Mahometanism fails as an unquestionable fulfillment of the symbol, the fact remains that something in that general period of the world must be its fulfillment. To say the least, the Mahometan effort to subvert the whole world to the worship of the prophet *may* be the thing represented. This false religion came into existence at the right time, swept the nations like a raging forest fire, and forced hundreds of thousands into submission. It would be remarkably strange if it were not included in a book of prophetic symbols touching the welfare of the church.

3. SOUNDING OF THE SIXTH TRUMPET
9: 13-21

13 And the sixth angel sounded, and I heard [3]a voice from the horns of the golden altar which is before God. 14 one saying to the sixth angel that had the trumpet, Loose the four angels that are bound at the great river

[3]Gr. *one voice.*

---

13 **And the sixth angel sounded, and I heard a voice from the horns of the golden altar which is before God,**—In the temple the golden altar was the altar of incense before the veil. (Ex. 40: 26.) See notes on 8: 2, 3. John sees this in heaven where God was seated upon his throne. (4: 1, 2.)

14 **one saying to the sixth angel that had the trumpet, Loose the four angels that are bound at the great river Euphrates.**—Since there is no vision intervening between the fifth and sixth trumpets, it is safe to presume that the fulfillment of the sixth vision was probably in the east also, and it will be found

after the events pictured in the fifth trumpet vision. It is unnecessary even to mention the conflicting views of expositors on this verse. As the word "angels" means messengers—agents through whom something is accomplished—and these four had been held in check for a time, it is evident that the command here means to release them for the accomplishment of what was designed. It seems wholly incredible that such a vision should not represent some great historical movement. If applying the fifth trumpet vision to Mahometanism was correct, then this doubtless refers to the Turkish power. A comparison of the vision with facts of history will make this apparent. Four "angels" here are called four "winds" in 7: 1. See Heb. 1: 7.

Since the power referred to was to operate on earth, it is most natural to understand "Euphrates" as applied literally and meaning the well-known river of that name east of Palestine. We have already learned that words may be used literally in passages of general symbolic character; an example already noted is Psalm 80: 8, "Thou broughtest a vine out of Egypt." Vine is figurative; Egypt is literal. Gibbon says that one of the greatest Turkish princes reigned in the eastern provinces of Persia one thousand years after the birth of Christ. For about a half century these people operated east of the Euphrates, accepting the Mahometan religion, and were finally authorized by the Caliph to cross the river to wage a war in defense of that religion. This explains "bound" and "loosed" in verses 14 and 15.

Commentators have had much difficulty in explaining who and what the "four angels" signify. The language implies that all four were turned loose at the same time. This does not harmonize with the view of some that the four divisions of the Turkish Empire were meant, for the reason that this division did not occur till A.D. 1092, which was some thirty years after the Turks had crossed the Euphrates on the mission designated. Probably the simplest solution is this: As the four quarters of the earth mean the whole, completeness or fulness, so the four angels would indicate the full power, which God would allow to be turned loose against the Eastern Roman Empire. This at least is in harmony with historical facts, which is much in its favor.

Euphrates. 15 And the four angels were loosed, that had been prepared for the hour and day and month and year, that they should kill the third part of men. 16 And the number of the armies of the horsemen was twice ten thou-

15 **And the four angels were loosed, that had been prepared for the hour and day and month and year, that they should kill the third part of men.**—The time of restraint before crossing the river was the time of preparation for the work. This preparation was complete when the Mahometan Caliph invested the Turkish leader as "temporal lieutenant of the vicar of the prophet." (*Decline and Fall,* Vol. V, pp. 510-512.) This occurred in A.D. 1055. Again expositors are hopelessly at variance on the meaning of the time expressed. The popular view is the day-year theory, by which the sum total of all the times mentioned is supposed to be the exact time from the crossing of the river to the fall of Constantinople in A.D. 1453. But the methods of calculation differ, though any of them may be made to give practically the time needed for the theory. Some use a thirty-day month and a 360-day year; others a solar year of 365¼ days. Some begin with the time the Turkish leader was invested with authority at Bagdad; others when he crossed the Euphrates. Doubtless such hairsplitting calculations are unnecessary. If the true explanation is that the sum total of all the times stated is the period meant, it is sufficient to know that with either of the calculations the result is substantially the time till the taking of Constantinople.

But another and perhaps simpler view is this: The destructive power which was to be permitted to overthrow the Eastern Empire of Rome was ready to begin at the exact time—hour, day, month, and year—that God's providence had determined. This view requires no exact time limit, and obviates the necessity of all calculations. And it does not interfere in any measure with the time factor as presented in the historical facts. The command to kill indicates that the vision represents a peculiarly destructive war. The "third part of men" here refers to the Eastern Empire and only one-third of that part of the Roman Empire. Not exactly one-third, but a large element. The one-third indicates that the destructive work was limited—could not kill all.

16 **And the number of the armies of the horsemen was twice ten thousand times ten thousand: I heard the number of them.**

sand time, ten thousand: I heard the number of them. 17 And thus I saw the horses in the vision, and them that sat on them, having breastplates *as* of fire and of hyacinth and of brimstone: and the heads of the horses are as the heads of lions; and out of their mouths proceedeth fire and smoke and brim-

—Literally two myriads of myriads, or 200 millions. Such an immense number—definite for indefinite—was doubtless intended to indicate an enormous army. Gibbon speaks of the "myriads of Turkish horses" and the blood of 130,000 Christians as "a grateful sacrifice to the Arabian prophet." (Vol. V, p. 512.) This shows that the Turkish army had a countless number of horsemen, and accords with the view taken of this vision. If this number indicates the result of one campaign, the total results over the period must have been appalling.

17 **And thus I saw the horses in the vision, and them that sat on them, having breastplates as of fire and of hyacinth and of brimstone:**—This is a description of how the horses and soldiers on them appeared to John as he beheld the vision. The breastplates appeared as if they were of fire, hyacinth, and brimstone; that is, red, blue, and yellow.

and the heads of the horses are as the heads of lions; and out of their mouths proceedeth fire and smoke and brimstone.—The horses with heads that looked like lions' heads, doubtless, was meant to indicate the fierceness and suddenness with which the Turkish army would strike its blows. Probably the roaring of the lion would also represent the loud noise as the firearms were discharged in their battles. The firing of guns from horseback would appear to those at a distance as coming from the horses' mouths. Here several expositors think we have a most remarkable proof that this vision refers to the Turkish power, though others think that the purpose was only to indicate that the wars in view were to be surpassingly fiendish. The latter is possible, but the facts are so significant that the former seems more probable. It is supposed that the invention or discovery of gunpowder was in the first half of the fourteenth century. That the Turks used artillery in their siege and capture of Constantinople, A.D. 1453, is the plain statement of Gibbon. He mentions three large cannons and says that "fourteen batteries thundered at once on the most accessible places," and that one of them possibly "discharged one

stone. 18 By these three plagues was the third part of men killed, by the
fire and the smoke and the brimstone, which proceeded out of their mouths.
19 For the power of the horses is in their mouth, and in their tails: for their
tails are like unto serpents, and have heads; and with them they hurt. 20

hundred and thirty bullets." (Vol. VI, pp. 388, 389.) Again the same author says: "From the galleys, and the bridge, the Ottoman artillery thundered on all sides; and the camp and city, the Greeks and the Turks, were involved in a cloud of smoke which could only be dispelled by the final deliverance or destruction of the Roman Empire." (*Ibid.*, p. 400.) The use of such cannon implies the use of smaller arms that were discharged with gunpowder.

18 **By these three plagues was the third part of men killed, by the fire and the smoke and the brimstone, which proceeded out of their mouths.**—"These three plagues" may mean that by the exploding of gunpowder—fire, smoke, and brimstone—the effect was produced. Of course, in such a battle many would be killed, but probably the thought has more direct reference to the destruction of the eastern Roman Empire, as being a one-third of the whole of the Roman Empire. Constantinople, founded by Constantine more than eleven hundred years before, as the capital of Rome, had withstood every assault up to this time. The siege with cannon delivered it into the hands of the Turks.

19 **For the power of the horses is in their mouth, and in their tails: for their tails are like unto serpents, and have heads; and with them they hurt.**—If the fire, smoke, and brimstone that, in the vision, seemed to pour out of the horses' mouths represent the use of firearms in taking a city, then it is easy to see how the power appeared in their mouths. The smoke from exploded gunpowder bursting from their guns would appear as if coming from the horses heads. How the power was also represented by their tails is not so evident. John did not see in this vision the ordinary cavalry soldiers with swords, spears, or bows, but horses with mouths from which there appeared to go fire, smoke, and brimstone, and with tails like serpents. The text says the power of this army was in the horses' mouths and tails. Elliott (followed by B. W. Johnson) attempts further to identify this symbol with the Turkish power by the fact that horsetails were emblems of authority carried by the Pachas—Turkish rulers. This

And the rest of mankind, who were not killed with these plagues, repented not of the works of their hands, that they should not [4]worship demons, and the idols of gold, and of silver, and of brass, and of stone, and of wood; which can neither see, nor hear, nor walk: 21 and they repented not of their murders, nor of their sorceries, nor of their fornication, nor of their thefts.

[4]See marginal note on ch. 3. 9.

view seems to overlook the fact that the text says power was *in* the tails "to hurt," not just an emblem of power. If there is any specific application for the expression, most expositors have failed to suggest it. Perhaps the serpentlike tails only signify the biting torture that would be felt by those who would have to suffer from the new kind of warfare indicated.

20 **And the rest of mankind, who were not killed with these plagues, repented not of the works of their hands, that they should not worship demons, and the idols of gold, and of silver, and of brass, and of stone, and of wood; which can neither see, nor hear, nor walk:**—The remaining two-thirds that were not killed in the Greek one-third of the Roman Empire did not repent. The language shows that, though they claimed to be Christians, they had so apostatized from the true teachings of Christ that they were both idolaters and morally corrupt. Of course this was also true, in fact, of the other parts of the Roman Empire. They were so wedded to their corrupt religious practices that they failed to realize that the awful Turkish scourge that had fallen upon them was probably God's providential punishment for their own sins. They learned no salutary lesson from their terrible calamities and sufferings. They worshiped departed spirits, a thing which is contrary to apostolic teaching. (1 Cor. 10: 20.) They also worshiped the idols made with their own hands from different kinds of materials, images that can neither see, hear, nor walk. Another plain sin. (Acts 19: 26.)

21 **and they repented not of their murders, nor of their sorceries, nor of their fornication, nor of their thefts.**—It is unnecessary here to offer detailed proof that the professed Christians were then guilty of these crimes to an alarming extent. The fact that the charge is here made is sufficient proof unless we want to deny the record. Of course, it does not mean that every one was guilty, but that these sins were scandalously prevalent. It is not a matter of wonder that such crimes would cause a just God to per-

mit such a disaster to befall them. In these expressions we have still another example that words may be used in their literal sense, even when in a passage that is highly symbolic.

SECTION SIX

REVIVAL OF TRUE CHRISTIANITY

10:1 to 11:14

Preliminary Note: In the first four trumpet visions we saw the overthrow of pagan Rome—a work finished in A.D. 476; in the fifth and sixth the Mahometan scourge and the destruction of the Greek or Eastern Empire—completed in the taking of Constantinople in A.D. 1453; the seventh trumpet, which is the announcement of the end of the world, is recorded in 11: 15-18. The things pictured in this section, 10: 1 to 11: 14, come between the sixth and seventh trumpets. This must be the time that includes the restoration of genuine Christianity. Departures from the true teaching began early, grew rapidly after the Roman Emperor, Constantine, recognized Christianty as the true religion. The selection of a universal bishop (pope) in the sixth century made a complete apostasy. Something more than eight centuries till the fall of Constantinople did not improve the church as 9: 20 and 21 show. The visions of this section were intended to encourage Christians then that truth would be restored; and to assure us, through the facts of history, that it has been.

1. THE LITTLE BOOK EPISODE

10: 1-11

1 And I saw another strong angel coming down out of heaven, arrayed with a cloud; and the rainbow was upon his head, and his face was as the

1 **And I saw another strong angel coming down out of heaven, arrayed with a cloud; and the rainbow was upon his head, and his face was as the sun, and his feet as pillars of fire;**—In this vision John sees an angel coming down from heaven to earth. Like the one mentioned in 5: 2, this one is a "strong" angel, probably indicating the greatness of the work he was to do. The description is somewhat similar to that of Christ in 1: 13-15, and some expositors think the angel represents Christ. Others think it refers simply to the power of Christ manifested in the work of the Reformation. Another view is that the angel represents Martin Luther as the leading character in giving the Bible back to the people. Perhaps it is only necessary to say that the

sun, and his feet as pillars of fire; 2 and he had in his hand a little book open: and he set his right foot upon the sea, and his left upon the earth; 3

angel may signify some great movement that had the approval of heaven, whatever may have been the agencies by which accomplished.

Clothed with a cloud indicates glory, and means that the work would be glorious. (Ex. 16: 9, 10; 24: 16.) The rainbow upon his head was a symbol of peace and mercy pointing to the character of the work to be accomplished. The face appearing as the sun naturally suggests the idea of light, which harmonizes with the vision of an open book. The work of the Reformation really consisted in giving the people the word of God—flooding the mind with divine light. It is uncertain just what may be signified by feet "as pillars of fire," but the expression harmonizes with the dazzling appearance of the heavenly messenger. The scene was profoundly impressive, and doubtless prepared John's mind to give the closest attention to what the angel commanded.

2 **and he had in his hand a little book open: and he set his right foot upon the sea, and his left upon the earth;**—What is signified by the "little book" has puzzled expositors much; but, if applying this vision to the Reformation movement is correct, then it is easy to understand that a book would be involved, for the Reformation largely pertained to the work of giving back to the people the word of God. The fact that the book was "open" clearly indicates that something was to be made known, or the book itself had a message of some kind. However, the text does not inform us what the book contained. The words "little" and "open" show that this book is different in some way from the "sealed" book of 5: 1. Verse 11, compared with 11: 1-13, makes it probable that the "little book" contained the revelation that was made to John about the restoration of the true church. The thoughts of this glorious work would be sweet, but experiences in doing it would be most bitter. Such are the facts as history shows.

John saw the angel placing one foot on the sea and the other upon the earth. On the significance of this expression commentators offer various views. The simplest and most plausible is that it intimates the general effect of the work the angel announced—

applicable to the entire world rather than limited work signified by the preceding trumpets. The symbol is certainly a proper one to indicate a diffusion of knowledge.

3 **and he cried with a great voice, as a lion roareth: and when he cried, the seven thunders uttered their voices.**—What the angel cried is not mentioned, but it was with a voice that roared like a lion. This may have been to indicate the power with which the great Reformation work should be done. As already mentioned, this work mainly had to do with a book. This meant the translation of the Bible and placing it in the hands of the people. Just preceding the Reformation the art of printing was discovered, and the Bible was the first book printed. Since the church in its apostatized condition was opposed to the distribution of the Bible among the people, naturally such distribution created a great disturbance, and produced the most bitter opposition to the reformers. Martin Luther, being the recognized leader in the work of placing the Bible in the hands of the people, of course came in for all the hatred and bitterness that a corrupt church could bring against one considered a heretic. The most natural application of the "seven thunders" is that they were uttered against the voice of the angel. That means that when the angel uttered his voice and John was authorized in the symbol to "measure the temple of God," the power opposed thundered against it with vehemence. All this plainly indicated that when the Reformation began the Roman Pope hurled against it his condemnation. What was done to Luther and his writings as well as other reformers are matters of history too well known to need recounting. To say the least, then, this application corresponds with the facts of history. The preaching of the word and defending the liberty to obey it resulted in the papal bulls of excommunication. In his life of Wickliffe, p. 198, Le Bas says: "The *thunders* which shook the world when they issued *from the seven hills* sent forth an uncertain sound, comparatively faint and powerless, when launched from a region of less elevated sanctity." (Quoted by Elliott, Vol. II, p. 112.) The term "seven" may here mean full or complete, and indicates the full condemnation the Roman pontiff pronounced

seven thunders uttered their voices. 4 And when the seven thunders uttered *their voices,* I was about to write: and I heard a voice from heaven saying, Seal up the things which the seven thunders uttered, and write them not. 5

---

against the reformers. Or, as suggested by some expositors, it may indicate that the thunders came from the seven-hill city. This would also identify the thunders with the papal authority.

D'Aubigné's History, Vol. II, pp. 114, 115, gives an account of a papal bull against Luther in which his writings that contained certain doctrines were to be burned, and Luther given sixty days to retract or be condemned as an obstinate heretic. Luther wrote Pope Leo X a letter in which he said, "Farewell, Rome." He denounced the Pope and on December 10, 1520, he publicly burned the bull the Pope had issued against him. (*Ibid.,* p. 150.) Surely the papal thunders had uttered their voices.

4 **And when the seven thunders uttered their voices, I was about to write: and I heard a voice from heaven saying, Seal up the things which the seven thunders uttered, and write them not.**—It is perfectly clear that John at first understood that the voices of the thunders were a part of the symbolism that was to be recorded, for his commission definitely required him to write what he saw. (1 : 11, 19.) It is also clear that the voices were speaking words, but strong like the voice of a lion. He was in the act of writing what the thunders said when a voice from heaven forbade it. This shows that God would not allow them to be recorded as a part of the revelation. To do so might have left the impression that they came from God; refusing them a place in the record shows that they came from some power which was in fact against God's will. This the apostate church of that day certainly was. The thunders claimed to be of heaven, but were not. In other passages in this book where John is commanded to write, the language shows plainly that the purpose was to give the faithful and true words of God. (14: 13; 19: 9; 21 : 5.)

The word "seal" sometimes means to approve (John 3: 33); it might also signify to hide or keep secret; but here to "seal up" with the additional words "write them not" simply means not to record them, for the reason that they are not true.

And the angel that I saw standing upon the sea and upon the earth lifted up his right hand to heaven, 6 and sware by him that liveth [5]for ever and ever, who created the heaven and the things that are therein, and the earth and the things that are therein, [6]and the sea and the things that are therein, that there shall be [7]delay no longer: 7 but in the days of the voice of the seventh angel, when he is about to sound, then is finished the mystery of God, according to the good tidings which he declared to his [8]servants the prophets.

[5]Gr. *unto the ages of the ages.*
[6]Some ancient authorities omit *and the sea and the things that are therein.*
[7]Or, *time*
[8]Gr. *bondservants.*

---

5 **And the angel that I saw standing upon the sea and upon the earth lifted up his right hand to heaven,**—These words show that John observed the angel as he assumed a position in accord with the solemn announcement he was about to make.

6 **and sware by him that liveth for ever and ever, who created the heaven and the things that are therein, and the earth and the things that are therein, and the sea and the things that are therein.**—The oath by him that liveth forever refers to God. It indicates that the angel was assuring John he had God's endorsement and verification of the truth of what he was about to say. The certainty of this was in the fact that God was able to confirm it, for he was the Creator of heaven, earth, and sea and everything in them. This was to give assurance to the churches then, and to others since, that the work depicted in this vision would actually be accomplished in spite of all the anathemas, excommunications, and papal thunders that could roar from the head of an apostate church. We should not forget that all these visions were intended, directly or indirectly, to protect and sustain the true people of God in facing the sufferings, persecutions, and death that might be inflicted by their enemies.

that there shall be delay no longer: 7 but in the days of the voice of the seventh angel, when he is about to sound, then is finished the mystery of God, according to the good tidings which he declared to his servants the prophets.—The margin, as well as the King James, says "time" shall be no longer. Certainly the literal meaning of the Greek word is "time." But we know that time did not end when the angel made his declaration, for two reasons: one is, that we are already several centuries this side of the Reformation; the other is, that the other features of this vision present things that were to occur before the seventh angel sounded. "Delay" no longer would mean that certain things would have to begin at once. If it meant that the Reformation—restoring the open Bible to the people—was to begin without delay, that was true in fact. But the seventh verse seems to connect the question of time—the period in view—with the sounding of the seventh trumpet. This was to bring the end, and has not yet transpired. (11: 15.) The Greek expression may be given thus: "time shall be not yet." That still presents a difficulty, for something must be added to complete the thought. Does it mean that a certain period of time will not end yet—until a specified work is done? Or, at a designated event, time shall not be prolonged? The latter seems the more probable view of the words. With this view accepted, the passage will yield this general thought: From the time that the Reformation began, the work to be accomplished through the Bible laid open to the world would not end till the seventh angel sounded; or, in other words, when that time comes the work for God in redeeming man will be finished and time or opportunity will not be prolonged beyond that event. Another way to express it is that "then is finished the mystery of God."

The angel also told John that finishing the mystery (divine purpose) of God was to be according to the good tidings declared by the prophets. That means it would be according to the promises about the overthrow of the "man of sin" and the final glorious triumph of the church. (Dan. 7: 24-28; 2 Thess. 2: 4-9.) From 2 Thess. 1: 7-10 we learn that the coming of the Lord will be at the judgment, when the wicked shall "suffer punishment, even eternal destruction from the face of the Lord." But when he comes (according to 2 Thess. 2: 8) he will destroy or slay the lawless one—"man of sin"; hence, the end of time, the purpose of God finished, and the judgment will all be at the same time.

Knowing Paul's promise that the "man of sin" would be destroyed by the Lord at his coming, some reformers were led to conclude that the return of the Bible to the people would soon bring that event. Elliott's Commentary (Vol. II, pp. 135-145) gives a number of examples, beginning with Luther himself. But, like many since, they probably expected the Bible to affect more people than it did. They were right in the fact that Christ will

8 And the voice which I heard from heaven, *I heard it* again speaking with
me, and saying, Go, take the book which is open in the hand of the angel
that standeth upon the sea and upon the earth. 9 And I went unto the angel,
saying unto him that he should give me the little book. And he saith unto
me, Take it, and eat it up; and it shall make thy belly bitter, but in thy

---

slay the "man of sin" at his appearing, but mistaken about his coming being soon, as we now know. Others since have also been mistaken in like ideas.

8 **And the voice which I heard from heaven, I heard it again speaking with me, and saying, Go, take the book which is open in the hand of the angel that standeth upon the sea and upon the earth.**—John himself now becomes a part of the scene—he is commanded to take the book out of the angel's hand. This, doubtless, indicated that he was to have some important part in the work of restoring the scriptural doctrine and practice. But as he had been dead about fourteen hundred years when the Reformation began, he did not do any of that work personally. Being one of the number through whom the true gospel was first promulgated, the restoration of that gospel gave him back his position of authority as one who ruled under Christ as King. (See Matt. 19: 28.)

9 **And I went unto the angel, saying unto him that he should give me the little book.**—These words show that John obeyed the voice he heard from heaven.

And he saith unto me, Take it, and eat it up; and it shall make thy belly bitter, but in thy mouth it shall be sweet as honey.—The command to eat the book was strange instruction; its double effect was equally strange. Of course, all this was to be carried out in the symbolic scene, and must represent some remarkable events on earth. To eat a book cannot be understood literally. We often speak of devouring a book by which we mean to give deep and earnest meditation upon its contents. The thoughts would give him joy, but practicing the teaching would bring persecutions, sufferings, and possible death. A similar thought is expressed by Jeremiah: "Thy words were found, and I did eat them; and thy words were unto me a joy and the rejoicing of my heart." (Jer. 15: 16.) This figure is based upon the fact that some food that is pleasant to the taste may give pain to the stomach.

mouth it shall be sweet as honey. 10 And I took the little book out of the angel's hand, and ate it up; and it was in my mouth sweet as honey: and when I had eaten it, my belly was made bitter. 11 And they say unto me, Thou must prophesy again [1]over many peoples and nations and tongues and kings.

[1]Or. *concerning* Compare Jn. 12. 16.

10 **And I took the little book out of the angel's hand, and ate it up; and it was in my mouth sweet as honey: and when I had eaten it, my belly was made bitter.**—This verse states that the effect which the angel said would follow his eating the book happened just as was said. This occurred in the symbol; the things represented are implied in the next verse.

11 **And they say unto me, Thou must prophesy again over many peoples and nations and tongues and kings.**—The teaching here would be the same whether the little book represents the Bible or the special things revealed in the eleventh chapter regarding the measurements of the temple and worship. The work of restoring a pure worship was based upon giving the people the open Bible; the things named in 11: 1-13 are a symbolic description of how that restoration would be effected, and the time during which it would continue. Learning from this vision what was to be done and its glorious benefits would be as pleasant to the weary mind as honey is to the taste. But doing the work would bring the bitterest experiences of persecution. This the reformers soon learned, as history abundantly shows.

As already mentioned, John would again prophesy when his teachings would be proclaimed. The work of bringing that to pass began with the reformers, but was completed later by a restoration to apostolic purity and simplicity. Peoples, nations, tongues, and kings show that the gospel was still to be universal for rulers and subjects. This implies one church, for the truth preached by the apostles had to be preached again. Not a new church, but a restoration of the original.

2. THE MEASURING THE TEMPLE, ALTAR, AND WORSHIP COMMANDED

11: 1, 2

1 And there was given me a reed like unto a rod: [2]and one said, Rise, and measure the [3]temple of God, and the altar, and them that worship

[2]Gr. *saying.*
[3]Or, *sanctuary*

1 **And there was given me a reed like unto a rod: and one said, Rise, and measure the temple of God, and the altar, and them that worship therein.**—In the preceding chapter the symbolic scenes were transferred from heaven to earth. This vision is also upon the earth. As John himself became a part of the vision of the little book, so he is a part of this vision. There appear before him the temple, altar, and worshipers with instruction to measure the three. While the old temple in Jerusalem had been destroyed for more than a quarter of a century, yet there was no more forceful way for John to understand the lessons than through that picture. Jewish minds had been accustomed for centuries to the temple system of worshiping God. Besides, before its destruction it had been used as a type of the church. (1 Cor. 3: 16.) Even the tabernacle which preceded the temple was definitely made, in its two parts, to represent the church and heaven. (Heb. 9: 1-9, 24.) John's being told to measure the temple, altar, and worshipers in the symbol meant that when the time arrived that this vision applied the church, the worship, and worshipers were to be measured. Once more we have in this text an example of a symbolic passage which contains both figurative and literal expressions. The words temple and altar are figurative; the word worshipers is literal. Measurements to be correct and valuable must be made by standard and accurate implements. In this case John was given a reed like a rod, something both accurate and convenient. Note that it was *given* him, not something he made; it must have been given by the angel, not by men. Since the purpose of measuring, according to verse 2, was to determine what was approved or acceptable to God, then the measuring instrument had to be of divine make. This was nothing else than the New Testament teaching that already had been given by the apostles. As it was perfect (2 Tim. 3: 16, 17), nothing else was allowed as a standard (Gal. 1: 8, 9).

therein. 2 And the court which is without the [3]temple [4]leave without, and measure it not; for it hath been given unto the [5]nations: and the holy city shall they tread under foot forty and two months. 3 And I will give unto

[4]Gr. *cast without.*
[5]Or, *Gentiles*

2 And the court which is without the temple leave without, and measure it not; for it hath been given unto the nations: —Since the word Gentiles means "nations," there is no difference between the King James and the Revised in meaning. The Gentiles could enter the outer court of the Jewish temple, but not the temple itself. In fact, only consecrated priests could enter that building. The altar referred to is the golden altar of incense inside the holy place of the temple. The Jewish priests were typical of Christians. (1 Pet. 2: 5.) As John in the symbol was told to measure the worshipers (priests) so in the thing represented only those professing to worship God were to be measured. The reason for this is that at the time the measuring was to be done the religious world was in a hopeless state of apostasy. The purpose of applying God's word to such false religions was twofold: first, to show that they were false; second, to show honest souls how to worship God in spirit and in truth. It was unnecessary to measure the irreligious; if they wanted to be saved, the law was in God's word already. But false teaching needed to be measured to show it a perversion of divine truth.

and the holy city shall they tread under foot forty and two months.—The material temple was in Jerusalem, the Jewish capital, and was considered a holy city. Like the temple, it is also a type of the church. (Gal. 4: 26; Heb. 12: 22.) The final state which we call heaven is referred to as the "holy city, new Jerusalem." (21: 2.) The words could not mean literal Jerusalem, for that has been "trodden down" by Gentiles practically all the time since it was taken by the Romans in A.D. 70 till the present, which is more than 1,260 years. To be trodden under foot would be fulfilled when Gentiles would corrupt and devastate the church. This had already been done when the measuring of the temple began with the Reformation. How long the church had thus been corrupted by worldly influences is stated here to have been "forty and two months." If taken literally, it would be three and one-half years or 1,260 days. This would be entirely too short a time to correspond with the period when the church was corrupted by worldly and human devices. With the year-day theory the time was 1,260 years. This is substantially the length of time that Roman Catholicism ruled with absolute authority, and therefore the time that religious corruption completely permeated church life.

It would not affect the argument if the exact date when the period began and ended could not be ascertained; the facts would still be true. The period evidently refers to the time during which the church was completely under the domination of the papacy; or, from the time the bishop of Rome became head of the church (pope) till his power was broken by the Reformation.

3. THE TWO WITNESSES
11: 3-14

my two witnesses, and they shall prophesy a thousand two hundred and threescore days, clothed in sackcloth. 4 These are the two olive trees and the two [6]candlesticks, standing before the Lord of the earth. 5 And if any

[6]Gr. *lampstands*.

3 **And I will give unto my two witnesses, and they shall prophesy a thousand two hundred and threescore days, clothed in sackcloth.**—Forty-two months, verse 2, and 1,260 days refer to the same period. This shows that months were counted as having thirty days. Three important things are mentioned in this verse: the witnesses, the time they were to prophesy, and the manner of their prophesying. Since the word witness means one who testifies, to prophesy simply means to give their testimony. They are further described in the next verse.

4 **These are the two olive trees and the two candlesticks, standing before the Lord of the earth.**—Expositors generally agree that what is said about the two witnesses is probably the most difficult passage in the whole book of Revelation. The theories suggested are hopelessly contradictory. One commentator (Alford) says: "No solution has ever been given of this portion of the prophecy." Some say that Enoch and Elijah are meant; others suggest Moses and Elijah. But no plausible reason has been assigned by anyone why Old Testament prophets should be re-

ferred to in a passage which clearly refers to a time subsequent to the great Roman apostasy. Most of the interpretations offered are not only indefinite in fact, but lack any evidence of showing that they fit the time necessarily required. This, of course, is fatal to them. Several expositors understand the two witnesses to mean the Bible—that is, the Old and New Testaments. This view appears to be the only one with enough plausibility to merit serious consideration. That the things stated harmonize with the facts of Bible power and influence during the long, dark night of papal domination preceding the Reformation is evidence that this view is most probably correct. To these facts we now give consideration.

The two witnesses are said to be "two olive trees and the two candlesticks." This certainly means that the witnesses are symbolically represented by the olive trees and candlesticks. The purpose of a candlestick is to give light. (Matt. 5: 15.) Anything that gives light may figuratively be called a candlestick. For that reason the seven churches (1: 20) are called candlesticks. For exactly the same reason David referred to God's word as a "lamp unto my feet, and light unto my path." (Psalm 119: 105.)

As lampstands (marginal translation) could only give light through the oil they contained, so the things which furnished the oil are also called the witnesses. In Zech. 4: 2-14 there is a similar symbol, but of one candlestick with seven lamps. The olive trees emptied their oil into the lampstands. They are explained to mean the two anointed ones. (Verse 14.) Zerubbabel is told that what he would accomplish would not be by might (any army) or by power, but by Jehovah's Spirit. (Verse 6.) In plain, simple words the meaning is that just as the oil supplied to the lampstands by the olive trees gave the light, so what he did would be by direction of the Spirit of God. So in the text in Revelation the thought is that the light given by the Bible is due to the fact that it was spoken by men inspired by God's Spirit. Since the candlestick which lighted the tabernacle stood in the holy place in front or before the mercy seat where God met the high priest in the atonement service, so here these candlesticks are represented as "standing before the Lord of the earth." This would, at least, imply that their testimony had God's approval. That is certainly true of the Bible.

The word "witness" means one who testifies, and testimony is what is said. The two divisions of the Bible are called the Old and New Testaments. Hence, they are witnesses in the sense that they present God's testimony. Being two distinct parts of the testimony, they fit the requirements of this symbol.

As already suggested, taking the 1,260 days literally—three and one-half years—would not be sufficient time for such momentous things as the symbol indicates; hence, the year-day theory, which means 1,260 years, seems a necessity. The text does not say that the witnesses testified only 1,260 years, but they testified that long "clothed in sackcloth." They had testified before that period began and again after they were killed and came to life. "In sackcloth" means that their testimony was hampered by dangerous obstacles in a dark and gloomy time. For true Bible teaching there have been no more mournful conditions than when the papal power virtually ruled the world. Possessing only handmade copies of the Scriptures was a natural handicap against their distribution. The teaching of the apostate church that only papal interpretations were authoritative naturally closed the door against personal study of the word. Bitter persecutions against those who refused submission to the Pope's authority complete the picture of gloom. Prophets clothed in sackcloth were a most appropriate symbol of the Bible struggling against such terrific odds.

Naturally all apostasies rise gradually, and fixing a definite date for their commencement is difficult and often impossible. It is certain that the great apostasy foreseen by Paul (2 Thess. 2: 3-12) began in the full sense when the "man of sin" was fully developed. That such a development was a real "antichrist"—against Christ—is an undoubted truth. Evidently the beginning of this great apostasy was the beginning of the 1,260-year period.

According to the general admission of church historians the first and basic departure from apostolic teaching was exalting one elder above the others and making him "the Bishop" of the congregation. This soon led to extending his authority over other congregations. This again led to ascribing superior authority to bishops of congregations in prominent cities. At this time they were called *patriarchs.* The contest for supremacy finally narrowed down to Rome and Constantinople, with Rome gaining the victory. Two

man desireth to hurt them, fire proceedeth out of their mouth and devoureth their enemies; and if any man shall desire to hurt them, in this manner must

---

dates especially have been urged as the time to place the beginning —A.D. 533 and 606. However, if no exact date can be fixed, the general facts are the same.

Elliott's commentary (Vol. III, p. 151) says that during the century A.D. 430 to 530 the Roman Papacy "*incipiently* assumed that principle of *domination over the ten kingdoms of Western Christendom,* as well as of *usurpation of Christ's place in the church, blasphemy against God,* and *hostility to God's saints,* by which it was afterwards more fully characterized." This gradual development of the man of sin is indicated in the following facts: Rome being the capital of the empire would naturally suggest the supremacy of her patriarch. Constantinople being the eastern capital naturally led to a rivalry for this honor. At the council of Chalcedon (A.D. 451) the Legates of Leo, patriarch of Rome, proclaimed him "head of all churches." In two councils at Rome, A.D. 494 and 495, the Roman bishop was declared to have "authority over the whole church." In A.D. 533 Justinian, the emperor of the eastern part of the empire, issued a decretal letter solemnly recognizing the Roman bishop as "head of the churches." The foregoing facts have been gleaned from Elliott's commentary, Vol. III, pp. 151 to 160. For reasons to be given in the notes on verses 8-13 A.D. 533 is accepted as the probable time to date the beginning of the 1,260-year period.

In A.D. 588 the patriarch of Constantinople, John the Faster, assumed the title of "Universal Bishop." Gregory the Great, who was at that time patriarch of the church at Rome, sent John and the emperor each a letter condemning their use of the title. Notwithstanding this condemnation, in A.D. 606 Boniface III induced Phocas, who reached the Roman throne through murder, to transfer the title from John the Faster to himself. This is probably to be considered but a wicked confirmation of the decree issued by Justinian in A.D. 533. The incident of A.D. 606 is reported by church historians generally.

5 **And if any man desireth to hurt them, fire proceedeth out of their mouth and devoureth their enemies; and if any man**

he be killed. 6 These have the power to shut the heaven, that it rain not during the days of their prophecy: and they have power over the waters to turn them into blood, and to smite the earth with every plague, as often as they shall desire. 7 And when they shall have finished their testimony, the beast that cometh up out of the abyss shall make war with them, and over-

---

shall desire to hurt them, in this manner must he be killed.—The Old and New Testaments as God's two witnesses, though testifying for 1,260 years in sackcloth, were to have God's protection and finally prevail. Their enemies, therefore, were to be devoured. Fire proceeding out of their mouth cannot be taken literally. God said to the prophet Jeremiah: "Because ye speak this word, behold, I will make my words in thy mouth fire, and this people wood, and it shall devour them." (Jer. 5: 14.) The evident meaning is that those who were enemies or rejected God's word would be punished finally as his word taught. The warning is repeated for emphasis with the statement that such enemies are to be killed "in this manner"—the manner God's word prescribes.

6 **These have the power to shut the heaven, that it rain not during the days of their prophecy**:—This language is probably an allusion to what was said about Elijah in 1 Kings 17: 1 and James 5: 17, 18. Withholding rain probably means that those who rejected or perverted the testimony of God's word would be deprived of blessings during the time of their wicked career as well as receive final condemnation.

and they have power over the waters to turn them into blood, and to smite the earth with every plague, as often as they shall desire.—The language here is doubtless an allusion to what Moses did in bringing plagues upon Pharaoh and the rebellious Egyptians. (Ex. 7: 17-20.) Again, we note that there is no reason for this language to be understood literally. That many calamities came upon the enemies of the true church during the long period of papal domination is, of course, certain. But since this text does not explain the things meant by these symbolic expressions, we do not attempt any definite application. However, the calamities came upon them as often as the witnesses desired—that is, just when in God's providence it was appropriate.

7 **And when they shall have finished their testimony.**—This does not mean the final end of their testimony, but the end of the

come them, and kill them. 8 And their [7]dead bodies *lie* in the street of the

[7]Gr. *carcase.*

testifying in sackcloth which resulted in their symbolic death. As subsequent verses show they came to life again, and of course continued their testimony.

the beast that cometh up out of the abyss shall make war with them, and overcome them, and kill them.—From Dan. 7: 3, 17, 23 we learn that "beast" represents a king or kingdom. The Greek word rendered "beast" means a wild and vicious animal. Here it must refer to some antichristian institution, for it fights against the two witnesses whom God raised from the dead and exalted to heaven. The beast here, we are sure, refers to the great apostasy described by Paul as the "man of sin"; plainly, it means the papacy. This will appear more certain as we examine references to the beast in subsequent chapters. (See 13: 1 and 17: 3.) From 20: 2, 3 we learn that the abyss is the proper abiding place of Satan; hence, the beast coming up out of the abyss indicates some unchristian institution under the influence of the devil because it came into existence by his power. The sad part of the picture here is that this devilish power or institution was to overcome the witnesses and kill them. Since we have decided the witnesses symbolize the word of God, killing them means the suppression of their testimony for a time; or, that they were to be rejected as true witnesses by some kind of legal enactment. As A.D. 533 has been shown to be the most probable time to date the beginning of the 1,260 years, the end of that period when the witnesses were to be slain would be 1793. If about that time the word of God was legally abolished, we have what fits the symbol perfectly, and additional proof that the dates accepted are correct.

Just as the "man of sin"—the papacy—was developed gradually, so the Protestant Reformation which broke the stranglehold of that "beast" came into existence gradually. All revolutions and apostasies arise that way. That the Reformation began in reality with Martin Luther in the sixteenth century is generally conceded, though preliminary work was done by others. Wickliffe in England in 1360 "appealed from the Pope to the word of God"; in the next century John Huss in Bohemia attacked "the scandalous lives of the clergy," and may be termed the "John the Baptist of the Reformation." (D'Aubigné's Reformation, Vol. I, p. 92.) But the Reformation really began with Martin Luther in Germany when he made his attack upon the sale of *Indulgencies,* the iniquitous barter, endorsed by the Pope, in which exemption from the penance prescribed for sin was sold for cash. On October 31, 1517, Luther posted his ninety-five propositions on the church door at Wittenberg, which was the most daring blow against papal authority that had ever been struck. It introduced perhaps the greatest religious struggle known to history to settle the momentous question—shall God's word (the two witnesses) be accepted as supreme authority, or shall mankind bow in subjection to a humanly originated papacy? From this time till the end of the 1,260 years the battle raged with fury, though the witnesses had already been testifying in distressing times. Killing the witnesses means either the complete destruction of the Bible or its suppression for a time. Verse 11 shows the latter to be what is meant. This could be done either by legally refusing to allow it read, or proclaiming it false.

The French Revolution introduced the "Reign of Terror," during which citizens were executed by the hundreds without justice or mercy. The nation was drenched in blood. The National Convention from 1792 to 1795 was a seething mass of the most revolting crimes. In 1793 in the convention Liberty and Reason had been celebrated as the real worship; "the ancient faith had been abjured"; the calendar had been changed and the traditions attached to it destroyed; the "Convention had substituted a divinity created in their own image" "for the supreme God of religious faith." (Guizot's France, Vol. VI, pp. 189, 190, 250.) Truly, God's witnesses may be declared legally dead under such circumstances. Since the "beast"—the papacy—caused the witnesses to testify in sackcloth, it may also be charged as indirectly causing their death, because France was up to that time dominated by Catholicism.

8 **And their dead bodies lie in the street of the great city, which spiritually is called Sodom and Egypt, where also their**

Lord was crucified. 9 And from among the peoples and tribes and tongues and nations do *men* look upon their [7]dead bodies three days and a half, and suffer not their dead bodies to be laid in a tomb. 10 And they that dwell on

---

Lord was crucified.—Leaving dead bodies to lie unburied in the street is both disrespectful and contemptible. The symbolic vision, as John saw it, indicates the great contempt which infidels who had decreed the abolishment of God would show for the Bible. The bodies lying in the street may also indicate that they could not get rid of the Bible though they officially rejected it. Since it was France that decreed the death of the witnesses, if the "great city" is to be taken literally it would refer to Paris, the capital. But elsewhere in this book the great city is used symbolically to indicate papal Rome. (See 14: 8; 17: 18; 18: 10.) In the last passage Babylon is used figuratively to represent the apostate church. Here we are told that spiritually the great city is also called "Sodom and Egypt"—that is, both of these cities are typical of it. Sodom represents corruption and Egypt bondage. Papal Rome, then, held its subjects in spiritual corruption and bondage. Then France turned infidel and rejected God's word that was spiritually crucifying Jesus afresh. (Heb. 6: 6.) Being a Catholic country, the witnesses were slain within the boundaries dominated by the papacy. The great city then probably refers spiritually to that apostate church rather than to any special earthly city.

9 **And from among the peoples and tribes and tongues and nations do men look upon their dead bodies three days and a half, and suffer not their dead bodies to be laid in a tomb.**—The legal abolishment of God's word was such a daring and unprecedented act that peoples from all nations would be amazed as they looked upon the situation—doubtless wondering whether the Bible would ever again be received as a supreme law. Here the year-day theory is probably the correct view. If so, the time is three and a half years. The French "Convention" continued for a little more than three years. The Constitution of 1793 was declared inapplicable and described as having been "dictated by tyranny," "accepted by terror," "an organized anarchy." (Guizot's France, Vol. VI, p. 235.) The new constitution was accepted in 1795. Refusing to allow dead bodies to be buried indicates that some individuals may have been in favor of the Bible during that

the earth rejoice over them, and make merry; and they shall send gifts one to another; because these two prophets tormented them that dwell on the earth. 11 And after the three days and a half the breath of life from God entered into them, and they stood upon their feet; and great fear fell upon

---

brief reign of terror, but the madness of the people prevented any chance to accept or practice its teaching.

10 **And they that dwell on the earth rejoice over them, and make merry; and they shall send gifts one to another; because these two prophets tormented them that dwell on the earth.**— Human weakness and sin make wicked people rejoice when their opposers are overcome. They are here represented as manifesting their joy by sending gifts one to another. This is a very natural way of expressing joy. The Bible condemns sin in most unsparing terms and it is no surprise that those who substituted liberty and reason for its divine precepts should rejoice at its legal suppression. It is not necessary to say that this language applied to all the earth, but only to that nation where the death of the witnesses was proclaimed. Nothing is more tormenting than condemnation coming from a divine source. Men may laugh at the Bible, yet they feel most deeply the sting of its rebukes.

11 **And after the three days and a half the breath of life from God entered into them, and they stood upon their feet;** —As God's power alone can raise a dead body, John declares that the bodies stood up because God sent the breath of life into them. So the word could testify only because it was the language of the Spirit of God; hence, when the Bible had been given liberty to testify again, it was attributed to God's giving them life. This symbolically is represented by the witnesses standing on their feet. The French National Convention lasted a little more than three years. Before ending in 1795 it "restored public worship." (*Standard History of the World,* Vol. VII, p. 3399.) In 1797 Napoleon concluded a treaty of peace with Pope Pius VI. (*Ibid.,* p. 3412.) This was about three and one-half years after the French Convention dethroned God and the Bible by decreeing the worship of Liberty and Reason. But, if the exact dates of the beginning and ending of the three and a half years cannot be fixed, the general facts here are substantial proof that the proper application of the symbol has been made.

them that beheld them. 12 And they heard a great voice from heaven saying unto them, Come up hither. And they went up into heaven in the cloud; and their enemies beheld them. 13 And in that hour there was a great earthquake, and the tenth part of the city fell; and there were killed in the earthquake [8]seven thousand persons: and the rest were affrighted, and gave glory to the God of heaven.

[8]Gr. *names of men, seven thousand.* Comp. ch. 3. 4.

and great fear fell upon them that beheld them.—To witness such a bodily resurrection would produce great fear upon those who saw it. This appeared to John in the vision. It indicates a profound fear that would naturally affect the people when the Bible was again received as the authoritative word of God. The wicked would tremble; the righteous would have a deeper respect for things divine.

12 **And they heard a great voice from heaven saying unto them, Come up hither. And they went up into heaven in the cloud; and their enemies beheld them.**—Clearly these are symbolic words. The picture is what John saw; what it represents is a different thing. John heard the call for raised witnesses to come up hither, and saw them ascend to heaven in a cloud. If we are correct in saying the witnesses represent the word of God, then their exaltation means their restoration as heaven's authoritative teachers. Their enemies beheld the witnesses ascend, which indicates that the infidel influences that attempted the destruction of the Bible were unable to prevent its return to its rightful place as authority.

13 **And in that hour there was a great earthquake, and the tenth part of the city fell; and there were killed in the earthquake seven thousand persons: and the rest were affrighted, and gave glory to the God of heaven.**—In the vision John saw an earthquake shake down a tenth part of the city and kill seven thousand, but it is not to be applied literally, for a real earthquake would not likely destroy exactly one-tenth and kill just seven thousand. That one-tenth might refer to one of the kingdoms composing the great Roman Empire is certainly possible, but more probable that it should refer to a large, but indefinite, part of spiritual Babylon—the papal church—as the part affected. Symbolically the earthquake indicates a great commotion among men, either political or religious. The principles of the Reformation which had

14 The second Woe is past: behold, the third Woe cometh quickly.

been working for more than two centuries were strengthened by religious toleration and the freedom of Bible study. When these principles of Protestantism came against the Catholic church, it produced the mightiest religious commotion in history. In the symbol John saw seven thousand killed. The number seven is conceded by practically all expositors to mean perfection or completeness. If to be so applied here, it would indicate that the Reformation, which restored the Bible to the people, would so completely destroy the papal power that no one would be forced to bow to her mandates. Subsequent history shows that to be the fact. That such a commotion with such results would produce profound fear of God is a natural conclusion. The words probably do not mean that mankind would fear in the sense of all rendering obedience, but rather in attributing such wonderful things to divine power.

14 **The second Woe is past: behold, the third Woe cometh quickly.**—Verses 12-14 are a very brief description of many centuries. After the exaltation of the witnesses to heaven—the Bible given back to the people by the Reformation—their testimony has been available, and will continue to be till Jesus returns for the judgment. As in the case of the apostasy, so the Reformation was a gradual work. The seeds were planted when the Bible began to be translated into various languages; the militant fight began when Martin Luther defied the Pope of Rome; it was finished when Protestantism with an open Bible was a recognized fact by the world in general. All that is involved in the church's history from that time till Jesus comes again is comprehended in verses 12-14, but no detailed visions are given to cover this period. An entirely different series of emblems begins with 11: 19. Here is the distinct division between the two grand parts of Revelation. In the latter half of the book is recorded the millennium or binding of Satan (20: 1-6) which, though briefly expressed, must come in the interval between the Reformation and the final judgment. Regardless of what view is taken of the binding of Satan, the fact that it is referred to as a thousand years shows it must be a long period. That the struggle in defense of Christianity against the apostate

church has been going on since the Reformation freed the Bible for general study is evident to all. This study we are still allowed to pursue without serious restraint, which is no mean proof that we are now in the midst of that period called the millennium. See notes on the text of that passage.

SECTION SEVEN

SOUNDING OF THE SEVENTH TRUMPET 11:15-18

1. THE FACTS STATED 11:15, 16

15 And the seventh angel sounded; and there followed great voices in heaven, and they said,

The kingdom of the world is become *the kingdom* of our Lord, and of his Christ: and he shall reign [9]for ever and ever.

[9]Gr. *unto the ages of the ages.*

15 **And the seventh angel sounded; and there followed great voices in heaven, and they said,**—We should not overlook the fact that these words describe what John saw and heard in heaven; they belong to the vision, but they announce some momentous event. Since there were only seven trumpets to sound, and this one was the last, it must indicate the ending of something. In 10:7 we are told that when the seventh angel "is about to sound, then is finished the mystery of God." This can have no other meaning than that the seventh trumpet sounds the end of time. It is the last trump to sound when the dead shall be raised. (1 Cor. 15:52; 1 Thess. 4:16.) The preceding verse says the third "woe cometh quickly." That means that when the events that were to come under the second woe had past, it would be only a short time till the end would come.

The kingdom of the world is become the kingdom of our Lord, and of his Christ:—The King James Version says "kingdoms"; but the Revised uses the singular "kingdom." Commentators agree that the Revised is correct. Unless this verse is properly understood there will be little prospect of rightly understanding much that is to follow in this book. Three questions deserve careful consideration: (1) What is meant by the kingdom becoming God's? (2) When will it become his? (3) Why is it referred to as the kingdom of both God and Christ? A kingdom in its fullness includes a king, territory, subjects, rule, and law. Sometimes, like other words, by a figure of speech (whole for part) it is used when only one feature is indicated. Thayer's Greek Lexicon, first definition, gives *royal power, kingship, domin-*

ion, rule as its meaning. Acts 1: 6 is given as an example. The Jews had the law of Moses, they were in the territory, they were the subjects; they wanted Jesus to restore the reign or *rule,* yet they said restore the kingdom. Evidently that is the meaning of the word in the verse we are considering. The sovereign dominion, royal power, will finally come back to the Father. Luke 16: 23 and John 19: 42 are plain examples of using the whole for a part. "Lazarus" stands for the spirit of Lazarus and "Jesus" means the body of Jesus.

Regarding the second question we should note: God was king over Israel before they demanded a man for a king. (1 Sam. 8: 4-9.) This kingdom (rule) was taken from the Jews because they killed Christ. (Matt. 21: 38-43.) Christ established a kingdom which began after his return to the Father, and Christians were citizens of it. (John 18: 36; Col. 1: 13; Rev. 1: 5-9.) The kingdom—royal dominion or rule—was to be taken away from the Jews and given to another nation—Christians. This reign since Pentecost has resided in Christ. After the judgment it will be returned to the Father. (1 Cor. 15: 24-26.) At the present time Christ has the legal right over all (1 Pet. 3: 22), but in the final state he himself will be subject to God. (1 Cor. 15: 27, 28.) During the present age Satan has usurped a wicked rule over the world, but this is not legally his and, therefore, has no bearing on the argument that Christ is now a reigning king.

Finally, it may be asked how it can be also called the kingdom "of his Christ," if the dominion will then be turned back to God? We may as well ask how the kingdom now can be called the "kingdom of God," if the dominion belongs to Christ. That it is called both now is evident from many passages. (Matt. 6: 33; 21: 43; John 3: 3; Matt. 20: 21; John 18: 36.) In like manner the final kingdom (heaven) is called the "kingdom of Christ and God." (Eph. 5: 5.) Rev. 22: 1 speaks of "the throne of God and of the Lamb." It is perfectly clear that in the broad general sense whatever is God's is also Christ's, but that does not conflict with the fact that Christ is now reigning and will turn that reign back to God at the judgment. That seems the evident meaning of the text in hand.

But if by any chance the passage should be applied to Christ's

16 And the four and twenty elders, who sit before God on their thrones, fell upon their faces and worshipped God, 17 saying,

rule before the final judgment, still there is nothing in the words to show that absolute righteousness will prevail. The reason for knowing that such a state will prevail in heaven is the fact that we are told that "flesh and blood cannot inherit the kingdom of God." (1 Cor. 15: 20.) The things that lead to sin will not be there, and all dying in sin will not be there. (Rev. 21: 8.) Such is not the case while we are on earth. Hence, the only application possible, if the text refers to Christ's reign on earth, is that it would mean a time when all could or would have a chance to serve him if they desired. This happens to be true now; but, for reasons already given, is not the application of the text. The distinction between all serving Christ and all having the *privilege* to do so will be fully developed when we discuss the millennium mentioned in chapter 20. Earthly kingdoms will not all be converted and become God's kingdom a thousand years before the final judgment; for the all-sufficient reason that after the thousand years are finished there will still be "nations" engaged in the great final battle just preceding the final judgment. (20: 7-11.) This is another reason why "kingdom" in 11: 15 refers to heaven instead of to a period of absolute and universal righteousness on earth preceding the judgment.

and he shall reign for ever and ever.—The expression "our Lord" refers to God, for the additional expression "his Christ" will admit of no other application. The pronoun "he"—singular number—must refer to God or Christ, not to both. For the reasons already given, and the fact that the reign is to be turned back to God at the judgment, it is evident that it refers to God.

16 **And the four and twenty elders, who sit before God on their thrones, fell upon their faces and worshipped God,** 17 **saying,**—Regarding the twenty-four elders see notes on 4: 4. These words picture what John saw in heaven; they are in the vision and only indicate that when the redemption of man has been accomplished the angelic creatures will ascribe all praise to God.

2. THE SONG OF THANKSGIVING
11: 17, 18

We give thee thanks, O Lord God, the Almighty, who art and who wast; because thou hast taken thy great power, and didst reign. 18 And the nations were wroth, and thy wrath came, and the time of the dead to be judged, and *the time* to give their reward to thy [1]servants the prophets, and to the saints, and to them that fear thy name, the small and the great; and to destroy them that destroy the earth.

[1]Gr. *bondservants.*

We give thee thanks, O Lord God, the Almighty, who art and who wast; because thou hast taken thy great power, and didst reign.—These words of praise to God are further proof that the pronoun "he" in verse 15 refers to God. The vision pictures a time when God's rewards had come to the righteous and his rejection of the wicked had taken place. The words "didst reign"—aorist tense in the Greek—indicate a completed past action; God had entered upon his final, eternal rule, and the heavenly creatures were ascribing thanksgiving to him because his reign had begun.

18 **And the nations were wroth, and thy wrath came, and the time of the dead to be judged, and the time to give their reward to thy servants the prophets, and to the saints, and to them that fear thy name, the small and the great; and to destroy them that destroy the earth.**—In their song of praise the elders look back to the final struggle when the wickedness of the nations caused the last great battle between right and wrong, vividly described in 19: 11-21, followed by the final judgment as pictured in 20: 11-15, and the proper rewards were given to both classes. The description of the righteous as prophets, saints, small and great, does not mean different rewards to different classes; it is only a rhetorical way of saying that the righteous of all classes will spend eternity with God and his Christ. Destroying the wicked who cursed the earth with their sins is the final proof that this section refers to the judgment and that glad day when all the redeemed enter upon the joys of their eternal home. The very thought should fill righteous souls with inexpressible ecstasy!

The logical division of the book at 11: 19 forces the following symbols to cover substantially the same time as the preceding series, for the end of the world closes both series. This is evident because 11: 18 says it is "the time of the dead to be judged," and

20: 12 says that John saw "the dead were judged out of the things which were written in the books." If the first series ends with the judgment, the second series would have no place in time unless they were presenting the same period from different viewpoints. More than once we will be called to note the fact that a new vision or set of symbols is carrying us back over ground already surveyed. Such reviews will either present the same event with a different scene or give a detailed description of what has had only brief mention.

Here the first set of symbols comes to an end. Evidently they were designed to encourage the saints to be faithful "unto death," by pointing out many of the struggles that would fall to the lot of Christ's followers. They were to impress Paul's declaration that "through many tribulations we must enter into the kingdom of God." (Acts 14: 22.) May our hearts rejoice in the glorious anticipation of the blessed eternal kingdom, while in another set of symbols we restudy the things that had to happen to God's children.

PART FOURTH

VISIONS OF THE WOMAN AND HER ENEMIES
11: 19 to 20: 15

SECTION ONE

THE DRAGON AND THE BEASTS
11: 19 to 13: 18

1. A PRELIMINARY VISION
11: 19

19 And there was opened the [2]temple of God that is in heaven; and there was seen in his [2]temple the ark of his covenant; and there followed lightnings, and voices, and thunders, and an earthquake, and great hail.

[2]Or, *sanctuary*.

19 **And there was opened the temple of God that is in heaven; and there was seen in his temple the ark of his covenant;**—Before beginning to open the seven seals (6: 1) there appeared to John, as recorded in chapters 4 and 5, some preliminary visions. These visions, too, were seen in heaven, and were evidently intended to assure John that what was about to be revealed concerning the future would certainly be accomplished. The temple was typical of the church. (Heb. 9: 1-9; 1 Cor. 3: 16.) Displaying the open temple with the ark inside, doubtless, was designed to show that the things to be presented in the following visions had special reference to the church and its worship. In the preceding series of symbols the church's struggles against paganism received the stronger emphasis, the references to the papacy being sketched briefly. In the following series the church's spiritual enemies are given major consideration.

and there followed lightnings, and voices, and thunders, and an earthquake, and great hail.—These things appeared to John as he beheld the vision. Since the whole scene was probably intended to impress John with the necessity of a pure church and pure worship, it was appropriate that he should see and hear such things as would indicate the necessity of reverencing God and his word. It is very similar to those manifestations of divine majesty that accompanied God's speaking the commandments on Mount

Sinai, and the plagues in Egypt. There were thunders, hail, lightnings, and earthquakes. (Ex. 19: 16-18; Psalm 18: 13.) At the opening of the new covenant law on Pentecost there were manifestations of his great power. (Acts 2: 1-4.) So before beginning these symbols, showing the struggles to maintain the apostolic church, a display of divine power was an appropriate thing. They might indicate commotion in the things fulfilling them.

2. THE WOMAN AND DRAGON DESCRIBED
12: 1-6

1 And a great sign was seen in heaven: a woman arrayed with the sun, and the moon under her feet, and upon her head a crown of twelve stars; 2

---

1 **And a great sign was seen in heaven: a woman arrayed with the sun, and the moon under her feet, and upon her head a crown of twelve stars;**—A "sign" is something to represent or signify something else. This very word shows that the vision John saw in heaven was a symbol of something. Sign is often used to indicate future events as Matt. 16: 3 clearly shows. The very language of this paragraph proves that its meaning here applies to the future.

The commentators generally agree that the woman in the vision represents the church. The relationship of a wife to her husband symbolically refers to the relationship of the saved to God or Christ. Of national Israel Isaiah said: "For thy Maker is thy husband; Jehovah of hosts is his name." (Isa. 54: 5.) Concerning Christ's relationship to the church Paul said: "For the husband is the head of the wife, as Christ also is the head of the church." (Eph. 5: 23.) In verse 32 he declares plainly that in using the illustration of husband and wife he spoke of Christ and the church. Changing the figure slightly, Paul refers to Sarah and Hagar as being the two covenants—one from Mount Sinai, the other from Jerusalem—and says that Christians are children of the free woman. (Gal. 4: 23, 24, 31.) There is no room for doubt here that the woman represents the church. Paul told the Corinthians that he had espoused them unto one husband. (2 Cor. 11: 2.)

The description of the woman shows that she represents the true apostolic church, as it was originally established, not the corrupt

and she was with child; and she crieth out, travailing in birth, and in pain
to be delivered. 3 And there was seen another sign in heaven: and behold, a
great red dragon, having seven heads and ten horns, and upon his heads

---

church that was developed later. Sun, moon, and stars constitute the sum of material light; so through the word of God is given to the church all the spiritual light there is. Hence, indirectly Christ's disciples are the "light of the world." (Matt. 5: 14.) Since Christ is the "sun of righteousness" (Mal. 4: 2), and the source of all our spiritual light, "arrayed with the sun" probably means the church clothed with Christ. As those in Christ have put him on, arrayed with Christ is a most natural meaning for the expression. The suggestion made by some commentators that the moon represents the Jewish covenant or law seems the most probable explanation for this expression. The moon is an inferior light-shining body—reflects its light; such were the Jewish scriptures. Seeing the moon under her feet would imply their inferiority. Crowned with twelve stars most likely represents the apostles, who next to Christ occupied the most honorable position in the church as leaders. Twelve indicates perfection, and the apostles were the perfect mediums through which the church received her light. The word "crown" here—Greek *stephanos*—means a crown of victory, not a ruling crown. The apostles victoriously revealed the truth.

2 **and she was with child; and she crieth out, travailing in birth, and in pain to be delivered.**—The peculiar condition of the woman indicates a time when the church was to increase its membership and implies that this vision takes us back to an early day in her history, if not to the very beginning. The success of the church in the first century is found in the New Testament. From that time on, of course, we are dependent on secular history.

3 **And there was seen another sign in heaven: and behold, a great red dragon, having seven heads and ten horns, and upon his heads seven diadems.**—There is no need to worry about the seeming incongruity of a dragon being "in heaven," or just what is meant by heaven, as some interpreters do; for what John saw is only a picture to indicate certain facts or events. This should be kept constantly in mind as the symbols are studied. The word "sign," as in verse 1, shows that something in the future is indi-

cated. The word "dragon" is used thirteen times in the New Testament and all are in this book. In verse 9 he is called "the old serpent" and "the Devil and Satan." Literally, it seems to denote some fabulous, serpent-form creature. Since the dragon is represented here as the deadly enemy of the woman and her offspring, the language appears as an allusion to Eve and the serpent in the Eden tragedy. (Gen. 3: 1-6.) But the description here indicates that Satan figures in the events only as an instigator of fight on the church, the dragon being some earthly agency or medium through which the actual opposition was to be made. Plainly stated, the spirit of the dragon is the devil; he inspires the dragon's acts.

The dragon is described as being great and red in color. This implies that his fight against the true church would be terrific and characterized with bloodshed. It is not unusual for fabulous creatures in mythology to be given some unnatural appearance, but there must have been significant reasons for picturing an enemy of the church in such hideous form. Seven symbolically represents completeness and heads indicate power or authority, but there is probably some additional reason why that number is used in this emblem. The full significance of this symbol will be seen only when compared with similar ones in 13: 1 and 17: 3. The word "horn" is an emblem of power and the number "ten" indicates its general or universal exercise. Some expositors explain "heads" to be symbolic of wisdom and the "horns" to indicate power. That, of course, is true in fact as applied to the dragon, and the numbers show the complete and extensive use of such powers. The diadems upon the seven heads show that the dragon was some kind of ruling institution.

It is a matter of common knowledge that the church was established within the Roman Empire, and was therefore politically subject to Roman law. That the church passed through many persecutions and suffered much from the Roman rulers is also a known fact. The natural conclusion, then, is that the first great power against the church was pagan Rome. Elliott's commentary (Vol. III, p. 15) gives documentary evidence that the dragon became a Roman ensign near the close of the second century. If so, it is another indication pointing to the Roman Empire as the church's first enemy—in the texts using the word dragon. Another proof

seven diadems. 4 And his tail draweth the third part of the stars of heaven, and did cast them to the earth: and the dragon standeth before the woman that is about to be delivered, that when she is delivered he may devour her

---

that pagan Rome was that first enemy is that John later saw a beast to which the dragon gave his authority (13: 1, 4), and this beast had seven heads. Diadems upon the heads would indicate at least that ruling authority was claimed. In 17: 12 the ten horns of the beast are said to be "ten kings." Horns, therefore, signify the power to rule. "Ten" may only mean the universal rule of the Roman Empire or different divisions of the empire that supplied this power. The leading facts are sufficient to identify the dragon as pagan Rome. John saw a monster in the picture, and there is no more necessity for every detail to represent some specific thing than for every item in a parable to indicate something definite in the application.

4 **And his tail draweth the third part of the stars of heaven, and did cast them to the earth:**—In the vision John apparently sees the dragon passing through the heaven sweeping down one-third of the stars with his tail. Perhaps all that was intended by this part of the symbol was to indicate what a terrific and powerful enemy the church would have to meet in the Roman Empire. This feature of the symbol harmonizes with the idea that the dragon is represented as a serpent. Since this work of the dragon seems to have occurred before the exaltation of the "man child" (verse 5), it may indicate different rulers that had been subjected to Rome when nations had been conquered by Roman arms, or it could refer to religious leaders who were killed or who apostatized. If this be the proper application, then the stars falling to earth indicated that rulers would lose their places of authority or deny the faith. The third part means not all, but a great number.

and the dragon standeth before the woman that is about to be delivered, that when she is delivered he may devour her child.—As the woman represents the church, the birth of a child indicates increase in the church by the addition of members. Of course, there had been a growth of the church since its establishment at Pentecost. The emblem here then must mean some time when there was about to be a great increase of the church, or when the increase became so influential that Rome felt the necessity of

child. 5 And she was delivered of a son, a man child, who is to rule all the [3]nations with a rod of iron: and her child was caught up unto God, and

[3]Or, *Gentiles*

its destruction. The persecution under Diocletian, the emperor, began in A.D. 303. The evident purpose was the destruction of Christianity. Gibbon says it was perhaps represented to Diocletian that "the glorious work of the deliverance of the empire was left imperfect, as long as an independent people was permitted to subsist and multiply in the heart of the provinces." (*Decline and Fall,* Vol. II, p. 62.) The twenty-third of February was the day appointed "to set bounds to the progress of Christianity," doors of church houses were broken open and volumes of the holy scriptures committed to the flames. (*Ibid.,* p. 63.) Gibbon further says that Diocletian was at length transported beyond bounds of moderation and declared "his intention of abolishing the name Christian." (*Ibid.,* p. 69.) In A.D. 311 Maximin, the Eastern Roman emperor, spoke of the "obstinate impiety of Christians" and readily consented to their banishment. (*Ibid.,* p. 78.) The dragon really stood ready to prevent the increase of the church.

5 **And she was delivered of a son, a man child, who is to rule all the nations with a rod of iron:**—In the symbol John now sees not only the woman, but also the son that was born. For reasons already presented the woman represents the church. Who or what is meant by the man-child has occasioned much disagreement among noted expositors. Some apply the words to Christ largely because the man-child was said to be caught up to God and to rule the nations with a rod of iron. The following reasons satisfactorily show that the words do not refer to Christ: (1) After Christ's ascension to heaven there was no occasion for his being rescued from the dragon. (2) The theory would make the church *produce* Christ, whereas the Bible makes him the founder of the church. (3) In verse 17 of this chapter the dragon is said to "make war with the rest of her seed, that keep the commandments of God." This language can only refer to members of the church. Then the man-child symbolically represents the increase of the church—those who through the church's activities became Christians. If there is an apparent lack of harmony in the man-child

representing members of the church and the woman the church, it is not a serious objection. Mother and child are of the same nature, and increase in the church leaves it the same institution. However, to use Paul's allegory (Gal. 4: 24-31), the woman may be said to represent the covenant and members the children of the covenant.

The expression "rule them with a rod of iron" in 19: 15 clearly refers to Christ, but the same expression in 2: 27 just as clearly refers to saints that keep Christ's commandments. This text, 12: 5, is unquestionably synonymous with 2: 27 and not with 19: 15. The word "rule" in all these texts (Greek *poimaino*) means to "shepherd," not the word (Greek *basileuo*) which means "reign." The thought is that those who keep Christ's commands will be able to shepherd or lead with God's word. A "rod of iron" would indicate that their dominion would be strong and dependable. Such is the nature of God's word.

and her child was caught up unto God, and unto his throne. —Since this cannot refer to Christ's ascension, it must mean some kind of glorious exaltation for Christians who had safely come through the persecutions. That this exaltation came soon after the decrees of Diocletian and Maximin that Christianity should be abolished is what the facts indicate as necessary to fulfill the symbol. In the vision the child appeared to John as ascending to the very throne of God to escape the wrath of the dragon. This means that the church with its increase in membership was to be exalted to a position where it would be protected instead of persecuted.

Gibbon says that "the defeat and death of Maximin soon delivered the church from the last and most implacable of her enemies." (*Decline and Fall,* Vol. II, p. 78.) He means the last of the enemy rulers in that age, for the beast to which the dragon was to give its authority was yet to arise. (13: 1, 4.) The sorrows as of a woman in travail had ceased. In A.D. 310 Galerius, the Eastern Emperor, issued his *Edict of Toleration* by which Christians were granted the right to worship God and conduct their own religious services. In A.D. 308 the Roman Empire was divided among six contending emperors. In A.D. 313 two of them, Constantine and Licinius, issued the celebrated Edict of Milan in which Christians were given complete liberty. By a victory over Licinius in A.D.

unto his throne. 6 And the woman fled into the wilderness, where she hath a place prepared of God, that there they may nourish her a thousand two hundred and threescore days.

323 Constantine became the sole ruler of the Roman Empire. By laws and edicts which he issued that were favorable to Christianity, and the calling of the church council at Nice in A.D. 325, he accepted Christianity as the true religion. It is even claimed he became a member of the church. Gibbon says the church considered Constantine as a "generous patron, who seated Christianity on the throne of the Roman world." (Vol. II, p. 273.) Surely the exaltation of the man-child symbol finds its appropriate fulfillment in this acknowledgment of Christianity.

6 **And the woman fled into the wilderness, where she hath a place prepared of God, that there they may nourish her a thousand two hundred and threescore days.**—John here, by anticipation, briefly refers to what he describes in verses 14-17. See those verses for comments.

3. THE WAR IN HEAVEN
12: 7-12

7 And there was war in heaven: Michael and his angels *going forth* to war with the dragon; and the dragon warred and his angels; 8 and they

7 **And there was war in heaven: Michael and his angels going forth to war with the dragon; and the dragon warred and his angels;**—After mentioning the flight of the woman, we have in this paragraph a statement of the sources of power, both wicked and good, with which this war was to be carried on. The words describe what John saw in the picture; they symbolically represent the efforts to destroy the true church. According to Dan. 10: 13; 12: 1, Michael is an angel of heaven that assists the righteous. Symbolically this indicates that in the struggles the church would be under the providence of God and led by those holding the testimony or words of Jesus. This evidently was designed to encourage the Christians to endure faithfully in spite of all persecutions. Verse 9 plainly says the dragon is the devil or Satan. Just as Jesus operates through his followers, so Satan operates through human agents. In this case pagan Rome is the instrumental drag-

prevailed not, neither was their place found any more in heaven. 9 And the great dragon was cast down, the old serpent, he that is called the Devil and Satan, the deceiver of the whole [4]world; he was cast down to the earth, and his angels were cast down with him. 10 And I heard a great voice in heaven, saying,

[5]Now is come the salvation, and the power, and the kingdom of our

[4]Gr. *inhabited earth.*
[5]Or, *Now is the salvation, and the power, and the kingdom, become our God's and the authority* is become *his Christ's*

on, the devil the influencing dragon. Hence, the visible war refers to the conflict between pagan Rome and the church.

8 **and they prevailed not, neither was their place found any more in heaven.**—This means that pagan Rome was to fail in her war on the church. In spite of bloody persecutions and a multitude of martyrs, the church still survived and won imperial recognition early in the fourth century. The decrees by Roman emperors to banish the Christian name from the earth had failed, as we have already seen. The devil through paganism continued to war against the church. Some forty years after Constantine recognized Christianity as the true religion, the Roman Emperor Julian withdrew privileges conferred by Constantine and was considered by the church as a tyrant. Gibbon says that "the genius of Paganism, which had been fondly raised and cherished by the arts of Julian, sunk irrevocably in the dust" under his successor Jovian; that under Jovian's reign "Christianity obtained an easy and lasting victory." (Vol. II, p. 521.)

9 **And the great dragon was cast down, the old serpent, he that is called the Devil and Satan, the deceiver of the whole world; he was cast down to the earth, and his angels were cast down with him.**—Here we have the direct statement that the devil is the indirect but real power that operated through paganism. John in the vision sees him and his angels cast down from heaven to earth. That represents the fact that paganism, which formerly ruled in the Roman Empire, had lost its seat of authority; Christianity had so prevailed as to overcome that influence. When the Christian religion became so influential as to affect the ruling house, all the agencies that were angels or helpers of paganism also lost place and power.

10 **And I heard a great voice in heaven, saying, Now is**

God, and the authority of his Christ: for the accuser of our brethren is cast down, who accuseth them before our God day and night. 11
And they overcame him because of the blood of the Lamb, and because of the word of their testimony; and they loved not their life even unto

come the salvation, and the power, and the kingdom of our God, and the authority of his Christ:—John heard a great voice coming from the place where he saw the dragon cast down. Verses 10-12 are a song of thanksgiving for the victory the saints gained over the pagan enemies. The word "brethren" in the next clause probably indicates that the rejoicing was done by the martyrs who had, under the fifth seal, inquired how long they must wait. See notes on 6: 9-11. Those exalted sing a song in celebration of victory. For other examples, see Ex. 15 and Judges 5. The victory over paganism was enough to cause rejoicing by the spirits of the martyrs as well as living saints.

The expression now is come "the kingdom" does not mean that the kingdom had not existed before that time. It can only be that it had come in the sense of prevailing over its enemies—come to its rightful position of authority to exist by permission of the empire. The saints had been saved a long time, yet the text speaks of salvation coming. Their Christianity had been preserved through persecutions. The authority of Christ had existed since Pentecost (Matt. 28: 18; Acts 1: 6-8), yet the passage says it now is come. These blessings had all come in the sense they were permitted to enjoy them in spite of all sacrifices they had made.

for the accuser of our brethren is cast down, who accuseth them before our God day and night.—Satan is here called an accuser of the brethren. This shows that through his agents he makes false charges against the true people of God. Seeing the dragon cast down indicates that paganism as the devil's agency lost its authority to persecute the church because Rome became, at least, nominally Christian. Day and night shows that Satan's work against righteousness is constant.

11 **And they overcame him because of the blood of the Lamb, and because of the word of their testimony; and they loved not their life even unto death.**—Clearly this refers to a time of martyrs. "Our brethren" who were accused by Satan are the ones indicated. The blood of Christ was not only the ground

death. 12 Therefore rejoice, O heavens, and ye that [6]dwell in them. Woe for the earth and for the sea: because the devil is gone down unto you, having great wrath, knowing that he hath but a short time.

[6]Gr. *tabernacle.*

of their justification, but that which stimulated them to a victorious struggle. The victory of Jesus even in giving his life was, by their faithfulness, made their victory. The word of their testimony means that in spite of their persecutions their testimony to Christ's words had not failed. They had not loved their lives so much that they would refuse to die for the truth. The supreme sacrifice was made for the church.

12 **Therefore rejoice, O heavens, and ye that dwell in them. Woe for the earth and for the sea: because the devil is gone down unto you, having great wrath, knowing that he hath but a short time.**—The great voice in heaven which John heard was exhorting those who dwell in the heavens to rejoice. It is true that "there is joy in the presence of the angels of God" even over one that repents (Luke 15: 10), but another application seems more probable for the verse in hand. The preceding facts represented by the woman-dragon symbols indicate things that happened to the church and pagan Rome. This is presumptive evidence that this part of the symbol should be so applied. In verse 5 the man-child (seed of the woman, verse 17) was caught up to God. This occurred when the church gained recognition from the Roman Empire. This was the "heavens" to which the church was exalted and furnished to them the occasion for the rejoicing here mentioned. Elliott (Vol. III, p. 33) quotes from Eusebius as follows: "Formerly we used to sing, 'We have heard what thou didst in our fathers' day.' But now we have to sing a second song of victory; our own eyes have seen his salvation." This is almost the language of verse 10.

Woe for earth and sea is what the voice announced would take place, not that it was asking for a woe to fall upon them. In these visions the world probably means the Roman world; earth and sea would mean the woe would come upon the whole Roman Empire. It would happen because the devil had come down—that is, paganism was operating under his influence. Satan was wroth—instigating the Roman Empire to engage in the most cruel measures—

because he knew that his time was limited. There are three ways in which he knew his time for action was limited: He would soon cease to operate, primarily through pagan Rome; under the reign of the beast his power was to be restrained for a thousand years; and at the judgment his influence over the righteous is to end. His career, then, is strictly a limited one.

4. THE WOMAN IN THE WILDERNESS
12: 13-17

13 And when the dragon saw that he was cast down to the earth, he persecuted the woman that brought forth the man *child*. 14 And there were given to the woman the two wings of the great eagle, that she might fly into the wilderness unto her place, where she is nourished for a time, and times,

---

13 **And when the dragon saw that he was cast down to the earth, he persecuted the woman that brought forth the man child.**—In the symbol John saw the dragon persecute the woman because he was cast down to earth. When Satan saw that his war on the church through the pagan empire was not effective because Christianity had been accepted by the emperor, he persecuted the church through other means. This fact will appear evident from the following verses.

14 **And there were given to the woman the two wings of the great eagle, that she might fly into the wilderness unto her place, where she is nourished for a time, and times, and half a time, from the face of the serpent.**—Whatever uncertainty there may be about the historical fulfillment of the symbols in this book, no position can be safe that conflicts with events known to have transpired already. The end of pagan Rome's persecution of the church, the establishment of the church in the empire, the rise of the papacy and the Protestant Reformation are plain facts that must be considered in interpreting prophetic symbols.

In the symbolic vision John sees the woman given two wings of an eagle by which she might fly into the wilderness. Similar words—"on eagles' wings"—are used regarding God's bringing Israel out of Egypt. (Ex. 19: 3, 4.) A wilderness would mean a place of safety, as was used by David and Elijah. (1 Sam. 23: 14, 15; 1 Kings 19: 4.) The woman here refers to the true church in its apostolic purity. The simple idea seems to be that the church,

and half a time, from the face of the serpent. 15 And the serpent cast out of his mouth after the woman water as a river, that he might cause her to be

in spite of the opposition, would be preserved as an institution. Hidden in the wilderness indicates that she would not appear as a visible body in congregational organizations, but the truth would still remain. Christ, as the head, could not be destroyed, and the New Testament, as its law, God would providentially preserve. Hence, though hidden from public view, the institution would remain. This is indicated in the expression that during the time in the wilderness the church would be "nourished"—that is, sustained. All that is necessarily meant here is that during the long period of obscurity the apostolic church would not become extinct. This is in accord with Daniel's statement that God would set up a "kingdom which shall never be destroyed." (Dan. 2: 44.) That means that no other kingdom would succeed it, or be built upon its ruins, as was the case of the four universal empires described by Daniel.

A careful comparison of 11: 2, 3; 12: 14; 13: 5 will show that twelve hundred sixty days, forty-two months, and time, times, and a half time all refer to the same period; hence, must all mean the same. But verse 6, when compared with verse 14, will show definitely that they do mean the same. That the expression is to be understood symbolically—a day for a year—and means 1,260 years seem certain. For reasons already given the probable time for the beginning of the 1,260 years was A.D. 533. See notes on 11: 3, 4.

From Christianity's exaltation by Constantine till the bishop of Rome was declared universal bishop was a period of 208 years. During that time Satan, called the dragon or serpent, continued to make war on the church—largely through the introduction of false doctrines and the exercise of human authority in religion. Gradually the church was corrupted until at the beginning of the 1,260 years the organization became the fully developed "man of sin" and the true church began its wilderness experience—lost to view as a visible organization.

15 **And the serpent cast out of his mouth after the woman water as a river, that he might cause her to be carried away by the stream.**—The woman "nourished" during 1,260 years

carried away by the stream. 16 And the earth helped the woman, and the earth opened her mouth and swallowed up the river which the dragon cast out of his mouth. 17 And the dragon waxed wroth with the woman, and went away to make war with the rest of her seed, that keep the commandments of God, and hold the testimony of Jesus:

---

means that the church was providentially kept alive in spite of Satan's persecutions, which in the symbol here are represented as a flood of waters being cast out of the serpent's mouth. David in referring to God's help in troubles said: "He drew me out of many waters." (Psalm 18: 16.) Jeremiah spoke of warring enemies as "an overflowing stream." (Jer. 47: 2.) This is a bold figure to represent the relentless hatred of Satan against the true church, and the fact that at no time will he cease his efforts to destroy it.

16 **And the earth helped the woman, and the earth opened her mouth and swallowed up the river which the dragon cast out of his mouth.**—the vision John saw was an onrushing flood about to overwhelm the woman when the earth with an open chasm swallowed up the water. The dragon is represented as the source of these floods of persecution. As already learned, the dragon is only the agent through which Satan operates. The lesson presented in this part of the symbol appears to be this: The true church, for the 1,260-year period, would be in obscurity—unseen as an organized body—during which time Satan would continue his efforts for its annihilation; but from unseen sources, like the earth swallowing up a flood, its complete destruction would be prevented. Jesus would still remain its head in spite of all pretenders; the gospel would be its law regardless of all false teaching; hence, as an institution, it would continue ready to appear in visible congregations, when the long period designated had come to an end. This verse guarantees that the church, as an institution, would not become extinct, though its true character and teaching would remain obscured for centuries. It is useless to try to point out certain events that prevented the annihilation of the church, for we now know from history that it was not annihilated.

17 **And the dragon waxed wroth with the woman, and went away to make war with the rest of her seed, that keep the commandments of God, and hold the testimony of Jesus:**—The first general effort to destroy the church was made through

the dragon beast—paganism. Failing to accomplish this result, the wrath and indignation of idol worshipers against the church would reach extreme limits. Satan being repulsed in his efforts to blot out the church as an institution changed his plans of attack. Evidently his method from that time on was to persecute the individual members of the church, here referred to as the "seed" of the woman. The statement of the woman being in the wilderness and the dragon "went away to make war" would indicate this change of method. This war was to be waged against "the rest" of her seed—that is, against individual followers of Christ who were trying to keep faithfully the commandments of God; those who in persecutions would not deny Christ's words; those martyred because they would not renounce their faith. Multitudes of these, during this long night of spiritual darkness, are solemn witnesses that what this symbol declares actually came to pass. The things here symbolically predicted are presented in detail in the following chapter.

This paragraph presents unmistakable evidence that the Catholic church cannot be the one here represented by the woman, for the woman being in the wilderness indicates that the true church was, as an institution, in obscurity during this 1,260-year period. The Catholic church claims a continued visible existence during that period; hence, cannot be the true church symbolized by the woman.

5. THE BEAST FROM THE SEA DESCRIBED
13: 1-10

1 and [7]he stood upon the sand of the sea.
And I saw a beast coming up out of the sea, having ten horns and seven

[7]Some ancient authorities read *I stood &c.* connecting the clause with what follows.

1 **and he stood upon the sand of the sea.**—This means that the dragon (Satan) stood upon the seashore ready to call the beast up from the sea. The King James Version says, "I stood," which would mean that John's position was or appeared to be by the sea when he saw the beast arise. Either view might be the correct one; hence, an immaterial matter.

And I saw a beast coming up out of the sea, having ten horns and seven heads, and on his horns ten diadems, and

heads, and on his horns ten diadems, and upon his heads names of blasphemy.

upon his heads names of blasphemy.—Chapter 12 presents the warfare which the dragon waged against the woman—that is, Satan's efforts to destroy the church; for verse 9 definitely declares the dragon to be the "Devil and Satan." In the two "beasts" of chapter 13 we have an explanation of how Satan waged his war against the church, they being the agencies through which the work was done. That the word "beast" means a wild or ferocious animal is clear both from the description and the things it was to do. This, it must be remembered, is only what John saw in the vision; it represents some institution whose destructive and deadly power would be used against the church.

This beast rose up out of the sea. Daniel saw four winds break upon the sea. (Dan. 7: 3, 4.) This means that the sea was lashed by stormwinds at the time. Rev. 17: 15 says, "The waters which thou sawest, where the harlot sitteth, are peoples, and multitudes, and nations, and tongues." The sea, as John saw it, denotes troublous times when people were greatly disturbed. This is always the case when a nation rises on the ruins of others. So this beast is a symbol of a kingdom that would arise when peoples would be disturbed like the waves of the sea.

In the symbol (12: 3) Satan himself is represented as a dragon with seven heads and ten horns; here the agency through which Satan operates appears as a terrible beast with seven heads and ten horns; the same beast is mentioned in 17: 3 with a like description. In 17: 9 we are told that "the seven heads are seven mountains, on which the woman sitteth." If the word "mountains" here is taken literally, it would be plausible to say it refers to the seven hills upon which Rome was built. But the statement (verse 3) that one of the heads "had been smitten unto death" and the "deathstroke was healed" can hardly apply to literal mountains. Verse 9 also says, "Here is the mind that hath wisdom." It required no special wisdom to know that Rome was built upon seven hills. Isa. 2: 2 speaks of "the mountain of Jehovah's house" and of nations flowing into it. Dan. 2: 35 says the "stone" that smote the image became "a great mountain." In these texts the word, "mountain" means God's kingdom; in Rev. 17: 9 it means forms

2 And the beast which I saw was like unto a leopard, and his feet were as *the feet* of a bear, and his mouth as the mouth of a lion: and the dragon gave him his power, and his throne, and great authority. 3 And *I saw* one

of government in the Roman world. Verse 10 says, "and they are seven kings." Since kings and kingdoms are used synonymously by Daniel (8: 17, 23), this might mean that the heads represented seven kinds of rulers, or seven forms of government. This would be another reason why the seven heads could not be seven literal mountains.

The beast John saw had ten horns; so did the fourth beast of Daniel's vision. (Dan. 7: 20.) If the fourth beast of Daniel's vision means Rome (the common view), then we have in the ten horns of both beasts another proof that the one John saw also symbolizes Rome. In describing the beast in Rev. 17: 12 the ten horns are said to be "ten kings." This probably refers to subdivisions in the Roman Empire after its pagan form had been overthrown. As a symbolic number "ten," doubtless, indicates completeness, and may be used here to denote that Rome's rule was general rather than limited to exactly ten minor kingdoms. A fuller discussion of the seven heads and ten horns is reserved till we reach the seventeenth chapter where the same beast again comes into the record. Then also we will examine the diadem (crowns) upon the horns and the names of blasphemy upon the heads.

2 **And the beast which I saw was like unto a leopard, and his feet were as the feet of a bear, and his mouth as the mouth of a lion: and the dragon gave him his power, and his throne, and great authority.**—Since the first three beasts that Daniel saw (Dan. 7: 4-7) were like a lion, a bear, and a leopard, and the fourth was an undescribed but "terrible" beast, then the first one that John saw must have been the same as Daniel's fourth. Being a composite emblem, it had parts to represent all three animals named by Daniel. As already mentioned, the beasts in Daniel's vision arose in succession. The fourth, therefore, resulted directly from those preceding and contained in its peculiar form the vital elements of all of them. Containing all the power represented by the three wild beasts made the Roman Empire the most "terrible" kingdom that had ever existed. As the church was established within its bounds, and was affected more by its power than any

of his heads as though it had been [1]smitten unto death; and his death-stroke was healed: and the whole earth wondered after the beast; 4 and they [2]wor-

[1]Gr. *slain.*
[2]See marginal note os ch. 3. 9.

other world nation, it unquestionably must have been included in any symbolic history of the church. The symbols of Revelation must be interpreted in harmony with well-known historical facts. The fact that the first beast represents the Roman Empire will be further evident when we study the second beast described in verses 11-18.

It should be noted that the text says that the dragon gave him his power, throne, and authority. The dragon is plainly declared to be the devil (12: 9); hence, he is the real source of opposition to the church. Therefore, whatever the Roman Empire did against the kingdom of Christ, it did as an agent, medium, or instrumentality of the devil. Any opposition to Christ or his church must come in some way from Satan; those persecuting the church are his servants.

3 **And I saw one of his heads as though it had been smitten unto death; and his death-stroke was healed: and the whole earth wondered after the beast;**—In 17: 10 it is said "and they are seven kings; the five are fallen, the one is, the other is not yet come." Whatever we may learn about this statement when we reach it, it is sufficient here to note that Rome was ruled by emperors in John's time. It was then a pagan empire. If this be what is meant by one of the heads (at least a plausible explanation), then that head receiving a death stroke means that that particular form of pagan Rome was killed. The most probable view here is that this part of the symbol was fulfilled when barbarian hordes from the north swept down upon the country and city and the empire came to an end in A.D. 476. This was begun by Alaric, king of the Goths, in A.D. 409 and finished by Odoacer at the date given. Thus ended the western part of pagan imperial Rome. The imperial form of government had received its deadly blow.

When the church later became a full-fledged apostasy, there was a practical union of church and state, with the church exercising the supreme power. At this time political Rome revived as a persecuting power of the true church; but its power was exercised in

shipped the dragon, because he gave his authority unto the beast; and they
[a]worshipped the beast, saying, Who is like unto the beast? and who is able
to war with him? 5 and there was given to him a mouth speaking great

a different way—it became the agent through which papal Rome (the apostate church) continued the persecutions. Rome as a secular power, doubtless, would have been consumed; permanently blotted out, like Babylon and Nineveh, had not the papacy healed her wounds by using her as the medium through which the true church was to be continually persecuted. It is an amazing thing that a persecuting power could receive such a blow and still survive in another form with its persecuting power unabated. It is no surprise that the whole world wondered after the beast.

4 **and they worshipped the dragon, because he gave his authority unto the beast;**—This is the language of John, and he means that when the people were astonished by what the beast did and worshiped him, they were worshiping the dragon—that is, they worshiped the devil whether they knew it or not. This was necessarily the case, for Satan gave the beast its power through pagan Rome as his agent; or, pagan Rome gave papal Rome its power.

and they worshipped the beast, saying, Who is like unto the beast? and who is able to war with him?—The power of Rome under the papacy was such that the people ascribed to it supreme authority. This they did by asking questions which meant that there was none like the beast or able to make war against him. This was nothing less than ascribing divine power to him. This is the way secular rulers of that time considered themselves, and such adulation was pleasing to them. Doubtless they made every effort to cultivate such sentiments in the hearts of the people. The power of political rulers under the domination of papal authority made their influence irresistible. Under such a system there could be neither political nor religious freedom. A power so unlimited had just the effect here indicated; ignorant people were ready to ascribe it to a supreme being.

5 **and there was given to him a mouth speaking great things and blasphemies;**—Nothing is said about who gave the beast such a mouth, but the natural presumption is that it was the dragon, the symbol of the devil, for in verse 2 we are told that he gave the

things and blasphemies; and there was given to him authority [3]to continue forty and two months. 6 And he opened his mouth for blasphemies against God, to blaspheme his name, and his tabernacle, *even* them that [4]dwell in the

[3]Or, *to do* his works *during* See Dan. 11. 28.
[4]Gr. *tabernacle.*

beast this power and authority. Such secular rulers as the symbols here describe would naturally be proud, boastful, and ready to claim divine powers. This, of course, was blasphemous. This is also characteristic of the second beast which, it is here assumed for the time, represents papal Rome. But that both beasts should have this same characteristic is not surprising. Their close relationship and interlocking interests would naturally lead them to manifest the same traits. Each operated through the other so that what was true of one was also true of the other in some measure.

and there was given to him authority to continue forty and two months.—Forty and two months are three and one-half years or 1,260 days. Reasons why this period should be considered symbolically and indicate 1,260 years have already been given. See notes on 11: 3, 4 and 12: 14. This time was the same that the two witnesses (God's word) would testify "in sackcloth" and the woman (true church) would remain in obscurity in the wilderness. This coincides exactly with the time that the papal power (Roman Catholicism) was to exercise supreme sway. Since this text is describing the relationship of secular and papal Rome, each operating through the other, it is natural that the former should be represented as being given authority to continue forty-two months. In the combination of church and state each would continue the same length of time.

6 **And he opened his mouth for blasphemies against God, to blaspheme his name, and his tabernacle, even them that dwell in the heaven.**—This repeats substantially what was said in verse 5, adding that the beast was actually doing what he was given a mouth to do. By the arrogant claims of authority the name of God was blasphemed, for only God has such power as the beast presumed to exercise. By "tabernacle," which was the ancient place of God's worship, the symbol indicates that such arrogance as the beast manifested blasphemed the worship of God. "Them that dwell in the heaven" probably refers to those in the church or the

heaven. 7 [5]And it was given unto him to make war with the saints, and to
overcome them: and there was given to him authority over every tribe and
people and tongue and nation. 8 And all that dwell on the earth shall [2]wor-
ship him, *every one* whose name hath not been [6]written from the foundation

[5]Some ancient authorities omit *And it was given . . . overcome them.*
[6]Or, *written in the book . . . slain from the foundation of the world.*

true worshipers of God. The beast then blasphemed God's name, the church, and the worship. Nothing of a divine nature was free from corruption and perversion by a church-state combination.

7 **And it was given unto him to make war with the saints, and to overcome them:**—It was given to the beast to overcome the saints by the same one that taught him to blaspheme. That was the dragon or Satan. See notes on verse 2. This is the same thing Daniel saw in his vision. (Dan. 7: 19-21.) However, Daniel represents this victorious power as being the little horn that came up among the ten horns in the fourth or Roman kingdom. Clearly this refers to the papacy, described as the second beast in Rev. 13. But we have already noted that secular Rome was largely the medium through which the apostate church operated; hence, what is ascribed to one may generally be ascribed to the other. Moreover, it may be true that, though two beasts appeared in John's visions, the main purpose was to reveal the war that the corrupt church would wage against the truth. This would justify applying to the means used anything the papacy did itself. That the saints were overcome to the extent that for the 1,260 years the church was unseen as an operative institution is a well-known historical fact. Specific instances of persecution against saints it is unnecessary to mention.

and there was given to him authority over every tribe and people and tongue and nation.—This language was substantially fulfilled if the beast here means political Rome; for the empire exercised a general, if not a universal, sway over men. But if the reference is also indirectly to papal Rome, it is also fulfilled; for the Catholic Church not only believed that it had the right to rule the world, but still believes it. Not only so, but during the 1,260-year period it practically exercised that authority. This text has to do with the beast's conduct during this period.

8 **And all that dwell on the earth shall worship him, every one whose name hath not been written from the foundation of**

of the world in the book of life of the Lamb that hath been slain. 9 If any man hath an ear, let him hear. 10 [7]If any man [8]*is* for captivity, into captivity he goeth: if any man shall kill with the sword, with the sword must he be killed. Here is the [9]patience and the faith of the saints.

[7]The Greek text in this verse is somewhat uncertain.
[8]Or, leadeth *into captivity*
[9]Or, *stedfastness*

---

the world in the book of life of the Lamb that hath been slain.—We are here told that all on the earth whose names are not in the book of life would worship the beast. This would be true indirectly, if the worship was rendered directly to the apostate church which is represented by the second beast. Of course, true saints did not worship the beast then and do not now. If only those whose names are not in the book of life worshiped him then those whose names are in that book did not worship him. The expression "written" in the book of life is figurative and means those who are saved and remembered as such by our divine Father. The words "from the foundation of the world," in the King James Version, modify the verb "slain"; in the Revised they modify "written." It is immaterial which is the correct reading. If the latter, the terms upon which men are saved was predetermined; if the former, then Christ's death was predetermined. In either case God's purpose was so certain to take place that it was spoken of as if already done, on the principle that God calls "things that are not, as though they were." (Rom. 4: 17.)

The Greek word for world—*kosmos*—means an "harmonious arrangement" of things, but in its use has a great variety of applications. The expression "from the foundation of the world" may be understood simply as "from the beginning." All the demands will be met by saying that after man sinned God purposed to save him through the death of his Son. Trying to make the words go further back involves the text in a difficulty for which man can offer no solution. The most natural explanations are probably the true ones.

9 **If any man hath an ear, let him hear.**—This means that those who are willing to be instructed should give heed to what had been said about the beast and the exhortation in the next verse. It was intended to encourage the saints in view of the dire

misfortunes which the symbols had indicated would come upon them.

10 **If any man is for captivity, into captivity he goeth: if any man shall kill with the sword, with the sword must he be killed.**—This is in perfect agreement with the words of Jesus: "For all they that take the sword shall perish with the sword." (Matt. 26: 52.) This is a general statement that the history of the world has verified abundantly. It harmonizes with another general statement that "whatsoever a man soweth, that shall he also reap." (Gal. 6: 7.) Nations recognize the law that "whoso sheddeth man's blood, by man shall his blood be shed." (Gen. 9: 6.) Here John evidently intended to encourage the saints by assurance that the nation that would inflict all these calamities would in turn be led into captivity—rewarded as her acts deserved. That political Rome led nations into captivity and papal Rome persecuted Christians are facts fully sustained. In both the spirit of this verse has been completely fulfilled. That both must pay for their crimes is as certain as that God's word is true.

Here is the patience and the faith of the saints.—In the things here pictured is the world's greatest test of Christian faith. No one has ever been called to suffer more than fell to the lot of the saints under the persecutions that came to the true church during the period when papal Rome exercised supreme power in connection with the Roman Empire. Nothing but the strongest faith can meet such tests.

6. THE SECOND BEAST DESCRIBED
13: 11-18

11 And I saw another beast coming up out of the earth; and he had two

---

11 **And I saw another beast coming up out of the earth;**—As John looked he beheld another beast that seemed to come out of the earth. We have already learned that, as a symbol, a beast represents a kingdom or institution of some kind. Sometimes the ruler, standing for the kingdom, is indicated by the beast. (See Dan. 7: 17, 23.) The first beast (verse 1) came up out of the turbulent sea, meaning that the secular Roman Empire came out of the agitated and disturbed state of men and nations. The second

horns like unto a lamb, and he spake as a dragon. 12 And he exerciseth all the authority of the first beast in his sight. And he maketh the earth and

arose out of the earth, which probably here represents the Roman Empire; that is, the papal or apostate church came into existence within the boundaries of that empire. It came quietly from a well-established state of things, like the solid earth, and was dominating the whole empire before the people realized that any change was taking place. This false church became so well established and powerful that 1,260 years were necessary to break its hold.

and he had two horns like unto a lamb, and he spake as a dragon.—That is, he had two horns like the horns of a lamb. The use of the word lamb indicates that the institution represented would have a show of humility; externally, at least, it would manifest the lamblike character, but would speak like a dragon. The pious exterior would be no evidence of godliness within. The beast's words—commands—would be harsh, arrogant, and imperious. Jesus had said that false prophets would come in sheep's clothing. (Matt. 7: 15.) Since the dragon has already been declared to be a symbol of Satan, it follows that the false teaching of the apostate church has Satan for its real source. A real lamb has two horns, but there may be no special significance in the number other than to show that the beast, in that particular, had the appearance of a lamb. As a symbol the word horn represents power. Two might indicate that this beast exercised both secular and spiritual power; the spiritual direct and the secular indirect—through the Roman Empire. These are true facts, even if not signified by the two horns, as the next verse definitely shows.

12 **And he exerciseth all the authority of the first beast in his sight.**—Exercising this authority in the sight of the first beast indicates that the first beast approved it, and that the second used the first as a medium through which to operate. Language could no more plainly indicate the close and harmonious relationship that existed between secular and papal Rome. These two beasts, though distinguished, are so similar in nature and work that they may be considered as two parts of one great power that was to persecute the true church. Or, the papal hierarchy may be considered as a continuation of the fourth universal empire—operating through Rome in its so-called Christian state.

them that dwell therein to [2]worship the first beast, whose death-stroke was healed. 13 And he doeth great signs, that he should even make fire to come down out of heaven upon the earth in the sight of men. 14 And he deceiveth

---

And he maketh the earth and them that dwell therein to worship the first beast, whose death-stroke was healed.—As the corrupt church spake like a dragon and exercised all the authority of imperial Rome, it is no surprise that it caused all (except those whose names were in the book of life, verse 8) to worship the rulers as representatives of the empire. When the pagan empire, through the invasion of the northern nations, came to an end in A.D. 476, it doubtless would have ceased forever, if it had not been perpetuated and revitalized by the apostate church in her borders. The imperial pagan head or form of government had received a death stroke, but we healed through a papal kingdom arising within its borders. Such a union of church and state was necessary to preserve the empire and protect the religious apostasy.

13 **And he doeth great signs, that he should even make fire to come down out of heaven upon the earth in the sight of men.**—The very nature of the beast, as revealed in this description, indicates that the "great signs" were only pretended miracles which he claimed to do. They would be such, however, that the ignorant and credulous people would be easily influenced to accept them as true. This beast and Paul's "man of sin" (2 Thess. 2: 3-12) evidently refer to the same thing—the papal hierarchy or Roman church. Paul declares that he operates "according to the working of Satan with all power and signs and lying wonders, and with all deceit of unrighteousness for them that perish." Jesus had predicted that there "shall arise false Christs, and false prophets, and shall show great signs and wonders; so as to lead astray, if possible, even the elect." (Matt. 24: 24.) Either these were "lying wonders"—false or pretended miracles—which Satan inspired the false church to perform, or they were real wonders which God permitted because people did not want the truth. In either case the element of falsehood entered into the program. Claiming to change the bread and wine into the actual body and blood of the Lord, the worshiping of relics, and other pretended

them that dwell on the earth by reason of the signs which it was given him to do in the sight of the beast; saying to them that dwell on the earth, that

miracles are ample proof that the Catholic church pretended to be a miracle-working power, and fulfills the demands of this text.

Some plausibility in claiming to make fire come down out of heaven could be made because Elijah in a real miracle at mount Carmel (1 Kings 18: 37, 38) did so, and the disciples James and John asked whether fire should be called down upon a certain Samaritan village (Luke 9: 54); but whatever effort the false church made was a deceptive trick of some kind. For in the next verse it is stated that the purpose of these pretended miracles was to deceive the people. Religious deceivers can resort to no more plausible scheme than some imitation of a real miracle.

14 **And he deceiveth them that dwell on the earth by reason of the signs which it was given him to do in the sight of the beast;**—The following will serve as evidence of false miracles which papal Rome has offered in proof of the claim that she is the true church. Gibbon in referring to Gregory the Great, who was Bishop of Rome, A.D. 590 to 604, says: "The credulity or the prudence of Gregory was always disposed to confirm the truths of religion by the evidence of ghosts, miracles, and resurrections." (Vol. IV, p. 422.) In a Catholic volume—*Pictorial Catholic Library*—is a section devoted to the "Apparition of Lourdes," in which the claim is made that the Virgin Mary appeared to a young girl several times in 1858. Finally she commanded the girl to drink from a spring that had suddenly burst from the earth. The water from the spring, it is claimed, has produced many cures. Such preposterous delusions are plain proof of the beast power trying to deceive the nations by false miracles. To this may be added the perpetual claim that the bread and wine of the communion are changed into the real body and blood of the Lord. This would require the continuous repetition of miraculous power. This false teaching alone is sufficient proof that the words of our text have been and are being fulfilled.

Doing these pretended miracles "in the sight of the beast," doubtless, indicates that secular Rome approved of what the apostate church did because of benefits received therefrom. During the

they should make an image to the beast who hath the stroke of the sword and lived. 15 And it was given *unto him* to give breath to it, *even* to the

1,260-year period the church and state had such common interests that it is practically impossible to separate them completely. Even the capital of the empire always remained the official residence of the Pope.

saying to them that dwell on the earth, that they should make an image to the beast who hath the stroke of the sword and lived.—Those deceived by the pretended miracles would be ready to obey the command to make an image to the first beast. The meaning of this part of the symbol is that the papal church required its subjects to give religious honor to the secular empire. Verse 12 says they were required to worship the first beast. Here, as in much of the book, expositors vary greatly. The presence of the masculine pronoun "who," some contend, indicates that the worship is of a man. If this is correct, worshiping Roman emperors may be the thing meant. Rulers represent governments and the worship of one implies the other.

As the two beasts must be taken symbolically, it is probable that "image" should be so applied. If so, the word doubtless has a broader application. Since the first beast (pagan Rome) was to receive a temporary death stroke and later revive, a possible, if not probable, meaning is that through papal Rome (Catholic Church) the empire received its dominion back, but in a so-called Christianized form. If so, this would be an image of its pagan form, because it exercised a similar power. This, at least, would meet all the demands of this symbol.

Elliott (Vol. III, pp. 227-239) holds that papal church councils, in which ecclesiastical laws were made, fulfill this symbolic prophecy. This view also carries much plausibility, for the church laws enacted in these councils were just as binding as the laws of ancient Rome; in fact, they were made and operated much like the political laws of the empire. Possibly all the preceding views may be involved in the word "image." But, regardless of its exact and proper application here, the general idea must be the close and cordial union between church and state.

15 **And it was given unto him to give breath to it, even to**

image of the beast, [10]that the image of the beast should both speak, and cause that as many as should not [2]worship the image of the beast should be killed.

[10]Some ancient authorities read *that even the image of the beast should speak; and he shall cause &c.*

the image of the beast, that the image of the beast should both speak, and cause that as many as should not worship the image of the beast should be killed.—According to the view that the "image" was the revived Roman Empire in its co-called Christianized form, this language would mean that the apostate church gave the empire this life, and authority to make laws and demand obedience on the penalty of death. As a matter of fact this is true, for the false church claimed authority over temporal rulers. But if the "image" refers to church councils, they too spake with the authority manifested in ancient Rome, and enforced their laws with the same irresistible power. Possibly being killed here, if councils be meant, does not mean physical death, but excommunication from the church; spiritual death, as the church viewed it. Whatever explanation be accepted the main thought is the domination which the church exercised over both its members and the government which it controlled.

From the time that the Emperor Constantine in the fourth century recognized Christianity as the true religion, the church's power was gradually extended till the full development of the "man of sin" had taken place, more than two centuries later; so, after the end of pagan Rome in A.D. 476, the reviving of the empire was also a gradual process. Near the end of the eighth century the church recognized it when Pope Leo crowned an emperor. Of this event Gibbon says:

"On the festival of Christmas, the last year of the eighth century, Charlemagne appeared in the church of St. Peter; and, to gratify the vanity of Rome, he had exchanged the simple dress of his country for the habit of a patrician. After the celebration of the holy mysteries, Leo suddenly placed a precious crown on his head, and the dome resounded with the acclamations of the people, 'Long life and victory to Charles, the most Augustus, crowned by God the great and pacific emperor of the Romans." (*Decline and Fall,* Vol. V, p. 43.) Thus it is clear that the beast ("man of sin" or apostate church) which arose in the Roman Empire did

16 And he causeth all, the small and the great, and the rich and the poor, and the free and the bond, that there be given them a mark on their right hand, or upon their forehead; 17 and that no man should be able to buy or to sell, save he that hath the mark, *even* the name of the beast or the number of

---

make an image of the first beast by creating from the old ruins a so-called Christian empire.

16 **And he causeth all, the small and the great, and the rich and the poor, and the free and the bond, that there be given them a mark on their right hand, or upon their forehead;**—The expressions, small and great, rich and poor, bond and free, are explanatory of the word "all," and mean that the authority here mentioned applied to all classes. The subject of the verb is beast introduced in verse 11. The word "mark," when taken literally, means some figure or token placed upon the object to indicate ownership or authority. The very nature of the case here demands that it be understood symbolically. It is, doubtless, used purposely to show the contrast between the true and pretended servants of God—the true and false church. To Israel God said his words would be "for a sign upon thy hand" and "for frontlets between thine eyes." (Deut. 6: 8.) It is no surprise, then, for members of an apostate church to carry a sign indicating their characteristics. The only way God's words could then or now be a mark or sign was their manifestation in the lives of his saints. When received into the mind ("frontlets between the eyes") and practiced ("sign upon the hand"), they would show those who had these signs to be true servants of God. Those who believed and practiced doctrines of the false church had the "mark" of the beast upon their hands and foreheads. Any outward tokens used by the false church were only symbols of the false doctrines believed.

17 **and that no man should be able to buy or to sell, save he that hath the mark, even the name of the beast or the number of his name.**—The word "even" supplied by the translators means that the "name" of the beast is the mark; but, omitting this word because there is nothing in the Greek for it, the text may mean that the mark, name, and number of the name are three distinct characteristics by which the beast may be identified. But if the mark means the doctrine and practice received from the false church, then the name and number would be additional features by

his name. 18 Here is wisdom. He that hath understanding, let him count the number of the beast; for it is the number of a man: and his number is [11]Six hundred and sixty and six.

[11]Some ancient authorities read *Six hundred and sixteen.*

which the identification might be confirmed. The name is to be determined through the proper application of the number.

Whatever these marks of identification may be, no one was allowed to buy or sell who did not have them. Whether the buying and selling are to be understood literally or symbolically is a question about which expositors are not agreed. That the Catholic Church did on occasions prohibit such commerce with heretics is evident from history. Elliott (Vol. III, p. 260) refers to the Synod of Tours, just when the Waldenses and Albigenses had begun to excite attention, under Pope Alexander III, as having "passed a law that no man should presume to receive or assist the heretics, not so much as to exercise commerce with them in *selling and buying.*" Naturally a church that believes it has the divine right to rule the nations of earth would claim the right to control the commerce of the world. But the view that these words should be taken symbolically seems more probable. The plain import, then, would be that only those with the mark of the beast would be allowed to preach or practice religious doctrines. This is evident from the fact that the Catholic Church refuses permission for her own members to hear others preach, but believes that she is the authorized custodian of divine things, and that all teachers should come to her for authority. In this the demands of the symbol are fully met.

18 **Here is wisdom. He that hath understanding, let him count the number of the beast;**—While it required divine wisdom to give this plan for identifying the thing represented by the beast, it also was necessary to have wisdom to learn what was meant. This is evident from the fact that those with understanding were urged to count the number. The number of the beast means the "number of his name," as appears from comparing verse 17. Elliott (Vol. III, p. 242) shows that it was not uncommon for the Greeks to express names by numerals; that is, the numerical value of the letters of a name were added together and the total number stood for the name. The language of this verse indicates

that to be the process meant in the command to count the number of the beast. Other names besides the correct one might have the proper numerical value; it would be strange indeed that, in the multitudes of names, others could not be found. But the name, when found, must fit an apostate church existing at about a certain period in the world. Moreover, an institution that had made an image of another one, and combined the secular and religious rule. Not just any name that had the right numerical value would do but only one that would fit the other descriptive features of the beast. The name then must correspond with the well-known facts of history.

for it is the number of a man; and his number is Six hundred and sixty and six.—Commentators have offered a variety of applications for the expression, "the number of a man." But the simplest and most natural one is, that the name of a man, the numerical value of which is 666, is so connected with the institution represented by the beast that it is a positive means of identification. After all is said, this seems the most plausible view of the text. Elliott, who is followed by several other expositors, explains in detail facts that seem conclusive evidence that *Latinos,* father of the Latin race, was the man meant. (Vol. III, pp. 245-255.) He quotes Irenaeus, a church father of the second century, who made the same application of the text. An objection is offered against the interpretation of Irenaeus because he spells the name *Lateinos* instead of *Latinos*. The objection, however, is without force, for he was using the Greek form of the word. Since Revelation was written in Greek that was the proper form to use. The numerical value of the letters in this name will appear from the following arrangement:

L	A	T	E	I	N	O	S
30	1	300	5	10	50	70	200=666

This solution has two important advantages: one is that the number is the name of a man—a thing the text seems to demand; the other is that it corresponds with what we now know to be facts —that is, that the Catholic Church arose in the Latin kingdom and is known as the Latin church, even its services being conducted in the Latin. As the number must represent a religious empire that was to exercise a power practically universal for 1,260 years, there is none known to history that will fit the requirements of the symbol except the Latin Church—the Roman Catholic. This conclusion is completely vindicated by the fact that the Roman Church still believes that universal dominion rightly belongs to itself. It cannot then be successfully denied that it was the church which did exercise that power during the period indicated. If so, our interpretation of the text is unquestionably the correct one.

As already suggested in the introduction (page xi), the use of symbols in describing their political and religious enemies was greatly to the church's benefit during the long period that the witnesses testified in sackcloth. Plainly naming the institution meant would doubtless have greatly increased persecution. Telling those who had understanding to count the number of the name implies that some Christians would be able to do it. Such saints then would understand what was meant, and it was better that their enemies did not know. With their experience as history before us, we should be able to understand also. Even if the expression, "six hundred and sixty and six," remains an unsolved puzzle, we know that in some way it describes a false religious power that was an enemy of the true church for the symbolic period of 1,260 days. This phase of the matter is definitely fixed by the language of the text.

The margin says that "some ancient authorities read *Six hundred and sixteen*." If this were the true reading, a different name might have to be found, but the general application of the passage would remain the same. However, the reading of sixteen instead of sixty-six does not appear to have any chance to be correct, according to the general views of critics.

SECTION TWO

THE SAINTS' ULTIMATE SUCCESS DEPICTED
14: 1-20

1. THE REDEEMED DESCRIBED
14: 1-5

1 And I saw, and behold, the Lamb standing on the mount Zion, and with

---

Note: The leading purpose of chapter 12 was to present Satan, symbolically described as a *dragon,* as the real enemy of the true church. As the author of evil he would naturally be the source of all opposition to the truth. Those through whom the opposition is manifested are but the agents through whom he works. In chapter 13 we have pictured, under the symbols of two beasts, the political and religious earthly agents that were to be the outstanding mediums for Satan's efforts. These were found to be the Roman Empire—pagan and "Christianized"—and the apostate church—the Catholic hierarchy. With such deadly struggles forecast, the saints would have been overcome with fear, if the symbolic story had ended at this point. Evidently the purpose of the present chapter was to encourage the Christians to faithfulness under all conditions by assurance that the truth would ultimately prevail, and the persevering be saved. While this was designed to benefit especially those who met the persecutions during the 1,260-year period, it will have the same effect in helping all Christians to endure to the end of life.

1 **And I saw, and behold, the Lamb standing on the mount Zion,**—We should be continually remindful that what John saw in the vision was the symbol; what it represents is a different matter. The two should not be confused. "I saw" means that another vision appeared. "The Lamb" refers to Christ (5: 6; 12: 11); it is here contrasted with the beast (13: 11) that had horns like a lamb, but spake as a dragon. The expression "mount Zion" is used only here and Heb. 12: 22. Jerusalem, because partly builded upon the literal mount Zion, is also referred to as mount Zion. It was the seat of government and place of worship for the old covenant, and typical of the church. (Gal. 4: 26.) Verses 2 and 3 strongly in-

him a hundred and forty and four thousand, having his name, and the name of his Father, written on their foreheads. 2 And I heard a voice from heaven, as the voice of many waters, and as the voice of a great thunder: and the voice which I heard *was* as *the voice* of harpers harping with their

---

dicate that his scene was in heaven. If so, mount Zion is used typically to represent the saints' final abode. Compare 4: 2, 3.

and with him a hundred and forty and four thousand, having his name, and the name of his Father, written on their foreheads.—The names of the Lamb and of the Father written upon their foreheads show that they were acceptable to both Christ and God. This and the place where they were standing clearly indicate that they were redeemed and had gained the ultimate victory —were safe from any further attacks from either beast. See notes on 13: 16 regarding mark of beast on forehead. In 7: 4-9 is also mentioned the same number as having been "sealed" from the twelve tribes, after which is mentioned a numberless multitude from all peoples—and Gentiles. In our present text only the 144,000 are mentioned. Whether they are the same that are mentioned in the seventh chapter or not is immaterial, for in both places the purpose is to encourage faithfulness by foretelling the final success true saints will have. The number is doubtless symbolical and means an incalculably large multitude.

2 **And I heard a voice from heaven, as the voice of many waters, and as the voice of a great thunder:**—Whether or not the whole vision was seen in heaven, "Zion" being used typically, the voice John heard came from heaven. From verse 3 the natural conclusion is that the voice was singing the new song before the throne. The language shows that it was a song of sublime powers. It filled the air as the roaring of mighty waters or the waves of the ocean. The sound was not the roaring of waters, but "as" or similar to such sound. Its majesty was also indicated by saying it was "as" the voice of a great thunder. Reverberating through the heavens like the peals of loud thunder.

and the voice which I heard was as the voice of harpers harping with their harps:—The King James Version represents John as saying he heard the harpers harping, but the Revised says the voice he heard was "as" harpers harping. This must be correct, for all three clauses are in the same grammatical construction, the

harps: 3 and they sing as it were a new song before the throne, and before the four living creatures and the elders: and no man could learn the song save the hundred and forty and four thousand, *even* they that had been pur-

---

word "as" being in all of them. John then said nothing about hearing harps, but only that the voice he heard was like the harping—possibly meaning that it was both grand and melodious. This passage gives no support for the use of mechanical music in worship for the following reasons: (1) What John heard was in heaven, not on earth. There is no proof that we are privileged to have everything in the church that will be in heaven. (2) There is nothing said about the 144,000 redeemed harping on harps. The word "as" settles that. (3) The plural number of the word "harps" shows that many harps were used, which would mean each had a harp, if it referred to the redeemed playing harps in heaven. In a congregation one instrument is used for all. There simply is not anything here to give the least support to mechanical music in church worship.

3 **and they sing as it were a new song before the throne, and before the four living creatures and the elders:**—For comments on the four living creatures and the elders see notes on 4: 4-7. "Before the throne" indicates that they were in the presence of God and the Lamb, which means that they were a part of the saved. This final glory of the redeemed is here pictured to encourage struggling saints; it is an assurance that their labors will not be in vain and that the righteous will ultimately win the victory. With the 1,260 years of terrible struggle between the church and her enemies, such encouragement was of the greatest importance. It is of great value to faithful Christians in all times; without such promises to strengthen us few would endure to the end.

and no man could learn the song save the hundred and forty and four thousand, even they that had been purchased out of the earth.—This means that none except the redeemed can fully appreciate the joys of salvation, and certainly we will not understand what heaven means until we reach it. We rejoice in pardon of sins and are made exceedingly happy in the anticipation of eternal life, but will have to wait for its realization till we meet our Redeemer over there. Only those who have passed through a

chased out of the earth. 4 These are they that were not defiled with women; for they are virgins. These *are* they that follow the Lamb whithersoever he goeth. These were purchased from among men, *to be* the firstfruits unto God

great sorrow can fully know what relief means; so only those who have been saved from a terrible misfortune can appreciate the blessing. Of course, nothing can approximate the sublime and transporting joy to be experienced by those who will be permitted to stand on the eternal Zion and dwell in the celestial city. A song of praise for such a blessing can only be sung by those who have been purchased from sin by Christ's blood. For this reason what John heard seemed to be a song, but a new one which even saints on earth could not understand.

4 **These are they that were not defiled with women; for they are virgins.**—That the saved in heaven will be those who have lived clean and chaste lives is certain from the general teaching of the Scriptures. But in view of the fact that the lessons in Revelation are mainly expressed in symbols, it is more reasonable to conclude that the impurity mentioned here is to be understood figuratively. In the Old Testament the abominable sin of literal adultery is made the figurative term by which idolatry is described. This use of the word is found in Jer. 3: 1-10. The Greek word for "virgins," though feminine in form, evidently has a masculine sense in this text; hence, it should be taken spiritually to indicate moral and spiritual purity. As the word "man" is often used to mean mankind, so the word "purity" with a masculine sense includes both men and women. It is doubtless the purpose of this verse to contrast true saints with those who follow the "Mother of Harlots." (17: 5; compare 2 Cor. 11: 2.)

These are they that follow the Lamb whithersoever he goeth. These were purchased from among men, to be the firstfruits unto God and unto the Lamb.—Jesus is represented as a good shepherd, and his disciples as sheep to follow him. (John 10: 11-15; compare Psalm 23.) Those finally saved will be the ones who have followed him, which can only mean those who have obeyed his commands. This truth is sustained by many texts of scripture. "Whithersoever he goeth" means doing any and all things he commands.

and unto the Lamb. 5 And in their mouth was found no lie: they are without blemish.

They were purchased or redeemed by the blood of the Lamb, as all the saved must be, but the 144,000 are represented as "firstfruits" unto God. They were not said to be redeemed because of their rank or station in life, but by the merits of Christ's blood. The Jews offered the first fruits of the harvests to the Lord. As the first fruits were also a guarantee of the full harvest later, so the great number that John saw were those who, as martyrs and other faithful ones, had been true to the Lord during the period when the saints were struggling against the two beasts mentioned in chapter 13, and their condition was a guarantee that all faithful followers of Christ will be saved finally.

5 **And in their mouth was found no lie: they are without blemish.**—Liars in heaven, of course, would be an intolerable thought. In 21: 8 we are informed that "all liars," along with other abominable characters, will have their part in the "lake that burneth with fire and brimstone." The Jews were not allowed to offer blemished animals in sacrifice to the Lord; neither can guilty sinners spend eternity in worshiping God in heaven. The redeemed in heaven will be without blemish. This, however, does not mean that they have never been wicked, for the very fact that they were redeemed implies that they had been sinners. In 7: 14 it is said, "They washed their robes, and made them white in the blood of the Lamb." Because of this and the fact that they came "out of the great tribulation" successfully, they are before the throne where they serve God day and night. (7: 15.) This is a symbolic scene indicating the way the saved will pass the time in eternity. It does not mean that the eternal age is yet begun, though the righteous dead are now in a state of happiness. This is the clear teaching of Jesus. (Luke 16: 19-31.)

2. THREE JUDGMENT ANGELS
14: 6-11

6 And I saw another angel flying in mid heaven, having [1]eternal good tidings to proclaim unto them that [2]dwell on the earth, and unto every na-

[1]Or, *an eternal gospel*
[2]Gr. *sit.*

6 **And I saw another angel flying in mid heaven, having eternal good tidings to proclaim unto them that dwell on the earth, and unto every nation and tribe and tongue and people;** —As already noted this chapter gives a brief general description of the success made by the saints during the time the church was to wage war with the two beasts, and of its final triumph at the end of the world. The events mentioned are few in number, general in character, and far apart in point of time. The first paragraph certainly includes the redeemed of the 1,260-year period, and may be all the redeemed up to the close of that dreadful time. "Another angel" means one in addition to all the others he had seen in previous visions; or, expressed differently, the meaning is that an angel gave him another vision. This text does not mean that the eternal good tidings—everlasting gospel—first began to be preached at the time referred to here; for the gospel of Christ began to be preached first on Pentecost according to the command of Jesus. (Luke 24: 46; Acts 1: 8.) The gospel of Christ is the "eternal good tidings" which was to be preached till the end of the world. (Matt. 28: 20.) This preaching which the angel flying in the heaven announced to John seems to mean that done after the beginning of the Protestant Reformation, when the Catholic Church lost her dictatorial power and preachers were allowed, under the flag of Protestant liberty, to preach the Bible to all nations. The great apostasy came gradually, and the Reformation spread gradually, but it gave the liberty and furnished the motive for world-wide evangelism. The angel flying through heaven probably indicates the rapidity with which the preaching of the Reformation would spread. After the long night of spiritual slavery—the 1,260 years of religious darkness—the reformatory work spread by leaps and bounds. Soon all nations were allowed the privilege of reading and obeying without hindrance—a blessed privilege that people still have.

tion and tribe and tongue and people; 7 and he saith with a great voice, Fear God, and give him glory; for the hour of his judgment is come: and [3]worship him that made the heaven and the earth and sea and fountains of waters.

[3]See marginal note on ch. 3. 9.

7 **and he saith with a great voice, Fear God, and give him glory; for the hour of his judgment is come:**—This is substantially what Peter said to Cornelius; namely, those that fear God and work righteousness are acceptable to him. (Acts 10: 35.) Solomon taught the same lesson in these words: "Fear God, and keep his commandments; for this is the whole duty of man. (Eccles. 12: 13.) The angel was not announcing a new truth, but only what had been true all the way along. The application of this truth was to be carried out by obeying the same gospel that had been preached since Pentecost. Judgment here does not mean the final judgment when all nations will appear before the Lord, but the special judgment upon the beast at the end of the 1,260 year period; the time when the Catholic domination was to be broken and men be allowed to obey the gospel; hence, the command for them to "fear God, and give him glory."

and worship him that made the heaven and the earth and sea and fountains of waters.—Paul declared that the "man of sin" would sit in the temple of God "setting himself forth as God." (2 Thess. 2: 4.) That means, of course, that he would demand that reverence and devotion for himself which belong only to God. The Pope claiming to be the authoritative representative of Christ on earth is the only one that qualifies as deserving this description. This blind worship of a man is the thing which gave him complete sway over men for the long period of religious ignorance. But that anti-Christian power was broken by the Protestant Reformation, and men were taught that they were to worship the Creator of the universe, not man. In the symbol John heard the angel say that the everlasting gospel would be preached again; past history shows that it has been preached. This fact will be fully demonstrated by symbols yet to be studied.

8 **And another, a second angel, followed, saying, Fallen, fallen is Babylon the great,**—This does not mean another event that occurred after the things mentioned in verses 6 and 7. Rather

8 And another, a second angel, followed, saying, Fallen, fallen is Babylon the great, that hath made all the nations to drink of the wine of the wrath of her fornication.

this verse tells what transpired that made the proclamation of the everlasting gospel possible at that time. Though expressed in the past tense, all this was future when John saw the vision. This form of expression is called the "prophetic past," which means that a thing is so certain to transpire that it is spoken of as if it had already come to pass. Isa. 9: 2, 6 contains examples of the same usage. This is the first occurrence of the word "Babylon" in this book. Literal Babylon had long since disappeared; hence, the word here must be understood figuratively. See 17: 5 and 18: 2. "Fallen" did not mean that spiritual Babylon would cease to exist when the everlasting gospel began to be repreached, for its destruction will be at the coming of the Lord. (2 Thess. 2: 8.) It was to fall in the sense that it would no longer be able to make the world bow to the papacy.

Just as Jerusalem, the capital of God's ancient people and the place where the gospel was first preached, was typical of the church (Gal. 4: 24-31), so Babylon that once captured Jerusalem was made a type of the apostate church. Literal Babylon took the city, destroyed the temple, removed the holy vessels, and put the people of God in bondage for seventy years. The antitypical Babylon, the papal hierarchy, through a perversion of the church, took away the true worship of God, and put the people in spiritual bondage to papal authority for 1,260 years. The Reformation ended that bondage, but did not destroy the papal system any more than freeing Israel from Egyptian bondage destroyed Egypt.

that hath made all the nations to drink of the wine of the wrath of her fornication.—This is also highly figurative language. Fornication, as we have already learned, is typical of false and idolatrous doctrine and practice. It is here also represented as wine. Drinking wine intoxicates and leads to folly and madness; practicing false doctrines leads to confusion and rebellion against God. Jeremiah spake of the city of Babylon thus: "Babylon hath been a golden cup in Jehovah's hand, that made all the earth drunken: the nations have drunk of her wine; therefore the nations are mad." (Jer. 51: 7.) Her antitype, papal Babylon, made

9 And another angel, a third, followed them, saying with a great voice, If
any man [3]worshippeth the beast and his image, and receiveth a mark on his
forehead, or upon his hand, 10 he also shall drink of the wine of the wrath of
God, which is [4]prepared unmixed in the cup of his anger; and he shall be
tormented with fire and brimstone in the presence of the holy angels, and in

[3]See marginal note on ch. 3. 9.
[4]Gr. *mingled.*

---

the nations drunk with her false doctrines. In due time God allowed Babylon to be punished and finally destroyed; he has already broken spiritual Babylon's stranglehold on the world and will destroy her at the Lord's coming. The "wrath" here mentioned refers to the punishment that would fall upon her and those she deceives or intoxicates with her false teachings.

9 **And another angel, a third, followed them, saying with a great voice, If any man worshippeth the beast and his image, and receiveth a mark on his forehead, or upon his hand,**—This angel refers to the corrupt and anti-Christian power as the "beast" which is mentioned in 13: 11. This was to encourage the struggling saints with the promise that their great enemy with his entire influence would finally be destroyed. He here specifically mentions all individuals who would accept and practice the false teaching of the apostate institution. For comments on receiving the mark of the beast see notes on 13: 16, 17.

10 **he also shall drink of the wine of the wrath of God, which is prepared unmixed in the cup of his anger;**—The figure here is that of drinking from a cup of poison that would make one stagger, reel, and fall. As drinking the wine of Babylon's false doctrines led to religious drunkenness and departure from truth, so drinking the "wine of the wrath of God" means to suffer eternal banishment from his presence. Wine unmixed here means that the punishment would be up to full measure. God's righteous indignation at sin would require that he allow wickedness to be properly rewarded. Paul so taught in 2 Thess. 2: 12. This is a strong incentive to righteous living.

and he shall be tormented with fire and brimstone in the presence of the holy angels, and in the presence of the Lamb:—The word "tormented" carries the idea of conscious pain, which in itself shows consciousness in the final state. Fire and brimstone are evidently used in a figurative sense to indicate the terrible

the presence of the Lamb: 11 and the smoke of their torment goeth up [5]for ever and ever; and they have no rest day and night, they that [3]worship the

[5]Gr. *unto ages of ages.*

punishment that the lost will have to endure. Anything requiring the use of such figures must be too dreadful not to escape. The language may be used with reference to the destruction of Sodom. (Gen. 19: 24.) Whatever this punishment may be, it will be unending. Mark refers to it as "where their worm dieth not, and the fire is not quenched." (Mark 9: 47, 48.) Matthew refers to "eternal punishment" in direct contrast with "eternal life." Eternal in both expressions is from the same Greek word. The punishment, therefore, is of the same duration as the life.

The angels and Christ being present need not be pressed to signify anything more than that they will be present when the wicked are sent away into their punishment. However, it may add to their torment for them to know that their punishment is according to the righteous judgment of Christ, and a justification of the rewards to the righteous. Blessings for the righteous demand punishments for the wicked, else righteousness would not be worth seeking.

11 **and the smoke of their torment goeth up for ever and ever; and they have no rest day and night, they that worship the beast and his image, and whoso receiveth the mark of his name.**—Smoke ceases to arise when the fire goes out. This is a symbol to indicate that their punishment would not end; the two expressions "for ever and ever" and "day and night" both show that to be the meaning. When the final sentence is passed, the destiny of the wicked is fixed forever. The remainder of the verse is a repetition of the description of those who will be finally rejected. The number John is here talking about are those who identify themselves with the apostate church in doctrine and practice. For comment on the mark and name of the beast see notes on 13: 16, 17.

3. STATE OF THE RIGHTEOUS DEAD
14: 12, 13

beast and his image, and whoso receiveth the mark of his name. 12 Here is

12 **Here is the patience of the saints, they that keep the**

the [6]patience of the saints, they that keep the commandments of God, and the faith of Jesus.

13 And I heard a voice from heaven saying, Write, Blessed are the dead

[6]Or, *stedfastness*

---

commandments of God, and the faith of Jesus.—The sufferings and persecutions which saints would have to endure in their struggles against the powers of the beast would require the strongest patience. The fact that they kept the commandments of God would be sufficient proof that they did have the required patience. Keeping the faith of Jesus means that they held to the faith Jesus required and did not deny him. The promise of the ultimate overthrow of their enemies would also be an incentive to sustain their faith and keep them patient.

13 **And I heard a voice from heaven saying, Write, Blessed are the dead who die in the Lord from henceforth:**—Angels flying in midheaven, as they appeared to John in the vision, had pronounced the doom of those who worshiped the beast. Next he hears a voice that seems to come from heaven commanding him to write a certain promise regarding the dead. It is not stated whose voice was speaking. John recorded not only what he *saw* in the visions, but also what he *heard*. The thing he was told to write was spoken by the heavenly voice; it was not a comment by John.

The blessing here pronounced was upon a certain class of the dead—those "who die in the Lord." This implies two things as necessary to secure this blessing: first, to come into the Lord, for no one can be in the Lord who does not come into him; second, to live faithfully in him till death, for no one can die in the Lord (be worthy of Christ's mercy and favor) unless he is faithful unto death. (Matt. 24: 13.)

The word "henceforth" in this verse has cost commentators no little time and trouble. The difficulty is in the fact that faithful Christians dying in the Lord in any age of the world will be ultimately blessed. Why then, say "henceforth"? Henceforth from what time, and why from that time? If henceforth be joined to the word "dead," it might mean that the righteous will be blessed in some signal way from the moment of death. This is most certainly true in fact, but true of all the righteous dead. The connec-

who die [7]in the Lord from henceforth: yea, saith the Spirit, that they may rest from their labors; for their works follow with them.

[7]Or, *in the Lord. From henceforth, yea, saith the Spirit*

tion here seems to indicate that this promise was intended to encourage those who would be victorious in their struggles against the beast. If this be the primary application, then it would be a wonderful help in enduring the persecutions to be assured of an ultimate blessing. From the time that such torments began, those dying in faithfulness would show such genuine Christian fortitude that there could be no question about their eternal happiness. Of course, the principle here taught will continue to be true of all righteous dead.

yea, saith the Spirit, that they may rest from their labors; for their works follow with them.—The Holy Spirit is meant here and the thought is that what the voice said was by the Spirit's direction. The faithful dead rest from their wearisome toil in preaching the gospel and living the Christian life while struggling against the power and influence of the papal beast. Looking forward to reward and rest are the two chief motives that make the burden of tiresome labor bearable. It is a fact that the good deeds one does continue to have their influence on others after his departure, but that does not seem to be the point made here. The statement is that "their works follow with them." This implies that the good of righteous deeds does not remain alone on earth to affect others, but follows with the dead to the judgment. Paul declares that at the judgment each will receive "according to what he hath done" (2 Cor. 5: 10), which means that man's faithfulness till death will be the ground upon which he will be saved; hence, the value of his labors will be with him at that day. Again we remark that this is true of Christians in all ages.

4. THE JUDGMENT HARVEST AND VINTAGE
14: 14-20

14 And I saw, and behold, a white cloud; and on the cloud I *saw* one

14 **And I saw, and behold, a white cloud; and on the cloud I saw one sitting like unto a son of man,**—In this paragraph the saints are further encouraged by a symbolic description of the final

sitting like unto a son of man, having on his head a golden crown, and in his hand a sharp sickle. 15 And another angel came out from the [8]temple,

[8]Or, *sanctuary*

judgment on both good and bad. Harvest is a common figure used to indicate the final separation of the two classes. "He will gather his wheat into the garner, but the chaff he will burn up with unquenchable fire" are the words of John the Baptist. (Matt. 3: 12.) "The harvest is the end of the world." (Matt. 13: 39.) The expression "like unto a son of man" is found in Dan. 7: 13 and Rev. 1: 13. Since verses 17 and 18 of the latter chapter clearly show Christ to be the one meant, it is safe to presume it means Christ in all three passages. Jesus frequently referred to himself as the "Son of man." (Matt. 8: 20; 9: 6; 10: 23; 11: 19.) The person John saw in the vision was either Jesus or one that represented him by resemblance. That this vision pictured the coming of Christ at the judgment is evident from what is said about the harvest and the vintage. That the symbol should represent him as coming on a cloud harmonizes with the plain language that describes his return. When he ascended "a cloud received him out of their sight," and two men (probably angels) told the apostles he would "so come in like manner" as they beheld him going into heaven. (Acts 1: 9-11.) Appearing upon a white cloud at the judgment is just what we would expect from what the Scriptures say of his return.

having on his head a golden crown, and in his hand a sharp sickle.—The crown upon his head indicates that Christ had become a victor—conquered his enemies and his truth was now ready to be finally vindicated. Since the whole vision includes the judgment, Christ's royal or kingly power is also implied. In Matt. 25: 31-46, where the judgment is described in plain words, Christ is represented as sitting upon the "throne of his glory" when the nations appear to hear their destinies declared. The word "throne" here does not signify Christ's *reigning,* but his *judging*—passing sentence upon the wicked and announcing the reward of the good. Sickle is the implement with which grain is cut, or vines are pruned. It is, therefore, an appropriate emblem to indicate the harvesting of the righteous or the cutting off of the wicked.

15 **And another angel came out from the temple, crying**

crying with a great voice to him that sat on the cloud, Send forth thy sickle, and reap: for the hour to reap is come; for the harvest of the earth is [9]ripe.
16 And he that sat on the cloud cast his sickle upon the earth; and the earth was reaped.
17 And another angel came out from the [8]temple which is in heaven, he

[9]Gr. *become dry.*

with a great voice to him that sat on the cloud,—This makes the fourth angel that is mentioned in this chapter. (Verses 6, 8, 9.) He appeared to John as coming out of the temple. (See 11: 19.) The most holy place of the temple represented heaven, the very dwelling place of God. This angel in the vision bringing the command from God to him who sat upon the cloud means that the time had come for God to announce the judgment. As only the Father, according to Christ's own words, knows the time for Christ's return (Acts 1: 7; Matt. 24: 36), the command for it would naturally come from the Father. The angel was only the messenger by whom the command was given. Using a great (loud) voice may indicate that it was designed for all to hear, for the judgment pertained to all.

Send forth thy sickle, and reap: for the hour to reap is come; for the harvest of the earth is ripe.—Send forth the sickle means do the reaping. The hour has come shows that the time God had in his own mind for the judgment and end of the work had arrived. It was fitting that the command to reap should be given to Christ, for he was the sower who scattered God's word as seed. He was the proper one to harvest it. All that will be saved will be through that word. The harvest being ripe means that everything is ready for gathering the saved into heaven's garner.

16 **And he that sat on the cloud cast his sickle upon the earth; and the earth was reaped.**—This verse tells us that the thing commanded was done—the earth was reaped. This part of the vision depicts the end of time and what will occur so far as the righteous are concerned.

17 **And another angel came out from the temple which is in heaven, he also having a sharp sickle.**—Again John sees another angel come out from the temple, which is plainly stated as being in heaven. A peculiarity of this angel is that he also is said to have a sharp sickle. Regarding the harvest and the end of the world,

also having a sharp sickle. 18 And another angel came out from the altar,
he that hath power over fire; and he called with a great voice to him that
had the sharp sickle, saying, Send forth thy sharp sickle, and gather the
clusters of the vine of the earth; for her grapes are fully ripe. 19 And the
angel cast his sickle into the earth, and gathered the [10]vintage of the earth,
and cast it into the winepress, the great *winepress,* of the wrath of God. 20

[10]Gr. *vine.*

Jesus said that "the reapers are angels." (Matt. 13: 39.) Perhaps the whole truth may be stated by saying that Jesus was to reap through the angels as his agents. The figure of the harvest, by its very nature, would include both good and bad—wheat and chaff; but that of the vintage refers only to the wicked. The point in the emblem is not the preservation of the clusters, but the pressing out of the juice which represents the condemnation of the wicked. This figure is thus applied by Joel. "Put ye in the sickle; for the harvest is ripe: come, tread ye; for the winepress is full, the vats overflow; for their wickedness is great." (Joel 3: 13.)

18 **And another angel came out from the altar, he that hath power over fire; and he called with a great voice to him that had the sharp sickle, saying,**—This is the sixth angel mentioned in this chapter. The brazen altar stood in the outer court before the temple. It was the place where burnt offerings were presented to God. The work to be done was destructive in its nature, and the altar of burnt offerings was the appropriate place from which the angel should come.

Send forth thy sharp sickle, and gather the clusters of the vine of the earth; for her grapes are fully ripe.—This means that the clusters were to be cut off and cast into the wine press. Being fully ripe means that wickedness had continued till it was the proper time to remove the sinners from the earth. Sin had reached the full limit to which God's mercy would allow it to come.

19 **And the angel cast his sickle into the earth, and gathered the vintage of the earth, and cast it into the winepress, the great winepress, of the wrath of God.**—In this symbol John saw the angel obeying the command and casting the clusters into the wine press. Crushing the grapes and the red juice flowing like streams of blood was a most striking emblem of destruction. It

And the winepress was trodden without the city, and there came out blood from the winepress, even unto the bridles of the horses, as far as a thousand and six hundred furlongs.

forcefully represented the overthrow and final rejection of the wicked. The vintage of the earth would be the wicked part of the earth. The wine press of God's wrath means that the wicked will be forced to feel the power of God's righteous indignation, when they find themselves rejected.

20 **And the winepress was trodden without the city, and there came out blood from the winepress, even unto the bridles of the horses, as far as a thousand and six hundred furlongs.**—In the vision John saw the juice pressed out with men's feet, which was the method used at that time. Wine presses were usually placed in vineyards, not in cities; hence the statement that it was without the city. Apparently there is no figurative significance in that fact unless it be the final separation of the wicked from the righteous. The city of Jerusalem represented the final city of God, the home of the saved, and of course the lost are without that city. The text says blood came out. In this expression the symbol—juice of the grape—is dropped and what it represents is stated. Blood, however, is but a symbol of the overflowing of the wicked—their final rejection.

The wine press was called great because of the immense number of the lost. The flowing of the juice, like blood in a great battle, looked to John like a great lake, sixteen hundred furlongs and up to the bridles of horses in depth. If this measurement means a square, the surface covered was two hundred miles square. It indicates the immense, even countless multitudes, that will be lost when God's wrath is finally poured out upon the wicked. This is the last, sad event in the experience of the condemned before entering their final state. It was designed to encourage the saints in their trials by the assurance that in God's own time they would be finally relieved of their persecutions—their persecutors would depart from them forever. The ultimate happiness of the faithful in Christ is the especial lesson pictured in the symbols of this chapter.

SECTION THREE

POURING OUT OF THE SEVEN PLAGUES

15: 1 to 16: 21

Preliminary Notes: 1. There are three sets of symbolic sevens, each one bringing the story to the end of time or the coming of the Lord. Since the prophetic history of the church from John's time was pictorially revealed in the book of seven seals, naturally the seventh seal would not be exhausted till the end. The seven trumpets came under the last seal and the sounding of the seventh one brings the end. (11: 15-19.) In like manner the plagues, under another set of symbols, complete the cycle, for 15: 1 says in them is "finished the wrath of God."

2. The fourteenth chapter was designed to encourage saints in their struggles by predicting the fall of Babylon (verse 8) and the final victory of the righteous (verse 13). Section three points out the means by which these glorious results are to be accomplished.

3. In view of the fact that these plagues were to be poured out upon the beast and his worshipers (16: 2, 10), it is evident that they represent a series of events that will ultimately end the papal hierarchy—accomplish the destruction of the "man of sin." This event will occur at the coming of the Lord. (2 Thess. 2: 8.) All this is proof that the plagues did not begin to be poured out till after the 1,260-year period, or the time when Rome's complete sway began to be destroyed.

1. AN INTRODUCTORY VISION

15: 1-4

1 And I saw another sign in heaven, great and marvellous, seven angels having seven plagues, *which are* the last, for in them is finished the wrath of God.

---

1 **And I saw another sign in heaven, great and marvellous, seven angels having seven plagues, which are the last, for in them is finished the wrath of God.**—This sign which John saw in heaven was one of marvelous beauty fitted to excite wonder and prepare the mind to appreciate the promise of victory over the beast. Appearing in heaven would indicate that this victory would come through the judgments that God would providentially bring

2 And I saw as it were a [11]sea of glass mingled with fire; and them that come off victorious from the beast, and from his image, and from the number of his name, standing [12]by the [11]sea of glass, having harps of God. 3 And

[11]Or, *glassy sea*
[12]Or, *upon*

upon the beast. Saying that these plagues are the last is explained to mean that when they are completed the wrath of God against the papal beast power will be finished. However long a time may be covered by the plagues, their finish means the end of the world.

2 **And I saw as it were a sea of glass mingled with fire; and them that come off victorious from the beast, and from his image, and from the number of his name,**—A similar vision is recorded in 4: 6 except that here the sea of glass is "mingled with fire." There it was "before the throne"; here it is in heaven, hence must have reference in some way to the saved. This is further evident by the fact that it is those who are victorious that are standing by it, or upon it, according to the margin. Compare the notes on 4: 6. On the expressions image of the beast and the number of his name see the notes on 13: 15-18. The victory mentioned here evidently refers to the fact that those standing by the sea of glass had successfully resisted all the schemes and devices of the papacy to force them to accept its doctrines and practices; this they did in spite of threats and persecutions. The fire may represent the persecutions in which they attained their glorious victory. (Acts 14: 22.)

standing by the sea of glass, having harps of God.—As the scene was laid in heaven and the persons were those who had gained a victory over the beast, it must refer to saints in glory, not to those in the church on earth. The word "harps," as a symbol, doubtless, means the praise that the redeemed will render to God. It certainly could not mean mechanical harps, for pure spirit beings would not need material harps. In Eph. 5: 19 Paul uses the Greek word *psallo* in a figurative sense, saying that it is done with the heart. Whatever spiritual faculties we have for praising God will be the heavenly harps. Whatever the meaning of this expression, it can have no reference to the church on earth. See notes on 14: 2.

they sing the song of Moses the [13]servant of God, and the song of the Lamb, saying,

Great and marvellous are thy works, O Lord God, the Almighty; righteous and true are thy ways, thou King of the [1]ages. 4 Who shall not fear, O Lord, and glorify thy name? for thou only art holy; for all the nations shall come and [2]worship before thee; for thy righteous acts have been made manifest.

[13]Gr. *bondservant.*
[1]Many ancient authorities read *nations.* Jer. 10. 7.
[2]See marginal note on ch. 3. 9.

3 **And they sing the song of Moses the servant of God, and the song of the Lamb, saying, Great and marvellous are thy works, O Lord God, the Almighty; righteous and true are thy ways, thou King of the ages.**—It does not seem reasonable that those who gained a victory over the beast should sing the same song that was sung when Moses led Israel out of Egypt. (Ex. 15: 1.) That they should celebrate their victory in an appropriate song like the Israelites did at the Red Sea is altogether reasonable; hence, the language probably means that they sang a song to the Lamb as the Israelites did to Moses. Both victories were accomplished through God's help and in a similar way. Since reference is made to the deliverance of the Israelites from Egypt it is natural for the song to speak of God as having almighty power and his works being great and marvelous. The Red Sea and Mount Sinai furnish examples. That God should be just or righteous, true in all his ways, is required by his very nature. Pharaoh with all his wickedness was as justly treated as the Israelites in their affliction. So the reverses that fell upon the beast power were but evidences of the just providences of God.

God is here referred to as the "King of the ages"; the margin says *King of nations,* and the King James Version *King of saints.* It is immaterial which is the true reading, for if God is King at all, he is King of all three. There is a broad general sense in which God has and will rule in all ages, though the specific reign in this age is given to Christ. Since this authority was given to him by the Father, and he operates through the Father's power, the direct reign will be given back to the Father in the final state. (1 Cor. 15: 24.)

4 **Who shall not fear, O Lord, and glorify thy name? for thou only art holy; for all the nations shall come and worship before thee; for thy righteous acts have been made manifest.**

—This means that all should fear his name because of his holiness. Then it is affirmed that all nations—that is, people from all nations—will come and worship before him. His righteous acts have been made known and those influenced by them to be faithful regardless of persecution will be permitted to worship before him in heaven and join in the song of praise.

2. THE SEVEN ANGELS COMMISSIONED
15: 5 to 16: 1

5 And after these things I saw, and the [3]temple of the tabernacle of the testimony in heaven was opened: 6 and there came out from the [3]temple the seven angels that had the seven plagues, arrayed [4]with *precious* stone, pure

[3]Or, *sanctuary*
[4]Many ancient authorities read *in linen,* ch. 19. 8.

5 **And after these things I saw, and the temple of the tabernacle of the testimony in heaven was opened:**—"After these things" means after the things mentioned in the vision described in verses 1-4. The tabernacle was erected in the wilderness and the temple was a permanent building on the same plan builded in Jerusalem. Both buildings were divided into two apartments—holy and most holy—the latter being typical of heaven. (Heb. 9: 1-7, 24.) The two names referred either to the whole building or to either apartment of it. The word tabernacle here probably means the entire building and the word temple means the most holy part. This represented the actual dwelling place of God. It was the place where God's law was kept and was filled with God's presence; hence, it was a testimony to God's presence. John saw within this place the vision.

6 **And there came out from the temple the seven angels that had the seven plagues, arrayed with precious stone, pure and bright, and girt about their breasts with golden girdles.**—Seeing these angels come out of the open temple indicated that they came from God's presence and shows that their mission to bring punishment upon the beast and his dupes was with divine approval. Seven is acknowledged as the number of perfection. Seven angels with authority to pour out seven plagues means that the punishment would be thorough and complete—God's wrath on the beast being finished with the last one.

and bright, and girt about their breasts with golden girdles. 7 And one of the four living creatures gave unto the seven angels seven golden bowls full of the wrath of God, who liveth [5]for ever and ever. 8 And the [3]temple was filled with smoke from the glory of God, and from his power; and none was

---

Whether the text should read "stone pure and bright" or "pure and white linen" (as in the King James) is a matter for textual critics. Evidently both expressions are found in some manuscripts. One would mean that their garments were adorned with precious stones; the other that they were clothed with pure white linen indicative of the purity of their mission. Precious stones would show the value of their work. There is no material difference which one is the true reading—both express a truth. Their golden girdle was like that worn by Christ in the vision of 1: 13. They were appropriately arrayed.

7 **And one of the four living creatures gave unto the seven angels seven golden bowls full of the wrath of God, who liveth for ever and ever.**—The four living creatures were introduced in vision in 4:6, 7. See the notes on those verses for an explanation. It is evident that they are some kind of heavenly beings in attendance upon God, and therefore suitable beings to deliver the plagues to the angels. Which one of the four acted in this event is not stated. The bowls were full of the wrath of God. Doubtless that expression was used in reference to the custom of drinking poison out of a bowl, and was intended here to indicate the punishments that would be poured out upon the papal beast. The figure of "pouring out" God's wrath is common to the Old Testament. See Psalm 79: 6; Jer. 10: 25; Zeph. 3: 8. The thought here seems to be: each angel received out of the sum of God's indignation against the beast power a measure of wrath into the bowl given him and poured it out at the proper time and at the proper place. In words without a figure, it means that punishments would fall upon the papal power.

8 **And the temple was filled with smoke from the glory of God, and from his power;**—This language indicates that the smoke came from the glorious power of God, and is, therefore, an appropriate symbol of divine power. Mount Sinai, when Jehovah descended upon it, was covered with smoke. (Ex. 19: 18.) When the tabernacle was put up the cloud filled it (Ex. 40: 34);

able to enter into the [3]temple, till the seven plagues of the seven angels should be finished.

1 And I heard a great voice out of the [3]temple, saying to the seven angels, Go ye, and pour out the seven bowls of the wrath of God into the earth.

[5]Gr. *unto the ages of the ages.*

the same was true when the temple was built later (1 Kings 8: 10). When Isaiah received his commission, he saw in a vision God sitting upon his throne and the house filled with smoke. (Isa. 6: 4.) Smoke here then represents the glorious power of God which was a guarantee that the plagues would be certain to fall as indicated in the symbol.

and none was able to enter into the temple, till the seven plagues of the seven angels should be finished.—The general application of these verses is to the plagues promised to the beast. Interpretations of special expressions must harmonize with the general idea. In the literal temple the most holy apartment represented God's dwelling place; hence, it was there that the high priest made the atonement in behalf of the people. No one being allowed to enter the symbolic temple till all the plagues had been finished indicates that nothing could prevent the falling of the plagues just as promised. The beast power had reached the point in wickedness when nothing but punishments would meet the demands of divine justice. The door would be closed against those who would petition in behalf of such a corrupt institution; its ultimate end must be destruction. The Lord's ears are open to the supplication of the righteous, but against those that do evil. (1 Pet. 3: 12.) This symbol presents the "man of sin" as doomed to destruction with no power to prevent, for there would be no means that would produce repentance and reformation. Since God is always ready to hear the righteous, we know the foregoing application of this text must be the right one.

1 **And I heard a great voice out of the temple, saying to the seven angels, Go ye, and pour out the seven bowls of the wrath of God into the earth.**—These words are a statement of the commission to the angels. They were spoken in the temple, indicating that the authority to execute their commission is from God. The word "earth" here is to be taken literally, for the angels who were to pour out the plagues were in heaven, and those upon

whom they were to fall were dwelling on the earth. The part of the earth in each case corresponds with those affected. This verse is but a general statement of authority being conferred upon the angels; the remainder of this chapter is a detailed description of how that authority was carried out.

3. THE FIRST FIVE PLAGUES DESCRIBED
16: 2-11

2 And the first went, and poured out his bowl into the earth; and [6]it became a noisome and grievous sore upon the men that had the mark of the beast, and that [2]worshipped his image.

[6]Or, *there came*

2 **And the first went, and poured out his bowl into the earth; and it became a noisome and grievous sore upon the men that had the mark of the beast, and that worshipped his image.**—This is what John saw in the vision, but what this represents as a symbol is another thing. There is perhaps no part of Revelation for which expositors have offered more different explanations than the seven bowls of God's wrath. That they represent punishments and calamities that were to befall the papal hierarchy is generally admitted, but the difficulty comes in trying to fix upon some historical events as the fulfillment of the symbols. If we are not able definitely to locate any event that is a sure fulfillment, we will still know that the symbols have been or will be fulfilled by some such events. The general facts about which there can be no reasonable doubt are these: (1) That a general series of calamities would befall the beast and his devotees that would culminate in his destruction. To misunderstand these or misapply the items will not change this fact. (2) These plagues were to affect directly the man of sin—the apostate church. (3) As they were to accomplish his destruction, they would naturally begin when his power was ready to wane. This would indicate that these plagues would not begin to be poured out till after the 1,260-year period had ended. The record says (13: 4, 5) that authority was given unto the beast to "continue forty and two months." These facts are certainly true, and would be sufficient for practical purposes, if no effort were made to find any historical fulfillment.

A noisome and grievous sore would be a physical malady that is particularly painful and tormenting. These words, doubtless, are to be understood symbolically—that is, some calamities would fall upon men that would be as disagreeable as the physical plagues mentioned. Surely there would be more calamities befall them than just one physical disorder. But whatever punishments were visited upon them, they would be as tormenting as a burning boil. Those to be thus tormented were men who had the "mark" and "image" of the beast. As already learned, this refers to those who have received the doctrines of the apostate church and practice them. See notes on 13: 15-17. Naturally this means that whatever the plagues might indicate, the events would occur in countries predominantly under the influence of Catholicism, either religiously or politically, or both. It should be remembered that this beast power was united so closely in both religious and political forms that each sustained the other and a plague upon one affected the other.

As a matter of historical fact the Roman apostate church began the loss of her universal sway over the nations about the time of the French Revolution, A.D. 1789 to 1794. Of all the conflicting views presented by expositors this appears to be the most probable, and is the view of several. Elliott (Vol. III, pp. 351-375) gives this application of the plague in detail. France, being a strong Catholic nation, was a suitable place for the events to happen. The *Standard History of the World* (Vol. VII, p. 3384) thus describes the unhappy state of France in this period:

"During the *Reign of Terror,* in 1793-94, unhappy France—torn by factions, rent by civil war, invaded by civil enemies, threatened by famine, suffering from bankruptcy, cursed by atheism—presented a picture beyond our powers of description."

On page 3386 it is stated that "infidelity and atheism reigned supreme," and that the leaders of the Paris Commune declared they intended "to dethrone the King of heaven as well as the monarchs of the earth." The national convention decreed "the abolition of the Christian religion in France and the substitution of the worship of reason instead."

The same authority, same page, thus states the treatment received by the Catholic Church:

3 And the second poured out his bowl into the sea; and [6]it became blood as of a dead man; and every [7]living soul died, *even* the things that were in the sea.

[7]Gr. *soul of life*.

"Gobel, the constitutional Bishop of Paris, and several other ecclesiastics were compelled publicly to apostatize from Roman Catholic Christianity and to accept the new worship of reason. While the cathedral at Notre Dame was thus profaned by being converted into a temple of atheism, the other Catholic churches were plundered and subjected to every kind of sacrilege, and the mass vestments and church ornaments and implements were carried through the streets in blasphemous processions."

The same writer says that the Reign of Terror cost the lives of more than a million Frenchmen. If such a moral and religious ulcer in the leading Catholic nation does not fulfill the demands of John's symbolic plague, it would be difficult to find anything in history that does. It would be remarkably strange that a situation without a parallel in history for moral and religious corruption should not be made a part of the symbolic imagery depicting the rise and fall of an apostate religion. That the papacy began at that time the downgrade which will ultimately end in its destruction is most certainly true; hence, it is the most probable application for the fulfillment of the first plague.

3 **And the second poured out his bowl into the sea; and it became blood as of a dead man; and every living soul died, even the things that were in the sea.**—John saw the second angel pour the contents of his bowl into the sea and it turned to the color of blood, and all living creatures in the sea died. It was not the warm flowing blood of a living being, but the dark coagulated blood of the dead. Very naturally this would destroy everything in the sea or upon the sea. This was only what John saw in the vision; what the symbol represents is the difficult problem the Bible student must try to solve. We have already learned (see preliminary notes on 6: 1-8) that modifying facts sometimes require certain words in a symbol to be taken literally and others figuratively. "Many waters" (17: 1) where the harlot sitteth is said in verse 15 to be "peoples, and multitudes, and nations, and tongues"; but the book nowhere gives a symbolic meaning for sea.

To say it must be given the same meaning as "waters" in 17: 15 is an assumption without proof. The words "earth" and "men" in the first plague (verse 2) are to be taken literally; for, whatever the plague meant, it was to affect people here on earth. That is where they dwell. Some commentators have suggested different figurative meanings for the word sea; but, in harmony with the application offered for the first plague, it seems more probable that it is to be understood literally here. The meaning then will be: some great calamities would take place upon the sea which would affect the papal nations adversely, and become one of the things that would help to bring about the destruction of the apostate church. This view harmonizes with plain facts of history, even if the word sea should be given some metaphorical meaning.

Elliott's commentary (Vol. III, pp. 378-380) describes the great naval war between France and England which began in the time of the French Revolution, 1793, and lasted more than twenty years. After naming about a dozen great engagements in which France and her allies lost heavily, Elliott says:

"Altogether in this naval war, from its beginning in 1793 to its end in 1815, it appears from James' *Naval History* that there were destroyed near 200 ships of the line, between 300 and 400 frigates, and an almost incalculable number of smaller vessels of war and ships of commerce. It is most truly stated by Dr. Keith that the whole history of the world does not present such a period of naval war, destruction, and bloodshed."

Such facts surely would justify the language of the symbol: the sea "became blood as of a dead man." Sweeping the navy of papal nations from the sea in such decisive victories is fittingly described by the words, "every living soul died," of the creatures in the sea. As Mr. Barnes so often says in his commentary, if the Spirit had desired to describe these historical facts in symbols, more appropriate language could hardly have been chosen. Regardless of how the plague is to be understood, these were heavy blows against those who had the "mark of the beast."

4 **And the third poured out his bowl into the rivers and the fountains of the waters; and it became blood.**—It should be re-

the waters; [8]and [6]it became blood. 5 And I heard the angel of the waters saying, Righteous art thou, who art and who wast, thou Holy One, because

[8]Some ancient authorities read *and they became.*

membered that whatever application may be given these symbols, the plagues represent events that were to fall upon the beast power as punishments. They would have to be where obedience to papal authority was rendered, and upon the worshipers in that system. As in the first two visions, the words "earth" and "sea" probably indicate the places where those plagues would be most heavily felt, so here rivers and fountains of waters, doubtless, refer to another place where the third plague would fall. If so, then the events indicated would happen in a section where rivers abounded. The statement that the water became blood as a result shows that the plague is to be understood as referring to destructive wars. Because John saw these visions in regular order does not mean that the events signified by one had to be past before those of another could begin. Events depicted by several may have occurred at the same time in different places.

Again we refer to Elliott (Vol. III, pp. 382 to 388), who describes another series of wars from 1792-1805 which were fought in the territory of the three rivers, Rhine, Danube, Po, and their tributaries. It must be admitted that these wars were at an appropriate time, and of the right character, to be the fulfillment of the symbol. If these wars do not fulfill the requirements of the vision, then something of a similar nature would have to be located at some other time. Nothing seems more probable, and certainly this view does no violence to the symbol.

5 **And I heard the angel of the waters saying, Righteous art thou, who art and who wast, thou Holy One, because thou didst thus judge:**—The expression "angel of the waters" is not easy of interpretation. That angels were sometimes given power to use or control certain elements is clear from 7: 1; 14: 18. In the text it seems more probable that the angel referred to is the one who poured out the plague upon the waters, the thought being that the angel declared the righteousness of God in the punishments indicated by this plague. They indicated that God is a righteous Judge.

thou didst thus [9]judge: 6 for they poured out the blood of saints and prophets, and blood hast thou given them to drink: they are worthy.
7 And I heard the altar saying, Yea, O Lord God, the Almighty, true and righteous are thy judgments.
8 And the fourth poured out his bowl upon the sun; and it was given

[9]Or, *judge. Because they . . . prophets, thou hast given them blood also to drink*

6 **for they poured out the blood of saints and prophets, and blood hast thou given them to drink: they are worthy.**—It is unnecessary to give any detailed account of the persecutions which the papal beast brought upon the true people of God. That this apostate church with her political power did shed the blood of saints we would know from what the angel here says, even if history recorded not a single instance. Since simple Christians and prophets (teachers of the word) had been killed, God allowed those persecutors to be given blood to drink—to suffer terrible bloodshed in the wars indicated. The angel declared that they were worthy—that is, they deserved the punishments they were getting because of their shedding the blood of saints.

7 **And I heard the altar saying, Yea, O Lord God, the Almighty, true and righteous are thy judgments.**—Under the fifth seal (6: 9-11) the martyrs were seen under the altar and they were crying with a great voice, asking how long till God would avenge their blood on those upon the earth. Here John hears another voice that appears to come from the altar endorsing the angel's statement that God's judgments are true and righteous. All this means that all the punishments indicated by these plagues that fell upon the apostate Roman church were a just and righteous retribution for sins against the church Christ established. It also placed the stamp of divine approval upon those who were martyrs for the word of God.

8 **And the fourth poured out his bowl upon the sun; and it was given unto it to scorch men with fire.**—The thing John saw was an angel pouring the contents of a bowl upon the sun which so intensified the heat that men were scorched. In the symbol the word "sun" is used literally; but in applying the symbol it must be used figuratively, for the reason that men do not live on the sun, as they do upon the earth or sea. Christ is referred to prophetically as "the sun of righteousness." (Mal. 4: 2.) In a dream Joseph

unto [10]it to scorch men with fire. 9 And men were scorched with great
heat: and they blasphemed the name of God who hath the power over these
plagues; and they repented not to give him glory.
10 And the fifth poured out his bowl upon the throne of the beast; and
his kingdom was darkened; and they gnawed their tongues for pain, 11 and

[10]Or, *him*

saw the sun, moon, and stars bowing to him. This was explained to mean his father, mother, and brethren. (Gen. 37: 9, 10.) As a symbol the sun represents a leader or prominent man. The simple and natural meaning of the fourth plague is that a great leader with irresistible power would bring great distress and suffering to men that might be likened to the burning rays of a scorching sun. The facts naturally indicates that he would be a military leader, and the sufferings would come through war.

According to the view taken of the preceding plagues, this one is probably another result of the French Revolution, and would naturally be expected to follow close after them. The military career of Napoleon Bonaparte came at the exact time to fulfill the requirements of this symbol. He was the most brilliant, successful, and scorching military sun the world had seen. His military talents were first recognized in 1793. After many successful invasions of other nations, he took the government of France into his own hands in 1799, becoming first consul for life. With unlimited power he became a constant menace to other nations. "Never before," says Elliott (Vol. III, p. 391), "had there been such a subversion of old dynasties, and changes in new ones, in the history of modern Europe." The nations that felt the scorching effect of his power were dominated by the papal system of religion. Surely no known historical event fits the symbol any better. It would certainly be remarkable if a career that so clearly affected the fortunes of the church would not be a subject to be depicted in a series of prophetic symbols. No other explanation seems as probable.

9 **And men were scorched with great heat: and they blasphemed the name of God who hath the power over these plagues; and they repented not to give him glory.**—Doubtless it would be impossible to learn how much suffering and bloodshed occurred in these wars. The natural effect that these calamities

they blasphemed the God of heaven because of their pains and their sores; and they repented not of their works.

---

would have upon wicked men would be to cause them to blaspheme God for allowing such misfortunes to fall upon them. They would charge that he alone had power to bring them. If they admitted that God had power to bring the plagues, and they were suffering from them, that should have produced repentance, but it did not. This shows that those with the mark of the beast were too fully steeped in false teaching to yield; so they repented not.

10 **And the fifth poured out his bowl upon the throne of the beast; and his kingdom was darkened;**—The preceding plagues were naturally preparatory to this one, which was a direct thrust at the very foundation of the system. The word "throne" means authority and this bowl was, therefore, intended to weaken the highest authority in the beast power. As the theory here accepted is that the beast represents the apostate or papal church, we conclude that the beast's throne means the authority of the Pope. This plague was greatly to weaken that power, but not to destroy it. That would not occur till the seventh plague had been poured out. The "man of sin" is not to be destroyed till the Lord comes. (2 Thess. 2: 3, 8.) This blow against papal authority would leave the Pope's subjects in distress and confusion, fittingly represented as spiritual darkness.

and they gnawed their tongues for pain, 11 **and they blasphemed the God of heaven because of their pains and their sores; and they repented not of their works.**—The words "pains" and "sores" seem to refer to the effects of the preceding plagues, indicating that this one only intensified their distress and misery already felt from plagues suffered. Gnawing their tongues signifies great suffering and deep anguish. The plague had the same effect in these particulars as the fourth had.

If no fact in history could be found to correspond with this symbol, we would know that something had occurred, and the symbol was true. That events transpired during the French Revolution and soon after it that weakened the power of Rome and strengthened Protestantism is too well known to need reciting. The language naturally implies that the fifth plague was poured out not long after the preceding ones. Elliott (Vol. III, pp. 395-408) offers the most plausible explanation. Briefly stated, he refers it to the time when the "Pope's temporal authority over the Roman state was abolished." After victories in northern Italy in 1796 and 1797, the French army under Napoleon was rushed toward Rome. The Pope (Pius VI) saved himself with a payment of some thirty million francs, and surrendered a hundred of the finest paintings and statues in the Vatican. But he lost his temporal power, was taken away as a prisoner, and soon thereafter died. In 1804 Pope Pius VII was summoned to Paris to crown Napoleon as emperor, or rather to give official sanction to his assuming the position. In 1801 Napoleon made an agreement with Pius VII by which the Roman Catholic Church was restored as the state religion of France, but Protestant worship was to be allowed. In 1809 Napoleon issued a decree, declaring the Pope's temporal authority at an end, but allowed him the Vatican and the position of spiritual head of the church. This intensely exasperated the Pope, who excommunicated Napoleon. The Pope was then taken a prisoner to France, and the states of the church annexed to that empire. These facts surely fulfill the demands of the symbol well enough to justify their acceptance as the things meant. The authority of the Roman Pontiff had been both changed and limited.

Notwithstanding these sufferings, they repented not, but still worshiped the beast. Peace was restored and the Pope returned to his place in Rome in 1815. The preceding year he issued a proclamation, declaring himself *"God's Vicar on Earth."* Soon after his return to Rome he refused tolerance to Protestant worship in France, and issued briefs against Bible societies, declaring the Scriptures themselves, unless accompanied with papal explanations, to be the gospel of men or the devil rather than of God. (See Elliott, Vol. III, pp. 418, 419.)

4. THE SIXTH PLAGUE DESCRIBED
16: 12-16

12 And the sixth poured out his bowl upon the great river, the *river* Eu-

---

12 and the sixth poured out his bowl upon the great river,

phrates; and the water thereof was dried up, that the way might be made ready for the kings that *come* from the sunrising. 13 And I saw *coming* out

the river Euphrates; and the water thereof was dried up,—Expositors are divided, in the main, between two views concerning the application of this plague, both appearing probable. As both harmonize with known facts, and either might have been the thing intended, we should not be dogmatic in our assertions. One view is that it refers to the same world power that was symbolized by the sixth trumpet (9: 13-19)—the Turkish Empire from which arose Mahometanism. The probability here is in the facts that the Euphrates River is mentioned in both passages and that the "false prophet," mentioned in verse 13, presumably is Mahomet, the founder of this false system of religion. Elliott and Barnes both defend this view and give historical events to indicate that Mahometanism about A.D. 1820 began a gradual loss of power, signified by the waters of the river Euphrates drying up. Probably the most plausible reason for this view is that such a great religious power as Mahometanism would hardly be left out of a system of symbols designed to portray the destinies of the church over a period when Mahometanism ruled so much of the world.

The other theory is that this plague was to affect spiritual Babylon, and this is based upon the supposed fact that the destruction of ancient Babylon furnished the imagery here. The intimation in Jer. 51: 36 was carried out when Cyrus drained the river Euphrates and entered the city of Babylon through its bed. As Babylon in this book (17: 3-5) clearly represents the false or harlot church, the drying of the Euphrates may prefigure its gradual decline and final overthrow. In the first few words of this paragraph we have portrayed the coming of the final great struggle between sin and righteousness, error and truth, in which the right will prevail. The time covered is from the early part of the nineteenth century till the coming of Jesus.

that the way might be made ready for the kings that come from the sunrising.—Again commentators are much at variance about who the kings are and the purpose of their coming. The word "king" sometimes stands for kingdom. (Dan. 7: 17, 23.) Possibly it here means the nations east of the Euphrates. If so,

of the mouth of the dragon, and out of the mouth of the beast, and out of the mouth of the false prophet, three unclean spirits, as it were frogs: 14 for

---

the application to the Mahometan races may be correct, in which case the drying of the river may mean the gradual loss of Mahometan power and the consequent coming to the gospel by people in such countries. If applied to papal Rome, the same thing would be true. In either case any weakening of enemies of the truth will lend it strength and lead to final victory. This is a general fact regardless of any special views of the details here mentioned. That we are now in the general trend of events leading to the "war of the great day of God" is evident from this paragraph, but how long will it be till that day arrives must be left to the infinite wisdom and power of God.

13 **And I saw coming out of the mouth of the dragon, and out of the mouth of the beast, and out of the mouth of the false prophet, three unclean spirits, as it were frogs:**—In this vision John saw the sources from which would come the enemies of the truth that will be united against it in the final struggle. They are enemies of the truth now, but will at last unite their forces in some way in a final desperate effort to destroy Christianity. Unclean spirits are in the next verse called "spirits of demons"—that is, evil spirits. They appeared to John as frogs, for which it is not easy to give a satisfactory reason; hence, no effort will be made here. Naturally unclean spirits would come from an evil source and operate through evil means. The dragon is called the devil (12: 9) and described as the deceiver of the whole world. Whatever means or agencies are used to propagate evil, the devil is the original source; he operates through them.

As the devil's first great persecutions against the church came through pagan Rome, the dragon here, doubtless, is a symbol for paganism, which may also be called idolatry. This would include any and all nations under the influence of idolatrous teaching. The application of the word "beast" in this verse depends upon whether or not the "false prophet" is to be identified as the second beast (13: 1-13), which we have already decided is papal Rome—the apostate church. If this identity be conceded, then "beast" in this verse must be something different from the Roman Church.

they are spirits of demons, working signs; which go forth [11]unto the kings of the whole [12]world, to gather them together unto the war of the great day of God, the Almighty. 15 (Behold, I come as a thief. Blessed is he that watcheth, and keepeth his garments, lest he walk naked, and they see his

[11]Or, *upon*
[12]Gr. *inhabited earth.*

Apparently nothing is left but to apply it to the political Roman Empire through which papal Rome exercised its power. If so, it would probably be the emblem for any and all corrupt political governments through which Satan can exercise his destructive power against the church. If the "false prophet" may refer to Mahomet and the system of Mahometanism, then the "beast" in this text would apply to the apostate church. Whatever may be the correct application of the three destructive forces, we are safe in saying that idolatry, corrupt political powers, and false religions in the name of Christ will be the combined forces Satan will use in his last effort to destroy Christianity. Coming from the mouths of the three indicates that these evil forces will be exercised through the teaching of false doctrines.

14 **for they are spirits of demons, working signs; which go forth unto the kings of the whole world, to gather them together unto the war of the great day of God, the Almighty.**—That these false religious powers would claim to perform miracles in support of their teachings is what would naturally be expected. It is plainly prophesied of the apostate church. (13: 11-13; 2 Thess. 2: 9-12.) By means of their false doctrines the nations of the world are to be so corrupted that they will be led to fight against the truth in the last war. When this time comes, which is here called the "great day of God," his wrath against evil on this earth will be finished. (15: 1.) When this time will be is known only to the Father himself. (Matt. 24: 36-39.)

15 **(Behold, I come as a thief. Blessed is he that watcheth, and keepth his garments, lest he walk naked, and they see his shame.)**—Suddenly or unexpectedly will the time arrive for this final blow—it will be the coming of the Lord. Paul said "the day of the Lord so cometh as a thief in the night." (1 Thess. 5: 2.) See also Rev. 3: 3, 13. To watch for an event means to be constantly prepared for it. Those who are faithful till death

shame.) 16 And they gathered them together into the place which is called in Hebrew [13]Har-Magedon.

[13]Or, *Ar-Magedon*

(Matt. 24: 13; Rev. 2: 11) will be happy, for they will not be taken unprepared. To keep his garments is a figurative expression. It probably means that as one who puts off his garments takes the risk of having them lost, leaving him naked, so one who lays aside his righteousness will find himself exposed to shame when the Lord comes. This verse is a parenthetical expression in which saints are warned and exhorted to faithfulness.

16 **And they gathered them together into the place which is called in Hebrew Har-Magedon.**—This verse does not describe the war of the great day of God, but simply mentions the gathering together for it. It is entirely unnecessary to suppose that this language means that all forces of good and evil will meet at any one place to engage in a physical warfare. This is symbolic language and only indicates that in the final struggle the forces of good will prevail. At his coming Jesus will slay "with the breath of his mouth" the man of sin (2 Thess. 2: 8), but how many or what means he will use is not revealed. He will only have to speak the word and events will transpire.

This verse mentions Har-Magedon as the place where this battle will be fought, but this is clearly a symbolic use of the term just as the final abode of the lost is called *Gehenna,* which literally means a valley east of Jerusalem where refuse was continually burned. Symbolically, it stands for torment and lamentation. It cannot mean that all the lost will dwell in that little place, but they will endure a continual punishment that is fitly represented by the perpetual burning in the literal Gehenna. In like manner Har-Magedon, referring to a famous battlefield where decisive victories were lost and won, figuratively describes the last decisive victory over the power of evil. The name means the mountain of Megiddo, but the battles were doubtless fought in the valley near that mountain. (2 Chron. 35: 22.) There Deborah and Barak defeated Sisera and his army (Judges 5: 19), and Josiah was slain (2 Kings 23: 29, 30). It was also referred to as a place of great mourning. (Zech. 12: 11.) Being such a noted place of Jewish wars, it becomes, like Marathon or Waterloo, emblematic of any decisive battlefield; hence, appropriately represents Satan's final defeat in whatever way that battle may be fought.

5. THE SEVENTH PLAGUE—THE END OF TIME 16: 17-21

17 And the seventh poured out his bowl upon the air; and there came forth a great voice out of the [3]temple, from the throne, saying, It is done:
18 and there were lightnings, and voices, and thunders; and there was a great earthquake, such as was not since [14]there were men upon the earth, so

[14]Some ancient authorities read *there was a man.*

---

17 **And the seventh poured out his bowl upon the air;**—Other bowls were poured out upon the earth, sea, rivers, and sun. This one upon the air may be designed to show that by affecting all major parts of the material universe the complete and final overthrow of wickedness is indicated by the plagues. In Eph. 2: 2 Satan is represented as the "prince of the powers of the air." From this some expositors conclude that Satan's defeat is the thing specifically meant. That idea, of course, is included in the other view. At any rate, this plague briefly describes the final struggle, and therefore brings the end of time. This is clearly indicated by the expression, "It is done," and the announcement in 15: 1 that the seven plagues will finish the wrath of God. The language of the paragraph harmonizes with this thought.

and there came forth a great voice out of the temple, from the throne, saying, It is done:—This voice which John heard coming out of the temple and from the throne shows that it was God announcing the time of the end. It was so certain to occur that it was announced as if already done. This is an example of the past being used prophetically for the future. See Rom. 4: 17.

18 **and there were lightnings, and voices, and thunders; and there was a great earthquake, such as was not since there were men upon the earth, so great an earthquake, so mighty.**—After the great voice announced "it is done," John heard voices, thunders, and the rumblings of the earthquake which, he said, would be greater than any that had ever been before. The scene was lighted up with the flashes of lightnings. Such a commotion of natural elements would fittingly indicate the end of the material

great an earthquake, so mighty. 19 And the great city was divided into
three parts, and the cities of the [1]nations fell: and Babylon the great was
remembered in the sight of God, to give unto her the cup of the wine of the
fierceness of his wrath. 20 And every island fled away, and the mountains
were not found. 21 And great hail, *every stone* about the weight of a talent,

[1]Or, *Gentiles*

world, and symbolize the destruction of that part of the religious world under the control of Satan. The end of the world could hardly be described in more forceful words. The scene will be one to strike terror to all wicked hearts.

19 **And the great city was divided into three parts, and the cities of the nations fell: and Babylon the great was remembered in the sight of God, to give unto her the cup of the wine of the fierceness of his wrath.**—Babylon being mentioned in the latter part of the verse indicates that the "great city" refers to Babylon. John saw, in the vision, the city divided into three parts. Since the symbol refers to the end of the world, and consequently the destruction of spiritual Babylon also, then the three-part division of the city could hardly signify anything more than the complete destruction of the papal church, the number three indicating fullness. With this view the cities of the nations would mean all lesser religious bodies that help to make up the sum total of false doctrines. They, too, will come to an end. Ancient Babylon persecuted God's people and in turn was destroyed; so spiritual Babylon has persecuted God's church since the apostasy arose and must be destroyed. God's fierce wrath must in due time be poured out upon her.

20 **And every island fled away, and the mountains were not found.**—This is but a part of the picture which John saw, and graphically portrays another feature of the final change at the end of time.

21 **And great hail, every stone about the weight of a talent, cometh down out of heaven upon men:**—This may be said in allusion to one of the plagues in Egypt. (Ex. 9: 22-26.) This indicates that the distress and torment of that day will be terrible. Hail of such size would produce great sufferings, and be terrifying in the extreme. Such undoubtedly will be the case when the awful scenes of the day of God's wrath appear.

cometh down out of heaven upon men: and men blasphemed God because of the plague of the hail; for the plague thereof is exceeding great.

and men blasphemed God because of the plague of the hail; for the plague thereof is exceeding great.—The wailing and blaspheming of the wicked at the judgment will do no good; it will be too late to reform and serve God. This chapter gives this summary statement of a succession of judgments upon wickedness in general, and the apostate papal church in particular. The false religions have been weakened by the earlier plagues, but the final overthrow, briefly depicted in the paragraph, will occur at the coming of the Lord. That which has been but barely hinted at here will be more fully described in the following chapters.

SECTION FOUR

BABYLON AND HER FALL MORE FULLY DESCRIBED

17: 1 to 19: 21

1. THE APOSTATE CHURCH THE "MOTHER OF THE HARLOTS"

17: 1-6

1 And there came one of the seven angels that had the seven bowls, and spake with me, saying, Come hither, I will show thee the judgment of the great harlot that sitteth upon many waters; 2 with whom the kings of the

---

1 **And there came one of the seven angels that had the seven bowls, and spake with me,**—The angel here being one of the seven whose work is described in the preceding chapter identifies this further revelation as directly connected with that in some way. As the three chapters of this section describe the fall and desolation of Babylon in detail, the only conclusion that seems appropriate is that they explain what was said to have occurred when the seventh angel poured out the seventh plague. (16: 17-21.) It may, therefore, be considered an extended symbolic view of what will take place when the last plague falls upon men. The language is in the past tense, but the incidents were then future—will not happen till Jesus comes again. Another example of the "prophetic past."

saying, Come hither, I will show thee the judgment of the great harlot that sitteth upon many waters;—The words "Come hither" represent one Greek word—an adverb; the meaning is that John was to give attention while he was shown the judgment that was to be inflicted upon the apostate church, here represented as a great harlot. In verse 15 the "many waters" are explained to be "peoples, and multitudes, and nations, and tongues." Since the apostate church is also called "Babylon the great," the image may have been drawn from the fact that the ancient city was situated upon the Euphrates and encompassed with many canals. (Jer. 51: 13.) These waters sustained the city; the city controlled the waters. In like manner the nations supported the apostate church, and the papacy ruled the nations.

2 **with whom the kings of the earth committed fornication,**

earth committed fornication, and they that dwell in the earth were made drunken with the wine of her fornication. 3 And he carried me away in the Spirit into a wilderness: and I saw a woman sitting upon a scarlet-colored

---

and they that dwell in the earth were made drunken with the wine of her fornication.—A pure woman is a symbol of the true church—God's faithful people—as the following texts will show: Gal. 4: 22-26; Eph. 5: 22-24, 31-33. An obedient wife to a loving husband is Paul's figurative description of the church as being true to Christ her head. An unfaithful wife typically represents an apostate church—those once God's people, but who have corrupted themselves with idolatry and human doctrines. The kingdoms of Israel and Judah were both called a backsliding people, and charged with having "committed adultery with stones and with stocks." (Jer. 3: 6-10; Ezek. 23: 37.) Because of their idolatry God allowed both kingdoms to be carried into bondage. The reason for the final rejection of the corrupt church is its idolatry and perversion of the truth. It is appropriately described, like the same sin among ancient Israel, as harlotry. This horrid sin is the disgusting symbol by which unfaithfulness to God is presented. Expositors generally agree that the word in the Bible refers to doctrinal corruption in most of its occurrences.

Kings here, doubtless, are to be taken literally, meaning that the rulers, representing the nations, were influenced and made the mediums through whom the perpetuation of these false doctrines could be made effective. To "commit fornication" means to practice the false teachings, and such people were affected by these practices as a drunk man is by wine. Intoxication by false doctrines is more deadly than that by wine. It not only dulls the senses, but closes one's eyes to the truth.

3 **And he carried me away in the Spirit into a wilderness:**—In a vision the great city's fall (16: 19) is now to be explained, and a change of scene is necessary. By the Spirit John's mind was transported to other symbols which give a detailed description of that fall. The event, of course, was future when John wrote, and is still future. Why these visions appeared in a wilderness is not stated. That the word wilderness, if any symbolic significance is intended, indicates the desolation that was to come upon the city seems the most probable view.

beast, [2]full of names of blasphemy, having seven heads and ten horns. 4
And the woman was arrayed in purple and scarlet, and [3]decked with gold
and precious stone and pearls, having in her hand a golden cup full of abom-

[2]Or, *names full of blasphemy*
[3]Gr. *gilded.*

and I saw a woman sitting upon a scarlet-colored beast, full of names of blasphemy, having seven heads and ten horns.—Unquestionably this woman is to be contrasted with the woman of 12: 1. The true and false churches are described by a variety of symbols. The former is called a temple, a city (Jerusalem), a household, a kingdom, and a true and pure wife. (1 Cor. 3: 16; Heb. 12: 22; Gal. 6: 10; Matt. 16: 18; Eph. 5: 22-23.) The latter John pictures as a beast, a city (Babylon), and an impure and faithless wife. (13: 11; 18: 2; 17: 5.) A drunken harlot with all the abominable wickedness that goes with such crimes is the disgusting view here given of the apostate church. John sees the woman sitting "upon many waters" (verse 1), and "upon a scarlet-colored beast" (verse 3). These are two views of the same woman. See next paragraph for an explanation of the beast.

4 **And the woman was arrayed in purple and scarlet, and decked with gold and precious stone and pearls,**—Scarlet color is a significant characteristic of royal apparel; rich jewels of gold, pearls, and precious stones are the natural adornment of earthly rulers. When enemies wished to ridicule the claim of Jesus that he was a king, they placed a scarlet robe upon him. (Matt. 27: 28.) Some think the red color in this symbol finds fulfillment in the Catholic Church's use of it in such things as the cardinal's red hats. Perhaps the harlot being so gorgeously decked and robed was only intended to indicate her claim of royal authority—the divine right to rule the world. No picture could more appropriately portray her false claim, for the dignitaries of no other church have been so gorgeously arrayed and richly decked.

having in her hand a golden cup full of abominations, even the unclean things of her fornication,—John sees the symbolic woman with a golden cup in her hand, which means she was appealing to all to drink of its contents. This is a figurative expression that means the apostate church was using every device possible to get all men to practice her false doctrines. The cup con-

inations, [4]even the unclean things of her fornication, 5 and upon her forehead a name written, [5]MYSTERY, BABYLON THE GREAT, THE MOTHER OF THE HARLOTS AND OF THE ABOMINATIONS OF THE EARTH. 6 And I saw the woman drunken with the blood of the saints, and with the blood of the [6]martyrs of Jesus. And when I saw her, I

[4]Or, *and of the unclean things*
[5]Or, *a mystery, Babylon the Great*
[6]Or, *witnesses* See ch. 2. 13.

tained corrupt and false teaching, fittingly represented by harlotry, and was therefore an abomination to God. The text calls them "unclean things," comparable to the unfaithfulness of a wife to her husband. There could be no stronger condemnation of a corrupt and perverted worship than such pretended honor to God.

5 **and upon her forehead a name written, MYSTERY, BABYLON THE GREAT, THE MOTHER OF THE HARLOTS AND OF THE ABOMINATIONS OF THE EARTH.**—The name written upon the forehead could be distinctly seen, and it enabled John to understand the character of the woman instantly. Doubtless the reason for its appearing in the symbol was to prevent anyone's misunderstanding the corrupt institution represented. Expositors are not agreed about the import of the word "Mystery." Some consider it a part of the name; others think it an introductory word by John himself, meaning that a mysterious name was written. This would imply that the name was to be taken figuratively—literal Babylon being taken symbolically to represent spiritual Babylon, the apostate Roman Church. In either view the true meaning would have to be found by learning the import of the symbol.

Concerning ancient Babylon Jeremiah said: "Babylon hath been a golden cup in Jehovah's hand, that made all the earth drunken: the nations have drunk of her wine; therefore the nations are mad." (Jer. 51: 7.) God permitted Babylon to punish Israel because of their sins, but promised that Babylon would be destroyed for her own sins. See verses 8, 9. This shows she was typical of the false church as our next verse indicates.

6 **And I saw the woman drunken with the blood of the saints, and with the blood of the martyrs of Jesus. And when I saw her, I wondered with a great wonder.**—John next sees the symbolic woman plainly drunk, not with wine, but with the blood

of the saints. The word "saints" here must be taken literally. The general statement "blood of the saints" is more particularly described as "blood of the martyrs"—that is, those who were slain because of their witnessing for the truth. The word "martyr" literally means a witness. The picture is that of victorious warriors inflaming their minds by drinking the blood of their victims. The meaning is, that the church that had become apostate through perverting Christianity with the commandments of men was so gloating over her persecutions of faithful saints that she was positively drunk mentally. John sees this abominable institution as the "Mother of the Harlots"—that is, the source from which would arise all churches that mingle the divine truth with human speculations.

Commentators have suggested many reasons why John wondered, but the simplest, and one that accords best with the angel's explanation in the next paragraph, seems to be this: he wondered what was signified by a drunken woman sitting upon a vicious wild beast.

2. THE MYSTERY OF THE BEAST EXPLAINED
17: 7-14

wondered with a great wonder. 7. And the angel said unto me, Wherefore didst thou wonder? I will tell thee the mystery of the woman, and of the beast that carrieth her, which hath the seven heads and the ten horns. 8 The beast that thou sawest was, and is not; and is about to come up out of the

---

7 **And the angel said unto me, Wherefore didst thou wonder? I will tell thee of the mystery of the woman, and of the beast that carrieth her,**—The angel's question shows he knew what was in John's mind, and his promise to explain is assurance that we are to receive a correct application of the symbol, as it applies to both the woman and the beast.

which hath the seven heads and the ten horns.—See notes on verses 10-12.

8 **The beast that thou sawest was, and is not; and is about to come up out of the abyss, and to go into perdition.**—The language here means that the wicked power represented by the beast John saw had existed, did not exist, but would come into existence again. This thought is repeated at the close of this verse

abyss, [7]and to go into perdition. And they that dwell on the earth shall wonder, *they* whose name hath not been written [8]in the book of life from the foundation of the world, when they behold the beast, how that he was, and is not, and [9]shall come. 9. Here is the [10]mind that hath wisdom. The seven heads are seven mountains, on which the woman sitteth: 10 and [11]they are

[7]Some ancient authorities read *and he goeth.*
[8]Gr. *on.*
[9]Gr. *shall be present.*
[10]Or, *meaning*
[11]Or, *there are*

and is referred to in verse 11. See notes on verse 10 for full explanation. The word "abyss" refers to the abode of Satan (see 9: 1, 2), and here the thought is that, when the beast returned in a new form, its power and presence should be attributed to Satan—that is, he would be the cause of its existence and the source of its power. The encouraging fact is here stated that this beast power would be destroyed, but when is not mentioned. On that point 2 Thess. 2: 8 shows it will be at the Lord's coming.

And they that dwell on the earth shall wonder, they whose name hath not been written in the book of life from the foundation of the world, when they behold the beast, how that he was, and is not, and shall come.—The events described would be so remarkable as to create surprise, challenge admiration, and lead to belief in the beast's power, except by those written in the book of life. Those who were faithful servants of Christ and worthy of everlasting life would not be deceived. See notes on 13: 8. The text indicates that the thing which would cause men to wonder was the fact that a power once formidable had become practically extinct, and yet was revived with terrific strength.

9 **Here is the mind that hath wisdom.**—This may mean either of the following: here is a symbol that will require wisdom to explain, or the explanation here given is a matter of divine wisdom. "Here is a meaning which compriseth wisdom," is the way Moses Stuart renders the expression. This implies that the explanation given by the angel might be understood some time.

The seven heads are seven mountains, on which the woman sitteth:—This language continues the description of the beast mentioned in verse 3. The similarity of the description here with that of the first beast in chapter thirteen (verses 1-10) seems to render it certain that the same power is meant in both passages.

The difference in the visions of the two chapters is this: the second beast (13: 11-18) represents papal Rome or the apostate church; in chapter 17 this church is represented by the drunken woman. In the former case two beasts appear in the vision; in the latter, one beast and a woman. The beast shows the rapacious nature of the church; the woman indicates the wiles with which the ignorant would be deceived. The visions vary; the facts are the same. The appearance of a drunken harlot sitting on the beast was to show the close relationship of the religious and political powers, and indicates that the apostate church was controlling the state, and operating through the means it supplied. This fact is evident from 13: 12 where it is stated that the second beast "exerciseth all the authority of the first beast," and required men to worship an image of the first beast. That the papacy claims the right to exercise or direct both religious and secular power, and did so during the time indicated by this symbol, is a matter of common knowledge that will hardly be denied. Elliott's commentary (Vol. III, p. 131) quotes the following from Flavio Blondus, a papal writer of the fifteenth century:

"The princes of the world now adore and worship as perpetual dictator the successor, not of Caesar, but of the fisherman, Peter; that is, the supreme Pontiff, the substitute of the afore-mentioned Emperor."

The Encyclopedia Britannica says the fourth Latern council (A.D. 1215), presided over by Pope Innocent III, passed the following law against heretics:

"It was there decreed that all rulers should promise to tolerate no heretics within their dominions, and that any prince who should refuse to comply with an injunction of the church to purge his dominions of heresy was to be punished with excommunication, and in case of contumacy to be deposed, if necessary by force by arms." (Vol. 13, p. 84, ninth edition.)

In November, 1302, Boniface VIII enunciated the doctrine of "papal supremacy," affirming "that the temporal sword wielded by the monarch was borne only at the will and by the permission of the Pontiff." (*Ibid.,* Vol. 19, p. 501.) This is enough to show that the apostate church claims the divine right to control and direct state rulers. Hence, it fits this phase of the symbol.

seven kings; the five are fallen, the one is, the other is not yet come; and

---

Since the beast here refers to imperial or political Rome, it is not improbable that the seven hills upon which the city was built may have suggested the idea of representing the seven heads as seven mountains. The mountains could hardly be taken literally for the reason that the next verse says five have fallen and one was yet to come. This could not be true of literal mountains. Isaiah (2: 2) described the kingdom Christ would establish as the "mountain of Jehovah's house"; Jeremiah (51: 25) represented Babylon as a "destroying mountain." Kingdoms or governments, then, are called mountains, but the Lord's mountain (kingdom) is superior to all earthly governments. The language, therefore, means seven different forms of government. On the surface the words seem to say that the woman was sitting upon all seven heads at one time, but verse 10 precludes this idea by saying that five had fallen when John saw the vision. The only sense in which she could have sat on all the heads at once was that following consecutively the last one included elements of all the preceding. In this sense, of course, it was a fact.

10 **and they are seven kings;**—This means that the seven heads also represent seven kings—that is, they are symbolical of kings as well as mountains. But Dan. 7: 17, 23 shows that prophetically king and kingdom mean the same. The king as supreme ruler represents the kingdom. This would be another way of saying the heads are emblems of seven kinds of royal governments.

the five are fallen, the one is, the other is not yet come;—Expositors present the widest variation of views on this verse; we have not space even to state them all. We mention three that appear to have received the most endorsements. (1) The beast is considered as the Satanic spirit of opposition as manifested in wicked kingdoms, beginning with Egypt, which was the first nation to persecute God's people. With some variation of opinion the others are thought to be Assyria, Babylonia, Medo-Persia, Greece, Rome, and Rome reconstituted after its fall. (2) Others take it literally and apply to the emperors individually. The same persons are not put in the list by all expositors who accept this the-

when he cometh, he must continue a little while. 11 And the beast that was,

ory. (3) Others think the heads mean different forms of the Roman government. Regardless of which theory may be accepted, those represented by the seven heads persecuted God's people and were instigated to do so by Satan. If the "woman" represents the papal apostate church, the position here taken, then it seems that the imagery applies to Rome in its various forms. This will eliminate the second theory, for this theory applies the seven heads to the imperial form exclusively. On the whole the third position seems most likely to be the correct view. There are two reasons that may be assigned for this: one is, that the imagery presents the struggle of the church against opposing powers, and Rome was in existence when the church was established; the other is that the picture of a beast with seven heads naturally signifies the same nation under different forms rather than different nations.

The different forms of the Roman government from its beginning till the establishment of the church are these: Kings, Consuls, Dictators, Decemvirs, Military Tribunes, and Emperors. The first five had passed away when John wrote the imperial form, the sixth, was then in existence. This harmonizes perfectly with the language of the text; and, being the facts concerning the Roman nation, would easily be so understood by John's contemporaries.

The seventh head to rise in the future from John's day is not so easily located. If the woman (papacy) is to be distinguished from the beast upon which she sat (and the imagery seems to require it), then the seventh and eighth heads should both be forms of political Rome.

and when he cometh, he must continue a little while.—The sixth head being the imperial form of Rome, the seventh could not arise till that fell. This occurred when pagan Rome ended in A.D. 476. The eighth head would necessarily have to be so-called Christianized Rome dominated by the apostate church. We have already seen that the papacy became a fully established institution in the sixth century. See notes on 11: 4. Whatever form of government controlled the Roman nations between A.D. 476 and the time the papal church began to dominate the political rulers was the time of the seventh head. Barnes' commentary (p. 430) ap-

and is not, is himself also an eighth, and is of the seven; and he goeth into

plies the seventh head to the Dukedom under the Exarchate of Ravenna, and quotes Gibbon as saying that during this period "eighteen successive exarchs were invested in the decline of the empire with the full remains of civil, or military, and even of ecclesiastical power." Whether this be true or not, whatever form of government existed at that time would fit the demands of the symbol. Such a form continued only a little while as compared with the preceding forms or that represented by the eighth head. Here is agreement again.

11 **And the beast that was, and is not, is himself also an eighth, and is of the seven; and he goeth into perdition.**—The thought here seems to be that the eighth head represents another form of government which prolonged the Roman world. Being "of the seven" means a head of the same beast of which the seven had been heads. Under the first six heads the beast had been different forms of paganism. In that form the beast ended in A.D. 476. After the "little while" of the seventh form of government, the Roman Empire was restored, being dominated by the papacy —hence, a politico-ecclesiastical power. On this point Elliott (Vol. III, p. 131) quotes Augustin Steucus, a Catholic writer, as follows:

"The empire having been overthrown, unless God has raised up the Pontificate, Rome, resuscitated and restored by none, would have become uninhabitable, and been a most foul habitation thenceforward of cattle. But in the Pontificate it revived as with a *second birth,* its empire being in magnitude indeed not equal to the old one, but in kind not very dissimilar; because all nations, from the east to west, venerate the Pope not otherwise than they before obeyed the emperor."

Surely a true picture of the woman directing the beast. The "mystery of lawlessness" that led to the "man of sin" in the sixth century began in Paul's day; the religious power that was finally so perverted as to create that apostasy began its open influence on the Roman Empire in the time of Constantine in the fourth century.

The promise that the eighth head form would go to perdition

perdition. 12 And the ten horns that thou sawest are ten kings, who have received no kingdom as yet; but they receive authority as kings, with the

---

may mean either that it would be finally destroyed or that it would lose much of its power when nations supporting it turned from it. The latter has already occurred through the Reformation work; the former will happen when the Lord comes.

12 **And the ten horns that thou sawest are ten kings, who have received no kingdom as yet;**—As the text defines "horns" to mean kings, this explanation must be accepted. The word king, as shown in Dan. 7: 17, 23, sometimes is used in the sense of kingdom—the ruler standing for the whole institution. Doubtless that is the sense of the word here, and means that minor kingdoms would come under subjection to the Roman power. These kingdoms had not come into that subjection when John wrote, for the reason that the papacy and the eighth head form of Rome had neither come into existence.

As usual expositors disagree on what kingdoms are meant here. Several accept the list made out by Sir Isaac Newton as follows: The Vandals, the Visigoths, the Suevi, the Allans, the Burgundians, the Franks, the Britons, the Huns, the Lombards, and the kingdom of Ravenna. Others accept the idea that "ten" is here a symbolic number—definite for an indefinite—meaning completeness and signifies the extensive and full sway which Rome would exercise over subordinate nations. This is probably the meaning. If so, it is unnecessary to find just ten kingdoms. Those mentioned, however, might be in the list; others also might be; or there might be more.

but they receive authority as kings, with the beast, for one hour.—This means that in their operation as kingdoms they were subject to the papal Roman Empire, received their authority from it. "One hour," of course, cannot be taken literally in such connection. As a symbol it indicates a short time and is similar to the "little while" in verse 10. This is a common use of the Greek word for hour. See 2 Cor. 7: 8; Gal. 2: 5; 1 Thess. 2: 17. It is a short time in comparison with the whole existence of the Roman kingdom, and indicates further that the beast power over these nations must end.

beast, for one hour. 13 These have one mind, and they give their power and authority unto the beast. 14 These shall war against the Lamb, and the Lamb shall overcome them, for he is Lord of lords, and King of kings; and they *also shall overcome* that are with him, called and chosen and faithful.

---

13 **These have one mind, and they give their power and authority unto the beast.**—Having one mind shows that whatever differences may have existed among these ten-horn nations, however they may have warred against each other, they were all Roman Catholics, and recognized her spiritual authority as the supreme power of government. The papacy received their endorsement and support.

14 **These shall war against the Lamb, and the Lamb shall overcome them,**—This shows that when these nations combined their power with Rome they would be fighting against the Lamb—that is, Christ. This, of course, was done in opposing Christ's true teaching, and persecuting his followers. The "Lamb shall overcome them" means that he will ultimately win a victory over them. This, in a measure, was accomplished when these nations turned away from Rome through the Protestant Reformation; it will be fully completed when the Lord comes, at which time the "man of sin" will be destroyed. (2 Thess. 2: 8.)

for he is Lord of lords, and King of kings;—That Christ is now, in his present position of head of the church, both Lamb and Lord is admitted without question; the Scriptures are too plain to be denied. That he is supreme above all earthly lords is also conceded by all. His present kingship is just as plainly stated and should be admitted. The church figuratively described is the kingdom. If Christ is the head of the body (church), then it must be true to facts to say that he is now a reigning king.

and they also shall overcome that are with him, called and chosen and faithful.—Naturally those who overcome will be those with Christ—those willing to suffer and endure as he did. Their success in overcoming will be proof that they have been called by him. Their faithfulness in meeting bitter sorrows and intense persecutions is unquestioned evidence that they were chosen. Jesus said: "If a man love me, he will keep my word." (John 14: 23.)

3. THE MYSTERY OF THE HARLOT
17: 15-18

15 And he saith unto me, The waters which thou sawest, where the harlot sitteth, are peoples, and multitudes, and nations, and tongues. 16 And the ten horns which thou sawest, and the beast, these shall hate the harlot, and shall make her desolate and naked, and shall eat her flesh, and shall burn her

---

15 **And he saith unto me, The waters which thou sawest, where the harlot sitteth, are peoples, and multitudes, and nations, and tongues.**—In verse 3 the woman was represented as sitting on the scarlet-colored beast. That was explained in the preceding paragraph. Verse 1 says she was sitting upon the sea. This paragraph explains that. The waters refer to a multitude of people of various nations who supported the papacy.

For clearness we again mention the fact that the apostate church is represented by the beast in 13: 11-18, but by the drunken harlot in 17: 1-7. This distinction should be remembered. It is common in scriptural figures for the same thing to be represented by several different symbols. Christ is called both Lamb and Lion to describe different characteristics. Both are appropriate, but must not be confused. So of beast and harlot. The former is an emblem of the persecuting spirit of the apostasy; the latter, the seductive wiles by which people would be led into false religious practices, called a "golden cup full of abominations" and "unclean things of her fornication." (Verse 4.)

16 **And the ten horns which thou sawest, and the beast, these shall hate the harlot, and shall make her desolate and naked, and shall eat her flesh, and shall burn her utterly with fire.**—This language indicates that political Rome (the beast) and the nations subject to it would hate the harlot (apostate church). This refers to a later period, for verses 13 and 14 show that their combined powers were engaged in war against the Lamb; at the time of this verse they were against the papacy, determined to make it desolate. This has been at least partly fulfilled in the fact that nations once subject to papal rule have become Protestant or rejected church rule in matters of state. Being despoiled of such glory and power is appropriately described as being made desolate and naked.

Eating her flesh and burning her with fire imply complete de-

utterly with fire. 17 For God did put in their hearts to do his mind, and to come to one mind, and to give their kingdom unto the beast, until the words of God should be accomplished. 18 And the woman whom thou sawest is the great city, which [12]reigneth over the kings of the earth.

[12]Gr. *hath a kingdom.*

struction, but are not to be taken literally. They probably indicate that when nations refused to be governed by papal authority the end of such rule over them was as complete as if a body had been eaten or a city burned.

17 **For God did put in their hearts to do his mind, and to come to one mind, and to give their kingdom unto the beast, until the words of God should be accomplished.**—This verse shows that in some way God was the moving cause (permitted or allowed) of these nations unitedly supporting the beast until the divine purpose was carried out in certain particulars. Then they became enemies of the harlot in accomplishing other purposes God had in view.

18 **And the woman whom thou sawest is the great city, which reigneth over the kings of the earth.**—In verse 5 the great city is described as Babylon. But this must be understood figuratively as meaning the papal church, which, like its prototype, ancient Babylon, must finally be destroyed.

4. THE FALL OF BABYLON DESCRIBED
18: 1-24

1 After these things I saw another angel coming down out of heaven,

The general idea of this chapter is that of a rich populous city being reduced to desolation. The fall of Babylon is the symbol by which is prophetically described the destruction of the apostate church. The vivid imagery, in the main, carries its meaning upon the surface. Only brief expressions from the text in 18: 1 to 19: 10 are given; hence, comparatively few notes will be necessary in explanation. The ideas of a wicked city and a dissolute woman are intermingled and carried to the end of the chapter.

(1) The Fall Announced (1-3)

After these things.—After the vision described in the last chapter John saw an angel in a halo of light descend from heaven.

having great authority; and the earth was lightened with his glory. 2. And he cried with a mighty voice, saying, Fallen, fallen is Babylon the great, and is become a habitation of demons, and a [1]hold of every unclean spirit, and a [1]hold of every unclean and hateful bird. 3. For [2]by [3]the wine of the wrath of her fornication all the nations are fallen; and the kings of the earth committed fornication with her, and the merchants of the earth waxed rich by the power of her [4]wantonness.

4 And I heard another voice from heaven, saying, Come forth, my people,

[1]Or, *prison*
[2]Some ancient authorities read *of the wine . . . have drunk.*
[3]Some ancient authorities omit *the wine of.*
[4]Or, *luxury*

This is assurance that the announcement he made will certainly be fulfilled.

"Fallen, fallen is Babylon."—This expression is borrowed from the Old Testament prophets who speak of ancient Babylon's fall. (Isa. 21: 9; Jer. 51: 8.) The tense here is "prophetic past" to indicate the certainty that the event would take place. For another example consult Isa. 9: 2, 6. The ruins of cities become the habitation of unclean and wild animals. Compare the language about literal Babylon. (Isa. 13: 20-24.)

All the nations are fallen.—This shows the reason for her fall—she made the nations drunk with her wine, and this will lead to their fall ultimately. By her perversion of the truth leaders have been seduced into sinful practices, here described as spiritual adultery.

Merchants of the earth waxed rich.—This includes all those who traffic in papal doctrines for gain. Those made the victims of this traffic will also fall when spiritual Babylon falls.

(2) God's People Told to Flee (4, 5)

Come forth, my people.—This is not the language of John, but the command of an angel of heaven. It is the same command that was given Israel regarding literal Babylon. (Isa. 48: 20; Jer. 50: 8; 51: 6.) The angel's command means that people should abandon all false doctrines taught by the mother of harlots, or any of her daughters. This is nothing less than a command to abandon sectarian teaching and practice. If any who have obeyed the gospel have wandered into human churches, they should come out at once. "My people" here probably does not mean Christians, but that noble honest number that really want to obey God—hence, by

out of her, that ye have no fellowship with her sins, and that ye receive not of her plagues: 5 for her sins [5]have reached even unto heaven, and God hath remembered her iniquities. 6 Render unto her even as she rendered, and double *unto her* the double according to her works: in the cup which she mingled, mingle unto her double. 7 How much soever she glorified herself, and waxed [6]wanton, so much give her of torment and mourning: for she saith in her heart, I sit a queen, and am no widow, and shall in no wise see mourning. 8 Therefore in one day shall her plagues come, death, and mourning, and famine; and she shall be utterly burned with fire; for strong is [7]the Lord God who judgeth her. 9 And the kings of the earth, who committed fornication and lived [8]wantonly with her, shall weep and wail over

[5]Or, *clave together*
[6]Or, *luxurious*
[7]Some ancient authorities omit *the Lord.*
[8]Or, *luxuriously*

anticipation, called God's people. (Compare Acts 18: 10.) That means they could become God's people in fact by coming out. Two reasons are assigned for their coming out: to prevent partaking of her sins and to escape the punishment sure to come.

Reached even unto heaven.—Her wickedness is known to God and he will not forget properly to reward her.

(3) Vengeance Pronounced (6-8)

According to her works.—Render to her double is language addressed to whatever powers God will use for administering punishment to the apostate church. It will be what her works deserve.

Mingle unto her double.—As her dupes drank from the cup of her false doctrines, so she must drink the cup of punishment. Her glorying in wantonness will be matched with torment and mourning.

In one day.—The harlot's boast "I sit a queen" finds its fulfillment in the papal claim of infallible authority, but her arrogant claims will end in one day—that is, suddenly. Paul represents the coming of Jesus as a "thief in the night." The plagues mentioned in verse 8 are such as naturally would come upon a city being destroyed; typically, they represent the complete overthrow and end of the apostate church.

(4) Extent of Babylon's Ruin (9-19)

Shall weep and wail.—Those who have been deceived by false doctrines shall weep and wail when in fear they look upon her destruction. They will be amazed at the sudden punishment of a city

her, when they look upon the smoke of her burning, 10 standing afar off for the fear of her torment, saying, Woe, woe, the great city, Babylon, the strong city! for in one hour is thy judgment come. 11 And the merchants of the earth weep and mourn over her, for no man buyeth their [9]merchandise any more; 12 [9]merchandise of gold, and silver, and precious stone, and pearls, and fine linen, and purple, and silk, and scarlet; and all thyine wood, and every vessel of ivory, and every vessel made of most precious wood, and of brass, and iron, and marble; 13 and cinnamon, and [10]spice, and incense, and ointment, and frankincense, and wine, and oil, and fine flour, and wheat, and cattle, and sheep; and *merchandise* of horses and chariots and [11]slaves; and [12]souls of men. 14 And the fruits which thy soul lusted after are gone from thee, and all things that were dainty and sumptuous are perished from thee, and *men* shall find them no more at all. 15 The merchants of these things, who were made rich by her, shall stand afar off for the fear of her torment, weeping and mourning; 16 saying, Woe, woe, the great city, she that was arrayed in fine linen and purple and scarlet, and [13]decked with gold and precious stone and pearl! 17 for in one hour so great riches is made desolate. And every shipmaster, and every one that saileth any whither, and mariners, and as many as [14]gain their living by sea, stood afar off, 18 and cried out as they looked upon the smoke of her burning, saying, What *city* is like the great city? 19 And they cast dust on their heads, and cried, weeping and mourning, saying, Woe, woe, the great city, wherein all that had their ships in the sea were made rich by reason of her costliness! for in one hour is she made desolate. 20 Rejoice over her, thou heaven, and ye saints, and ye apostles, and ye prophets; for God hath judged your judgment on her.

[9]Gr. *cargo.*
[10]Gr. *amomum.*
[11]Gr. *bodies.* Gen. 36. 6 (Sept.).
[12]Or, *lives*
[13]Gr. *gilded.*
[14]Gr. *work the sea.*

so great and proud. Those who have made gain trafficking in human practices in religion will mourn because their source of income has been cut off. There will no longer be anyone to be deceived. The articles of merchandise mentioned symbolize every kind of religious device used to deceive those ignorant of God's word. The things desired by the religious merchants are gone forever. Naturally such characters will cry, "Woe, woe," when spiritual Babylon falls. The smoke and blaze seen in a burning city are a weak but fitting emblem to indicate what will happen when apostate religion is forced to end its wicked work.

(5) An Outburst of Praise (20)

Rejoice over her.—This language is in direct contrast with the preceding description of the effect on those who made gain out of similar practices. The number of the righteous who will rejoice at the end of spiritual Babylon will include apostles and prophets and all other Christians. The meaning is that God's judgment in the

21 And [15]a strong angel took up a stone as it were a great millstone and cast it into the sea, saying, Thus with a mighty fall shall Babylon, the great city, be cast down, and shall be found no more at all. 22 And the voice of harpers and minstrels and flute-players and trumpeters shall be heard no more at all in thee; and no craftsman, [1]of whatsoever craft, shall be found any more at all in thee; and the voice of a mill shall be heard no more at all in thee; 23 and the light of a lamp shall shine no more at all in thee; and the voice of the bridegroom and of the bride shall be heard no more at all in thee: for thy merchants were the princes of the earth; for with thy sorcery were all the nations deceived. 24 And in her was found the blood of prophets and of saints, and of all that have been slain upon the earth.

[15]Gr. *one.*
[1]Some ancient authorities omit *of whatsoever craft.*

case will be what the suffering of saints will demand as a just reward.

(6) Sudden and Complete End Symbolized (21-24)

Cast it into the sea.—John next sees an angel cast a large stone into the sea. A similar act was performed to indicate the fall of ancient Babylon. (Jer. 51: 63, 64.) The sinking of the stone represents the sudden and complete fall of the apostate church; not by a slow decline, but because of a violent force against it.

Shall be heard no more.—Music which is the natural sign of joy will cease; no one in the city will have anything to produce gladness. All kinds of crafts will have no chance to operate, and machinery will cease to be heard. Lights will go out and social events will no longer occur.

All the nations deceived.—The reason for such desolation and ruin will be that false religion has received the nation with sorceries—all kinds of tricks, impositions, and false claims to divine power. Another reason is that in bloody persecutions this spiritual Babylon has slain saints and prophets of God. The word "all" here is used in an accommodated sense, meaning that a multitude had been slain in perpetuating the papal system.

5. THANKSGIVING BECAUSE OF BABYLON'S FALL 19: 1-10

In the preceding chapter three angels picture in vivid colors the fall of spiritual Babylon, and tell what the effects will be upon those deceived by her false religion; in this paragraph we have recorded the thanksgiving that will be expressed by the heavenly hosts.

1 After these things I heard as it were a great voice of a great multitude in heaven, saying,

Hallelujah; Salvation, and glory, and power, belong to our God: 2 for true and righteous are his judgments; for he hath judged the great harlot, her that corrupted the earth with her fornication, and he hath avenged that blood of his [2]servants at her hand.

3 And a second time they [3]say, Hallelujah. And her smoke goeth up [4]for
ever and ever. 4 And the four and twenty elders and the four living creatures fell down and worshipped God that sitteth on the throne, saying,
Amen; Hallelujah. 5 And a voice came forth from the throne, saying,

Give praise to our God, all ye his [2]servants, ye that fear him, the small and the great.

[2]Gr. *bondservants.*
[3]Gr. *have said.*
[4]Gr. *unto the ages of the ages.*

(1) THE SONG OF TRIUMPH (1-6)

After these things.—After the symbolic act and words of the third angel (18: 21-24), John heard another loud voice, as of a great multitude, coming from heaven. The invitation was extended to saints, apostles, and prophets (18: 20) to rejoice over the harlot's desolation. These verses contain the response to that invitation.

Hallelujah.—This word means "praise ye Jehovah," and the song ascribes salvation, glory, and power to God. This is right because only by his permission can any blessing be received.

True and righteous.—The final punishment of the great harlot will come because she corrupted the earth with her false doctrines and because she caused the blood of saints to be shed. Her punishment will avenge that blood. A righteous God will allow only righteous punishment. A second time John heard the redeemed saints say, "Hallelujah."

For ever and ever.—Smoke continuing to go up without end means that this refers to the final punishment after the judgment.

Fell down and worshipped God.—On the twenty-four elders and four living creatures see notes on 4: 4-8. In addition to apostles, prophets, and saints, the spirit beings around the throne of God rejoice over the final victory of the church. They give credit to God for the overthrow of Babylon. Another voice that appeared to come from the throne invited all servants of God to give him praise.

6 And I heard as it were the voice of a great multitude, and as the voice of many waters, and as the voice of mighty thunders, saying,
Hallelujah: for the Lord our God, the Almighty, reigneth. 7 Let us rejoice and be exceeding glad, and let us give the glory unto him: for the marriage of the Lamb is come, and his wife hath made herself ready.
8 And it was given unto her that she should array herself in fine linen,

---

God, the Almighty, reigneth.—John next heard a voice as if coming from a multitude that sounded like many waters and mighty thunders; a grand chorus of all the spiritual hosts of heaven saying that God reigneth. This harmonizes perfectly with Paul's statement that at Christ's coming and judgment the kingdom will be delivered back to the Father. (1 Cor. 15: 23, 24.) Then Christ will also become subject to the Father, and God will become all in all (verse 28), and his endless reign will begin.

(2) The Marriage of the Lamb (7-10)

Let us rejoice.—The reason given here for rejoicing is that the "marriage of the Lamb is come, and his wife hath made herself ready." The meaning is that the coming of the Lord to receive the prepared church is similar to a bridegroom coming for his bride. Marriage, as a symbol or illustration, is used four times in the New Testament, but each time to teach a different lesson—that is, some phase of marriage is used to illustrate a special feature of the relationship of saved people to Christ. (1) Rom. 7: 4 and Eph. 5: 22-32 show that the relationship of individuals, and the church as a whole, to Christ now is comparable to the natural relationship of marriage; therefore the saved are correctly represented as being spiritually "married" to Christ. (2) In Matt. 22: 1-14 the idea of a marriage feast is presented, and saved people are represented as guests. Nothing in the parable represents the wife, for the reason that the parable is constructed to teach the necessity of proper character. This is better done by the idea of guests suitably dressed. (3) In Matt. 25: 1-13 the lesson is sufficient preparation for the Lord's coming in order to be ready. This is best presented by representing the saved as wise and foolish virgins. But in the parable these virgins are not the bride; in the application they represent the two elements of the church. Again, the bride is left out of the parable, yet the church is the bride or wife. (4) In our text the lesson is the joy of being prepared for that eternal home

bright *and* pure: for the fine linen is the righteous acts of the saints.
9 And he saith unto me, Write, Blessed are they that are bidden to the marriage supper of the Lamb. And he saith unto me, These are true words of
God. 10 And I fell down before his feet to [5]worship him. And he saith
unto me, See thou do it not: I am a fellow-servant with thee and with thy
brethren that hold the testimony of Jesus: [5]worship God: for the testimony
of Jesus is the spirit of prophecy.

[5]See marginal note on ch. 3. 9.

Jesus has prepared for his own. This is like the joy of a bride going to the home prepared for her. These are the lessons based upon marriage as a symbol, and must not be confused, for all of them are true. When this passage is used as proof that the church is not "married" to Christ now, the figures are jumbled and Rom. 7: 4 and Eph. 5: 22-32 are ignored.

In 2 Cor. 11: 2 Paul says, "For I espoused you to one husband." This is no contradiction of what has been said; for, if obedience to the gospel is represented here as an *espousal,* it would only be another comparison with the natural marriage which would, in some way, be similar to the spiritual. It would not set aside any of the four mentioned, but just add a fifth, or another text to those given. The Revised text of Rom. 7:4 gives "joined to another" instead of "married to another." But the illustration is marriage, and verses 2 and 3 are talking about being freed from, and joined to, a husband. Joined to Christ then means as a spiritual husband. It must be allowed that these verses so present the case or Paul has used language that does not mean what it says.

Fine linen, bright and pure.—As a bride adorns herself with fine linen, so Christians adorn themselves with "righteous acts."

Blessed are they.—That is, blessed are those bidden to the "marriage supper of the Lamb." Those bidden are those who have washed their robes in Christ's blood (7: 14), and are faithful unto death (2: 10). Here again the saved are presented as guests at a feast; the idea of bride or wife is not in this verse, though mentioned in verse 7. "Marriage supper" clearly indicates the joys of heaven. Wedding feasts soon end; the joys of heaven are eternal. The angel next asserts that what he said were the true words of God; a solemn confirmation of fact.

Fell down before his feet.—This was the customary way in showing great respect for a superior. John was overcome by the majesty of the scene and the deep significance of the words he heard, and gave way to this Eastern custom. The speaker, who doubtless was an angel, promptly forbade it on the ground that he was a fellow servant with John. As the papal church, symbolized by the harlot, worships saints, this incident may have occurred in the vision to teach that it is sinful to worship any creature. At least that is the lesson taught by it.

The spirit of prophecy.—The angel not only declared himself the fellow servant with John, but also "with thy brethren." In 22: 9, a parallel passage, he says "with thy brethren the prophets." The meaning is that this angel held a similar position with John and other prophets in making known the will of God; that no one should worship a fellow servant. The angel then adds "worship God." The testimony to Jesus is the spirit of prophecy. That testimony is given by those endowed by the spirit, whether angels from heaven, prophets of old, or the apostles. They are servants; God is the object of worship.

6. A VISION OF THE VICTORIOUS ARMY
19: 11-16

11 And I saw the heaven opened; and behold, a white horse, and he that sat thereon [6]called Faithful and True; and in righteousness he doth judge

[6]Some ancient authorities omit *called*.

---

11 **And I saw the heaven opened; and behold, a white horse, and he that sat thereon called Faithful and True;**—In 18: 1 to 19: 10 we have a most vivid picture of the final overthrow of evil under the symbol of Babylon. In this paragraph John is allowed to see a vision describing the Lord's victorious army in this last struggle. This is not a new and later event, but a pictorial representation of the Lord's part in the one just described. In this book we are frequently brought back to events already related for the purpose of giving additional information.

The white horse, as we have already seen, is a symbol of successful or victorious warfare. See notes on 6: 2. Faithful and true are characteristics of Christ (1: 5; 3: 14), and, in connection with other expressions in this paragraph, make it certain that the rider on the horse represents him. But for reasons given in the

and make war. 12 And his eyes *are* a flame of fire, and upon his head *are* many diadems; and he hath a name written which no one knoweth but he himself. 13 And he *is* arrayed in a garment [7]sprinkled with blood: and his

[7]Some ancient authorities read *dipped in*.

notes on 6: 2 the rider there is not Christ. These texts then are not parallel.

and in righteousness he doth judge and make war.—The prophets declared that "righteousness shall be the girdle of his waist, and faithfulness the girdle of his loins." (Isa. 11: 5.) His decisions will all be just and his warfare in defense of the truth always right.

12 **And his eyes are a flame of fire, and upon his head are many diadems;**—His eyes were sharp, piercing, and bright, indicating his power to penetrate and see every object. He had on his head, not the "crown"—victor's wreath—but the "diadem"—symbol of his regal authority. "Many" diadems indicate the universal nature of his rule, and the complete victory he was to gain over all in the last conflict. This idea is expressed more fully in verse 16.

and he hath a name written which no one knoweth but he himself.—John saw the name, for it was written, but where it was written is not stated. No one knew it means that no one could understand what it signifies. It probably is the same as the "new name" (2: 17), which will be given those who overcome, and therefore will not be known till the final state is reached. This implies that it expresses some heavenly relationship which men in the flesh cannot understand.

13 **And he is arrayed in a garment sprinkled with blood:**—The King James Version has the word "dipped" in place of "sprinkle." This is a matter of textual criticism, and the Revisers have decided in favor of "sprinkle" as the correct reading. Some expositors explain this as referring to the blood shed in the last war, some of which would be sprinkled on the garment of the victorious rider of the white horse. This would indicate that the last conflict would be a destructive victory over the Lord's enemies. Others think the reference is to the shed blood of Christ through which he will gain the final overthrow of wickedness. If this is the reference, the word "sprinkle" is still appropriate. Peter speaks of

name is called The Word of God. 14 And the armies which are in heaven followed him upon white horses, clothed in fine linen, white *and* pure. 15

the "sprinkling of the blood of Jesus Christ." (1 Pet. 1: 2.) As the first covenant was dedicated by the sprinkling of blood (Heb. 9: 18-20), so the new covenant by the blood of Christ, figuratively called the "blood of sprinkling" (Heb. 12: 24) because that was the literal way the blood of animals was applied.

and his name is called the Word of God.—Some commentators think this cannot be the same as the name mentioned in verse 12 or the new name of 2: 17, for the reason that this one had already been given and could not therefore be "new." To this others reply that it is not known by man in the sense that no one can fully comprehend its meaning—that is, no one can understand the full import of God's Son being called the "Word." Of course this is true in fact, and may be the correct view of the expression, though hardly probable. See verse 12.

14 **And the armies which are in heaven followed him upon white horses, clothed in fine linen, white and pure.**—We should remember that the text describes what John saw in the vision; what it represents is another matter. There are two important questions regarding this heavenly army: (1) Who are included in it? (2) What part will they take in the conflict? Without doubt the passage refers to the coming of Christ and the last struggle between sin and righteousness. Some think this army will be composed of angels only and base their conclusion on Matt. 16: 27; 25: 31; 2 Thess. 1: 7. Others think it includes the martyrs and means the same as those mentioned in 6: 9-11; 14: 1-5; 20: 4. Still others think this army will include the redeemed saints as well as those martyred. It should be observed that this army clothed in white linen has no implements of war, which indicates that they are present as witnesses, not as actual fighters. There will be no fighting in the ordinary sense of that word, for all the wicked people in the world are no match for divine power. Under the withering touch of divine power 185,000 in the Assyrian army perished in one night without the touch of human hands. (2 Kings 19: 35.) So the almighty power of Jesus, when he comes, will destroy Satan's army—a victory sudden and complete. The angelic hosts of heaven will be present to rejoice.

And out of his mouth proceedeth a sharp sword, that with it he should smite the nations: and he shall rule them with a rod of iron: and he treadeth the [8]winepress of the fierceness of the wrath of God, the Almighty. 16 And he hath on his garment and on his thigh a name written, KING OF KINGS, AND LORD OF LORDS.

[8]Gr. *winepress of the wine of the fierceness.*

15 **And out of his mouth proceedeth a sharp sword, that with it he should smite the nations:**—Jesus said his kingdom was not to be defended with a carnal sword. (John 18: 36.) Paul declares that Christians fight with the "sword of the Spirit, which is the word of God." (Eph. 6: 17.) The thing that proceeds from the mouth means words. God's words are even sharper than a literal sword. (Heb. 4: 12.) From all this it is evident that smiting with the sword in this emblem represents the victory Christ will gain by his word. As the worlds were created by the word of God, so by the word of Christ wickedness will be banished. This agrees perfectly with Paul's statement that when Jesus comes he will slay the lawless one ("man of sin") with "the breath of his mouth." (2 Thess. 2: 8.) Not carnal bloodshed; but Christ will speak the word and divine power will do the rest. This text shows that wicked nations will be here when Jesus comes else there would be none for the Lord to smite.

and he shall rule them with a rod of iron: and he treadeth the winepress of the fierceness of the wrath of God, the Almighty.—Ruling with a rod of iron means in strict justice, whether in imparting favors or in inflicting punishment. This thought is expressed a number of times. (Psalm 2: 7-9; Rev. 2: 27; 12: 5.) The setting of the expression in this text shows that it means a just reward to the wicked. The preceding expression speaks of "smiting the nations," and the following one says that he will tread the winepress of God's wrath. Verses 17-21 show that the "winepress" of God's wrath refers to the final punishment of the wicked, a scene pictured in Jude 14, 15. The meaning is that as the treader presses out the wine from the grapes, so Jesus will inflict the fierceness of God's wrath against the wicked, but with absolute justice.

16 **And he hath on his garment and on his thigh a name written, KING OF KINGS, AND LORD OF LORDS.**—

Seeing this title written upon the garment further identifies the rider of the white horse as Christ. Just as the kingdom (mountain of the Lord's house) is above or greater than all other kingdoms (Isa. 2: 2), so Christ's position as King is superior to all other kings. Legally and rightly that has been his position since he took his seat (throne) at God's right hand. (Eph. 1: 19-23; Acts 2: 36.) This symbol represents him as still having that authority when he comes to execute God's wrath upon the wicked.

7. RESULTS OF THE CONFLICT DESCRIBED 19: 17-21

17 And I saw [9]an angel standing in the sun; and he cried with a loud voice, saying to all the birds that fly in mid heaven, Come *and* be gathered together unto the great supper of God; 18 that ye may eat the flesh of kings, and the flesh of [10]captains, and the flesh of mighty men, and the flesh of horses and of them that sit thereon, and the flesh of all men, both free and bond, and small and great.

19 And I saw the beast, and the kings of the earth, and their armies, gathered together to make war against him that sat upon the horse, and

[9]Gr. *one.*
[10]Or, *military tribunes* Gr. *chiliarchs.*

17 **And I saw an angel standing in the sun; and he cried with a loud voice, saying to all the birds that fly in mid heaven,**—The sun is the brightest shining orb in the world, and an angel so brilliant as to be distinguished when standing in the sun is beyond human description. This angel announced the result of the final conflict in a most impressive symbol. The fowls here mean birds of prey—those that eat flesh, and the image is that of such birds hovering over a battlefield ready to consume the bodies of the slain.

Come and be gathered together unto the great supper of God;—In verse 9 the saved are invited to the "marriage supper of the Lamb," which evidently means the rewards to be given finally to the faithful; here the "supper of God" means that the punishment of the wicked will be like giving to birds of prey bodies slain in battle. The picture of bodies thus consumed is the horrible emblem of the final destiny of the lost.

18 **that ye may eat the flesh of kings, and the flesh of captains, and the flesh of mighty men, and the flesh of horses and of them that sit thereon, and the flesh of all men, both free**

against his army. 20 And the beast was taken, and with him the false prophet that wrought the signs in his sight, wherewith he deceived them that
had received the mark of the beast and them that [1]worshipped his image:
they two were cast alive into the lake of fire that burneth with brimstone: 21

[1]See marginal note on ch. 3. 9.

and bond, and small and great.—John sees in the symbol the birds assembled to the battlefield to consume leaders, common men, and even animals. This means that the wicked of all classes will suffer the final banishment from God's presence. There will be no chance for rulers to escape any more than the common man; young and old will meet the same fate.

19 **And I saw the beast, and the kings of the earth, and their armies, gathered together to make war against him that sat upon the horse, and against his army.**—In 16: 13-16 John sees three unclean spirits coming from the dragon, the beast, and the false prophet to gather the kings of the whole world together for the last struggle—"the war of the great day of God." Here he sees that battle and its results. The hosts on both sides are assembled. This emblematic language means that evil on earth will be ended by the Lord at his coming, not that a real flesh and blood battle will be fought. This will include all kinds of evil represented by the beast and kings of the earth.

20 **And the beast was taken, and with him the false prophet that wrought the signs in his sight, wherewith he deceived them that had received the mark of the beast and them that worshipped his image:**—On the identity of the beast and false prophet, see notes on 16: 13. The fact that this language shows the false prophet wrought pretended miracles in the sight of the beast and deceived them who had received the "mark of the beast" indicates that the false prophet is the same as papal Rome. If so, then the "beast" would be political Rome in its so-called Christianized form while dominated by the papacy. This shows that in the last conflict corrupt political powers and false religions will both be used by Satan in his final effort to destroy Christianity. In the symbol John sees them both taken—defeated. The false prophet is a general expression broad enough to include all false teachers, and by implication all false systems of religion.

they two were cast alive into the lake of fire that burneth

and the rest were killed with the sword of him that sat upon the horse, *even the sword* which came forth out of his mouth: and all the birds were filled with their flesh.

---

with brimstone:—This means the end of these two kinds of wicked powers and the final punishment of those who supported them. The lake of fire refers to the last and complete torment of those banished from God forever. (Mark 9: 47, 48; Rev. 14: 10, 11; 20: 14, 15.) The last reference says the lake of fire is the second death which will take place when death and Hades are cast into that lake. This is final in showing that this paragraph refers to the separation of the good and bad at the judgment.

21 **and the rest were killed with the sword of him that sat upon the horse, even the sword which came forth out of his mouth: and all the birds were filled with their flesh.**—This is what John saw in the vision. Seeing the armies that followed the beast and false prophet killed with a sword and the birds feeding upon their flesh means that those who practice sin in corrupt politics or religion will be condemned to everlasting punishment. Thus again in this symbol we have seen the final conflict between sin and righteousness end in the vindication of Christ and his teaching. A decision from which there is no new hearing.

SECTION FIVE

THE "MILLENNIUM" AND THE JUDGMENT 20: 1-15

PRELIMINARY CONSIDERATIONS

Verses 1-10 have been made the battle ground for more conflicting theories, perhaps, than any other passage of scripture. This fact suggests caution and modesty in approaching it as commentator. Where so many have fallen must be dangerous ground. A few introductory considerations may aid in reaching satisfactory conclusions.

1. The word "millennium" is not in the Bible, but by common use has been given a permanent place in religious literature. It is a Latin word, meaning "a thousand years," and is generally substituted for that expression which is used six times in this passage. This is the only place in the Bible where this period is mentioned. If a distinct age in which Christ will reign personally on earth, it is remarkable that neither he nor any of the apostles in their plain teaching said anything about it. Why should so important a matter be mentioned only in a book of symbols and in a highly figurative passage?

2. The popular notion that the millennium is a period of absolute and universal peace, righteousness, and felicity is pure assertion; the word has no such meaning. The assumption is based upon the statement that Satan is to be "bound" during that period, which is supposed to mean literal binding and a complete destruction of his influence. Neither of these conclusions is true. If any wicked people are left on earth in the millennial age, Satan's personal binding would be of no special benefit; for his servants here could still torment and deceive the righteous. The wicked are his "ministers" now (2 Cor. 11: 15), and will be while here. At Christ's coming all the wicked are to be destroyed (19: 19-21) and the righteous living and dead are to receive immortal bodies (1 Cor. 15: 51, 52; 1 Thess. 4: 16, 17). If he comes to establish the millennium, then there can be no literal kingdom, for there will be none in the flesh either to rule or be ruled. Hence, the literal throne of David idea is false; the passage must be explained figuratively.

3. Many, including some pioneer preachers of the church of Christ, seemed to think the millennium would be introduced and perpetuated by the gospel prevailing over evil; that it would continue to win its way to men's hearts till all evil would be rooted out by the inherent power of the truth. The rapidity with which the restoration work succeeded probably led to this idea; but it evidently was a delusion. The notion overlooked the setting of this millennial passage, as well as man's ability to reject any and all kinds of moral influences. The history of mankind for nearly sixty centuries is unmistakably against such a view.

4. Whatever the millennium may be, it precedes the final judgment. This is conceded by all. If the judgment occurs at Christ's coming (a fact taught by the Scriptures), the doctrine that he comes to inaugurate the millennium is of necessity false. Peter makes the "coming of the day of God" the time when the heavens will be dissolved by fire and the elements melt with fervent heat. (2 Pet. 3: 12.) Paul says Christ will be revealed from heaven "in flaming fire" to render vengeance upon the disobedient and be "glorified in his saints." (2 Thess. 1: 8, 9.) The rewarding of both bad and good will be at the judgment. (2 Cor. 5: 10.) Jesus plainly teaches that both classes will be raised at the same time. (John 5: 28, 29.) These passages show clearly that the coming of Christ, the resurrection of both righteous and wicked, and the judgment will all occur after the millennium, which renders a thousand years reign of Christ on earth an impossibility.

Jesus divides "all that are in their tombs" into two classes: those raised to life—eternal salvation—and those raised to judgment—condemnation. The following conclusions are evident: If Jesus comes *before the millennium,* none can be raised *bodily* after it; for all are to be raised to be rewarded when he comes. Hence, the theory that only the wicked dead will then be raised is not true. If he comes *after* the millennium, none can be raised *bodily* before it, and the view that only the righteous dead will then be raised is also untrue. In either case the premillennial view of this passage is false. This fact will be more fully developed as we examine the language of the text.

5. To know the true setting of this passage is necessary to its correct understanding. The symbols in 20: 1-9 do not reveal

events that are to follow chronologically after those of 19: 19-21. These verses described the casting of the beast and false prophet into the "lake of fire"; 20: 10 tells of Satan being cast into the same place—that is, it completes the story partly told in 19: 19-21 and must refer to the same time. The millennial passage is a recapitulation of things described in preceding chapters with different symbols. Reviewing the same periods with changed scenes is common to this book. The seven seals that closed with the end of the world stop with 11: 18. The vision of the pure woman (true church) in her struggles against the dragon, beast, and false prophet, under the emblems of pouring out bowls of wrath, covers practically the same time, and the same final end is shown in 16: 17-21. Next the destruction of the false church, represented as a drunken harlot and a great city, is symbolically pictured in chapters 17 and 18, followed with a song of triumph by the redeemed. (19: 1-10.) In 19: 11-18 is told the means by which this overthrow of evil is to be accomplished. Finally 19: 19-21 and 20: 10 describe this overthrow and bring us for the third time to the end of the world, for the "lake of fire" in 20: 14 is defined as the "second death."

The evident purpose of 20: 1-10 is to give a brief review of Satan's overthrow from the time his power was restrained until banished in the lake of fire forever. This recapitulation is appropriate here because it was Satan who did and will furnish the beast and false prophets with the power by which they operate against the truth. Christ's personal coming ends the career of these three enemies; this event is *after*, not *before*, the "millennium."

1. THE BINDING OF SATAN
20: 1-3

1 And I saw an angel coming down out of heaven, having the key of the

---

1 **And I saw an angel coming down out of heaven,**—Perhaps it is well to observe again that we are here dealing with a symbolic vision that appeared to John. As noted several times before, the vision and the thing it represents must be kept distinct. As in other visions an angel is the medium of revealing the scenes, which guarantees that true facts are represented.

abyss and a great chain [2]in his hand. 2 And he laid hold on the dragon, the old serpent, which is the Devil and Satan, and bound him for a thousand

[2]Gr. *upon.*

having the key of the abyss and a great chain in his hand.—"Key" represents the angel's authority to open and close doors, but here must mean his right to force Satan to remain in his own place and be restrained from the unlimited use of his power which he had been exercising during the long period of papal usurpation. Being bound with a "great chain" signifies this restraint. No reasonable person will contend that the words "key," "abyss," and "chain" are to be understood literally. All that is necessarily implied is that the followers of Christ would have such protection against Satan's power that they would be free to obey Christ, if they desired. Anything more than this would ignore man's responsibility for his conduct, and make God a respecter of persons. No doctrine that conflicts with these two principles can be true as long as man dwells in the flesh.

2 **And he laid hold on the dragon, the old serpent, which is the Devil and Satan, and bound him for a thousand years,**—In the vision John saw the binding actually take place, but the thing it represents was far in the future when he wrote. See notes on 4:1, 2. He figuratively describes the dragon as the "old serpent" which is doubtless an allusion to the serpent in Eden. Then he drops the figure and plainly states that the dragon represents Satan. Beginning with deceiving Eve in the garden, it has been his business to deceive mankind ever since. His effort then was and ever afterward has been to discredit or pervert God's word—make people believe that God does not mean what he says, or means what he does not say.

Satan being a spirit, the only "chain" that can effectively bind him—restrain or defeat him—is God's word. In what was the world's greatest battle between right and wrong, Jesus defeated the devil at every turn with "it is written." (Matt. 4.) When God's word has free course in directing human life, the individual can safely protect himself against any device of Satan. When mankind has the right to use that protection at will, Satan is "bound" in the only way that is consistent with man's nature. Satan's binding

years, 3 and cast him into the abyss, and shut *it,* and sealed *it* over him, that

---

does not mean the destruction of all evil; though under restraint, Satan still operates through his angels who pose as ministers of righteousness. (2 Cor. 11: 13-15.)

The duration of this binding is stated as a thousand years. Is this a symbolic or literal number? As usual expositors are disagreed. To apply the day-year theory would give the enormous amount of 365,000 years. This appears wholly out of proportion with other numbers in this book that seem to fit the theory. If to be taken literally, the exact beginning and ending of the period could not be fixed definitely. With these difficulties to meet, it seems better to consider it a symbolic number. Other numbers such as 3, 7, 10, and 12 appear to carry a spiritual significance. In Ezek. 39 we have a description of the overthrow of Gog, and verse 9 says the Israelites should make fires of their weapons for "seven years." Certainly this means the complete destruction of their implements of war, not that it would take seven literal years to burn them. Through Moses God threatened Israel with seven times more, or seven times, punishment if they persistently rebelled against him. (Lev. 26: 18, 21, 24, 28.) Evidently this does not mean exactly seven times, for their sins required punishment far more times than seven. It means that they would be fully punished as their sins deserved. So the definite number—1,000 years —is probably used for a long but indefinite period. "Showing lovingkindness unto thousands" (Ex. 20: 6) means showing it to all of the class mentioned; "thousands of thousands" (5: 11) means a countless number. So in this text the word "thousand" most likely means an indefinite length of time, but long enough for the symbols to find complete fulfillment.

3 **and cast him into the abyss, and shut it, and sealed it over him,**—In vision John saw the woman driven into the wilderness for 1,260 day-years (12: 1-6), yet that did not occur till several centuries later, when the apostate church was fully developed. Shutting and sealing the abyss indicates the certainty of the influence of Satan's power being restrained. The true church apparently disappeared as one does who goes into a wilderness; but, though unseen as an organized body, it still existed in the hearts

he should deceive the nations no more, until the thousand years should be finished: after this he must be loosed for a little time.

and lives of individual faithful saints. So Satan during the thousand years has his power restrained, yet he still has through his unseen agents and workers means for deceiving those who are willing. During the 1,260-year period he exercised a practically unlimited power through the papacy and the kingdom it controlled. The millennium—the period of his being bound—must of necessity begin *after* that power was broken; and, for the same reason, it must have begun *when* that power was broken.

that he should deceive the nations no more, until the thousand years should be finished:—As the purpose of the binding was to prevent Satan's deceiving the nations, then the binding would consist in changing the situation which made the deception easily effective. During the papal supremacy the Bible, man's only real protection against the devil's power, was practically taken away from the people. With the Bible removed, it was no trouble for him to deceive the nations by superstition, false miracles, and pretended infallibility. When the Protestant Reformation broke the Roman religious yoke of bondage by giving the Bible back to the people with liberty to read and obey it without human dictation, Satan was bound in the fair meaning of the text. Through this right has come the privilege of restoring and maintaining apostolic congregations, which is a most fortunate and happy time for those who really desire to be pleasing to God. For emphasis the main thought is repeated. The millennial period is not a time of absolute and universal righteousness upon earth but a time of such restraint of Satan's power that all may have the privilege to serve God as the Scriptures teach, if they so desire. It is a period in direct comparison with the previous one of supreme papal authority. With this view we must conclude that we are now in the millennium. When it will end we do not know. This position, at least, has the plausible advantage of harmonizing with plain facts of religious history and leaves man free and responsible for his own conduct—a thing that must be true while men are in the flesh.

That this view may be clearly understood, a brief review of the main changes in church history is here repeated. It required about 300 years for the church to pass through the pagan Roman persecutions and receive recognition from the Emperor Constantine. Something over 200 years more were necessary to develop the papacy—Paul's "man of sin." (2 Thess. 2: 3.) This came through the slow process of corrupting divine truth with the "precepts of men"; or, viewing it from another standpoint, exalting men to unscriptural positions until the bishop of Rome was declared the Universal Bishop of the church. This was followed by the 1,260 years of papal rule, after which began the millennium. Any true interpretation must harmonize with these well-known historical facts.

after this he must be loosed for a little time.—That is, after the millennium ends, Satan must be loosed, not permanently, but for a "little time." There is no way to determine how long the "little time" may be, but it is the period that divides the millennium from the final judgment. It may be short in comparison with the 1,000 years, or with the whole history of the church up to that time.

2. THE MILLENNIUM DESCRIBED
20: 4-6

4 And I saw thrones, and they sat upon them, and judgment was given

---

4 **And I saw thrones, and they sat upon them, and judgment was given unto them:**—In the vision John saw thrones and persons sitting upon them, and describes in the next statement who they were. The word "judgment" is evidently used in the sense of rule which is the idea implied in the word "thrones." It means that those whom John saw were reigning in some sense. The particular sense will be discovered in the remainder of the paragraph. It is clear from the language that verses 7-10 logically followed verse 3 to complete the story begun with 19: 19. The narrative is interrupted at verse 3 and this paragraph is interposed to describe things that would transpire during the thousand years which had just been mentioned. It is an explanation of how Satan's binding, the first big event in his overthrow, would affect the church during the millennial period.

Both judge and rule carry the idea of authority to command, approve, or condone. One can reign in a secondary sense when he is

unto them: and *I saw* the souls of them that had been beheaded for the testimony of Jesus, and for the word of God, and such as [1]worshipped not the beast, neither his image, and received not the mark upon their

authorized to state or enforce the laws of the actual ruler. In this sense the apostles rule under Christ as our king. He conferred upon them the right to express the conditions of pardon which he gave them—thus to remit and retain sin. (John 20: 21-23.) In harmony with this is the reply of Jesus to Peter's question in Matt. 19: 27, 28. He said: "Ye who have followed me, in the regeneration when the Son of man shall sit on the throne of his glory, ye also shall sit upon twelve thrones, judging the twelve tribes of Israel." "The regeneration" means the Christian dispensation—that is, the time when men can be regenerated or born again. The apostles had followed Jesus; hence, they were given the right to rule by his authority. There can be no mistake about this, for in Luke 22: 28-30, a parallel text, Jesus said he appointed them a kingdom "that ye may eat and drink at my table in my kingdom." This refers to the Lord's Supper and shows that the apostles were in the kingdom while they lived on earth. If so, then they sat upon the thrones and judged while on earth. But Jesus said they would do this while he was sitting upon the throne of his glory. This incidentally shows that Jesus began his reign on Pentecost, as taught in Heb. 10: 12, 1 Cor. 15: 25, and disproves his supposed millennial reign on earth.

There is also a figurative sense in which Christians may rule: either by influencing others to correct living, or to condemn by implication the disobedient through faithfulness to God. Such is the teaching of Matt. 5: 16; Heb. 11: 7. Nothing is more certain than that the lives of men, both good and bad, continue to rule in the hearts and lives of others long after death. See 2: 26, 27; 14: 13; Heb. 11: 7. It is a solemn thought to know that the final salvation or damnation of men can depend upon how their lives, as examples, have ruled over others.

and I saw the souls of them that had been beheaded for the testimony of Jesus, and for the word of God, and such as worshipped not the beast, neither his image, and received not the mark upon their forehead and upon their hand;—This tells who were sitting upon the thrones. The definite statement is that

John saw "souls"; no mention whatever of "bodies." Selecting the term "souls" could not have been accidental, and certainly indicates that the resurrection in this passage is not that of bodies. This alone is fatal to the idea that Jesus will come personally at the beginning of the 1,000 years. By a figure of speech soul sometimes stands for the whole man, but in such passage a soul in the body—a living man—is clearly indicated. See Acts 2: 41; 27: 37. The Greek word for soul (*psyche*) often means life, as the following texts will show: Matt. 6: 25; 10: 25; 16: 26, 27. The "souls" John saw symbolically represented the lives of the classes which he immediately mentions. They reign with Christ because their lives are imitated by saints on earth who, like themselves, would die before becoming traitors to the faith, or by accepting false doctrines. Those on the thrones are further described as "souls" of those who had been "beheaded for the testimony of Jesus, and for the word of God," which means they had been killed because of their belief in Christ and refusal to deny him or God's word. Beheading, which was a common form of dispatching the condemned, probably stands for all kinds of martyrdom. It may be questioned whether the whole description here applies to martyrs only, or includes a second class of such as would not worship the beast and his image and refused to receive his "mark." The grammatical construction will allow either view; hence, neither one can be declared as absolutely certain. It is immaterial, however, which is accepted; for in either case they were saints who distinguished themselves by enduring persecution or death for the church. Only the lives of servants of God who have distinguished themselves would fit the symbol of reigning spiritually for a thousand years.

Another distinguishing feature of these who are here said to reign is the fact that the thing which gave them their position is that they resisted the power and influence of the beast. They must have lived then before Satan was bound—that is, when the apostate church exercised supreme power. Their millennial reign is put in direct contrast with the period in which they suffered. This is no mean proof that the millennium—time when Satan is bound—began when the papacy lost its supreme power. This is also proof of two important facts—namely, that we are now in the mil-

forehead and upon their hand; and they lived, and reigned with Christ a thousand years. 5 The rest of the dead lived not until the thousand years

lennium and that Christ did not come at its beginning. On the "mark" of the beast see notes on 13: 16, 17.

and they lived, and reigned with Christ a thousand years.—"They lived" does not mean that souls were brought to life, for souls do not die in the literal meaning of death. Those who obey Christ can never die (John 5: 25), but bodies of saints and sinners will die. Spiritually they *continued* to live in the sense that their work was vindicated and their names honored through those who perpetuated the same truth for which they suffered or died. Figuratively, that would be as though they had been raised and were reigning in person. This, as a fact, was true of the apostles and other martyrs long before the papal beast came into existence. This passage, however, speaks of a special class of martyrs that fought the corruptions of the apostate church. We know that the apostles, though dead in body, do *reign* with Christ on earth now. Why not allow that those who were a later set of martyrs do the same?

It is also a fact that living Christians whose lives are sufficiently noted reign, which, of course, is with Christ. So teaches Paul in Rom. 5: 17; 1 Cor. 4: 8. Such lives cannot be without influence after death. This is the direct promise of Heb. 11: 4.

5 **The rest of the dead lived not until the thousand years should be finished.**—"Lived not until the thousand years should be finished" implies that they would live after that time. "Lived not" evidently is in contrast with "they lived" (verse 4), which, in the latter part of verse 5, is called "the first resurrection." An important question here is this: Will the living again of the "rest" (an implied second resurrection) come immediately after the thousand years end or some time later? It must be remembered that a comparatively short period, called a "little time" (verse 3), will intervene between the thousand years and the judgment. In this period Satan will be "loosed," which means that wickedness will again prevail and all his evil forces will be marshaled for the last struggle against the church. The vital point that *must* be considered is, will the second resurrection occur at the beginning of the

"little time" or at its close? This cannot be ignored in any fair interpretation of this millennial passage.

There is probably no text in Revelation about which commentators are more hopelessly disagreed than this verse. Only four views seem to have enough plausibility to merit consideration. They are: (1) That it refers to the bodily resurrection of all the wicked dead at the end of the thousand years, or, maybe, at the end of the "little time." The advocates of this theory do not seem very definite on the exact time. (2) That the word "rest" means the remainder of the same class—that it includes all the righteous dead except the martyrs and others distinguished for service to God. (3) That it refers to the noted persecutors of saints—such as Nero—who will figuratively be raised in the lives of their imitators during the "little time." (4) That it refers to all the dead—both good and bad—who will be raised bodily at the judgment.

The first theory is a premillennial view. The decisive fact that proves it wrong is that Jesus himself places the bodily resurrection of both saint and sinner at the same time. (John 5: 28, 29.) Until this passage is proved false, that point is settled.

If the second theory means that the inconspicuous righteous dead will be raised at the end of the millennium, it is pertinent to ask for a reason. If the passage has noted saints reigning during the millennium when Satan is bound, it would hardly be consistent to represent inconspicuous saints as reigning during the "little time" while Satan is loose. If such saints are to be raised at the judgment, then the theory is true so far as the resurrection of the righteous dead are concerned. But it does not express all the truth on the question, for all the dead—righteous and wicked—will be raised then.

Regarding the third theory, it may be remarked that it would be no violation of either facts or consistency to represent noted church persecutors as being figuratively raised in the lives of those who imitate them in wickedness in the "little time." However, this would forbid the resurrection to be understood as that of the body. It would be the "souls" of the wicked, similar to the "souls" of the martyrs in verse 4, and therefore, obviate any charge of logical inconsistency.

An apparent objection to the fourth theory is that it violates the law of consistency by making the "first" resurrection figurative and the "second" (which is implied) literal. It is enough to reply that if verse 6, which mentions *first* resurrection, refers to the body, it also mentions *second* death which refers to the soul. But there is no unvarying law that prevents words being used in a figurative and literal sense in the same passage. Usually they should be given the same sense, but plain facts may require a different sense. Jesus uses "born" in John 3: 6 in both a literal and figurative sense. In John 5: 24, 25 "life" and "live" unquestionably imply a spiritual resurrection, while the language in John 5: 28, 29 just as clearly means a literal one. There is, then, really no inconsistency in saying that the "first" resurrection is a moral, spiritual, or figurative one and the "second" (implied) is a literal one. Verses 11-15 of this chapter are a vivid description of a literal resurrection of all classes at the judgment. This is at least strong presumptive proof that the fourth view is correct. It is consistent with words of Jesus and probably the true meaning.

To make the first resurrection a literal one involves the following insuperable difficulties, based upon Jesus' words in John 5 that all will be raised at the same time: If Jesus comes *before* the millennium, all the righteous and wicked will be raised then; hence, there can be no wicked left to be raised at the end of the millennium. If he comes *after* the millennium, then there will be no righteous dead raised at its beginning. If he comes after the "little time"—that is, at the judgment, then there will be none of either class raised either at the beginning or end of the millennium. In either case the premillennial theory is bound to be false. That Christ's personal coming will be at the judgment is the plain teaching of 2 Thess. 1: 7. If the first and second resurrections come at the beginning and end of the millennium, and are to be literal resurrections of the body, then there will be three literal resurrections unless there should be none at the judgment. To deny a literal resurrection of the body at the judgment conflicts with verse 13 of this chapter, for there can be no question about what it teaches.

This is the first resurrection.—That is, of those mentioned in verse 4, not the "rest" of verse 5.

should be finished. This is the first resurrection. 6 Blessed and holy is he that hath part in the first resurrection: over these the second death hath no [3]power; but they shall be priests of God and of Christ, and shall reign with him [4]a thousand years.

[3]Or, *authority*
[4]Some ancient authorities read *the*.

6 **Blessed and holy is he that hath part in the first resurrection: over these the second death hath no power;**—Those who faithfully contended against the beast, false prophet, and all wicked doctrines till death certainly were entitled to the salvation Jesus promised. (Matt. 24: 13.) They not only reign during the millennium, but are made sure against being hurt by the second death. The members of the church at Smyrna were urged not to fear what the devil would do to them, and promised that if they were faithful unto death they would "not be hurt of the second death." (2: 10, 11.) The reason for that is that they are in a state where Satan's power can never reach them. If raised bodily and reigning personally, as the literal kingdom theory demands, he could reach them unless their ability to sin has been removed. If so, then the devil could not deceive them when loosed for a season, as verse 8 says he will do.

but they shall be priests of God and of Christ, and shall reign with him a thousand years.—Those here who are guaranteed freedom from the second death not only resisted false teachings "unto death," but were faithful worshipers of God. Hence, figuratively they are represented as reigning and also officiating in the services of God—they are kings and priests. Peter declares that saints are "an elect race, a royal priesthood, a holy nation." (1 Pet. 2: 9.) A royal—kingly—priesthood agrees exactly with John's description in this book. (1: 6.) The idea is a kingdom of priests. Since Peter and John both teach that Jesus had already made that kingdom, then we know that the reign of "souls" in the millennium is through those on earth who imitate their fidelity. Any interpretation that conflicts with John's own words about the kingdom must be wrong. John the Baptist is called Elijah. (Matt. 11: 12-14.) He came "in the spirit and power of Elijah" (Luke 1: 17)—another way of saying that Elijah was raised from the dead in the person of John. Ezekiel represented the restoration of the Jews from Babylon to their own land as a coming "out of your graves." (Ezek. 37: 12-14.) Those who are old may be "born again," and those naturally alive may die, be buried, and raised without changing their physical state. (Col. 2: 12.) Who can deny the metaphysical use of terms, especially in a book filled with symbols?

3. SATAN OVERTHROWN AND CONDEMNED
20: 7-10

7 And when the thousand years are finished, Satan shall be loosed out of his prison, 8 and shall come forth to deceive the nations which are in the four corners of the earth, Gog and Magog, to gather them together to the

---

7 **And when the thousand years are finished, Satan shall be loosed out of his prison,**—The view here advocated is that the binding of Satan means the return to the people the right to read and obey the Bible without human dictation; his loosing, then, would be his regaining in some way the power to prevent or hinder such voluntary obedience.

8 **and shall come forth to deceive the nations which are in the four corners of the earth, Gog and Magog, to gather them together to the war: the number of whom is as the sand of the sea.**—Though we do not know how or exactly what means he will use, yet it is not improbable that increasing infidelity, superstition, and idolatry will be main contributing factors. Whatever is involved in his loosing, it is safe to say that wickedness will prevail as never before. In this "little time" will occur the events recorded in 19: 17-21 and 20: 7-10; it will be Satan's last struggle against the church in which not only he but his chief aides—beast and false prophet—will be overcome and banished to the lake of fire. (19: 20; 20: 10.) This victory will not be gained by a carnal sword, but by the word that proceeds from the Lord's mouth. (19: 15.) These enemies will be slain and the war against the church ended by the brightness of the Lord's coming and the breath of his mouth (2 Thess. 2: 8) as suddenly as the 185,000 in the Assyrian army were slain by an angel of the Lord. (2 Kings 19: 35.) In the time preceding the thousand years Satan deceived the nations largely through false religious doctrines and practice, virtually suppressing the Bible by demanding the acceptance of papal interpretations. That similar means will be used to deceive

after the thousand years is certainly probable. The existence of nations to be deceived after the millennium is proof that the nature of mankind then will be the same as now, and harmonizes with the question, "When the Son of man cometh, shall he find faith on the earth?" (Luke 18: 8.) "In the four corners" means that the nations will be scattered over the whole earth as now. This is further indicated by the fact that the number shall be "as the sand of the sea."

According to the doctrines of the premillennial coming of Christ, nations to be deceived by Satan after being loosed presents insolvable problems. The theory calls for the banishment of the beast and false prophet and the death of all the wicked (19: 19-21) at Christ's coming; the wicked dead to remain unraised (20: 5); the righteous dead to be raised and with the righteous living all to receive spiritual, incorruptible, and immortal bodies. (1 Cor. 15: 44, 54.) The theory requires all these resurrections to be of the body. The following difficulties are apparent for which no solution can be offered other than pure guesses: Will children be born during the thousand years? If so, will they inherit incorruptible and immortal bodies from their parents? If so, how can beings with such bodies be deceived by Satan? If they can be deceived with such bodies, how can they be safe during the millennium when many of his devices are recorded in the Bible? Can they receive corruptible and mortal bodies from parents with incorruptible bodies, without a fundamental law—seed bearing after its kind—being violated? Will their birth of parents put them in the kingdom? If not, how will they get in? If by obedience to the gospel, that is no improvement on the church. It is hard to see how Satan when loosed can deceive people with incorruptible and immortal bodies.

The wicked dead for whom the theory provides no resurrection till Satan is loosed at the end of the thousand years are already deceived, having lived and died in his service. So they cannot be the nations he will deceive. It is a significant fact that the advocates of a literal reign of Christ on earth have no solution but guesses for these problems. Nothing is satisfactory but to make the millennial reign figurative, and the coming of Christ and the bodily resurrection of the dead at the judgment.

war: the number of whom is as the sand of the sea. 9 And they went up over the breadth of the earth, and compassed the camp of the saints about, and the beloved city: and fire came down [5]out of heaven, and devoured them.

[5]Some ancient authorities insert *from God.*

On Gog and Magog see notes on 16: 14-16. The reference here in verse 8 and in 19: 17, 18 are both made in allusion to Ezek. 39: 11-18 and show that this paragraph is parallel with Rev. 19: 17, 18; hence, it follows that 19: 17-21 and 20: 7-10 contain a complete story of the defeat of the enemies of the church that will occur after the millennium. Read the passages in connection, omitting 20: 1-6, and this fact will appear evident.

9 **And they went up over the breadth of the earth, and compassed the camp of the saints about, and the beloved city:**— The figure here is that of contending armies. Satan's forces are represented as coming from all directions to besiege the beloved city. The imagery is borrowed from Israel's encampments, systematically planned for defense and convenience. Divested of all figures, the thought is that wicked powers will make a general attack on the church, under the influence of Satan. To make the final struggle a carnal battle against literal Jerusalem is to miss the symbolic teaching of the passage. Spiritual Jerusalem—the true church—will be scattered over the earth just as are forces of evil, and the conflict will rage everywhere.

and fire came down out of heaven, and devoured them.— Fire has been a common instrument when God visited capital punishment on incorrigible sinners. Note the destruction of Sodom (Gen. 19: 24); Nadab and Abihu (Lev. 10: 1-3); Korah, Dathan, and Abiram (Num. 16: 35). Christ will come "in flaming fire" and the earth shall be burned up in the day of the Lord's wrath. No emblem could more appropriately indicate the sudden and complete overthrow of Satan and his servants than to say fire came down from heaven and devoured them. The defeat of the same enemies referred to in 19: 21 is said to be accomplished by the sword "which came forth out of his mouth." The wicked at the judgment are to depart "into eternal fire." Symbols must be construed in harmony with plain truths literally stated.

10 And the devil that deceived them was cast into the lake of fire and brimstone, where are also the beast and the false prophet; and they shall be tormented day and night [6]for ever and ever.

[6]Gr. *unto the ages of the ages.*

10 **And the devil that deceived them was cast into the lake of fire and brimstone, where are also the beast and the false prophet;**—Jesus said the fire was prepared for "the devil and his angels." (Matt. 25: 41.) In vision John had seen the beast and false prophet cast in this lake; now he sees the devil cast in with them. This is another proof that this paragraph is a completion of the story in 19: 19-21.

and they shall be tormented day and night for ever and ever.—This means endless duration, and agrees with the plain statements of Jesus in Matt. 25: 46 and Mark 9: 48, 49. Whether the "fire" is to be construed literally or figuratively is immaterial; the lesson taught is intense and endless punishment. No more expressive emblem could have been used.

4. THE UNIVERSAL JUDGMENT
20: 11-15

11 And I saw a great white throne, and him that sat upon it, from whose face the earth and the heaven fled away; and there was found no place for

11 **And I saw a great white throne, and him that sat upon it,**—In this paragraph John describes the great judgment scene, closing with the final disposition to be made of the wicked. The word "throne" means authority to exercise power of some kind. It may indicate either reign or judgment; here the latter is certainly indicated. This is the same throne mentioned by Jesus in Matt. 25: 31 in describing the final judgment; it is there called the "throne of his glory." From the language there we know it will be Jesus himself who will sit upon the judgment throne. It is called the judgment seat of God in Rom. 14: 10, and the judgment seat of Christ in 2 Cor. 5: 10. This is not a contradiction, for God and Christ are one in the purpose of saving men. Then the Father hath committed judgment to the Son (John 5: 22), and Christ's judgment is, therefore, the judgment of the Father also.

from whose face the earth and the heaven fled away; and there was found no place for them.—The disappearing of the

them. 12 And I saw the dead, the great and the small, standing before the throne; and books were opened: and another book was opened, which is *the book* of life: and the dead were judged out of the things which were written

---

heaven and the earth is what John saw in the picture; and their disappearance was final. Whether this is to be understood symbolically to indicate a complete change of religious systems or the final change in the material world, as described in 2 Pet. 3: 7, 10-12, is an immaterial matter; for the judgment will bring a radical change in both. The old system in both will disappear forever—their purposes will have been accomplished.

12 **And I saw the dead, the great and the small, standing before the throne;**—Jesus said there would be gathered before him all nations. In the emblem John sees the scenes enacted as predicted. "The great and the small" is a general expression that includes all, both evil and good. This is in perfect agreement with plain statements in nonfigurative language. Jesus said "all nations" would appear before his throne; Paul says we shall "all" stand before the judgment seat; and that "each one" may receive the things done in the body. This makes it universal.

and books were opened: and another book was opened, which is the book of life:—Both Old and New Testaments use the figure of man's name and deeds being recorded in a book. The following passages give clear proof of that fact: Ex. 32: 32; Mal. 3: 16; Phil. 4: 3; Rev. 3: 5; 13: 8; 18: 8; 21: 27. The thought is that God's infinite memory will enable him to reward properly both bad and good just as if a written record had been kept. His knowledge of men's acts is just as accurate as a perfect writing. Some commentators interpret the "books" to mean the record God keeps of men's conduct, and the "book of life" to be the roll or record of the names of the righteous. But since we are to be judged by the words of Jesus (John 12: 48), it seems more probable that one of the books, at least, should represent the Bible which contains the law by which mankind shall be judged. The other two could be the record of man's deeds and a register of the names of the saved. Whatever distinction we make in the application of the books, it is certain that men are to be judged in harmony with God's law and according to their deeds. A failure to have our

in the books, according to their works. 13 And the sea gave up the dead
that were in it; and death and Hades gave up the dead that were in them:
and they were judged every man according to their works. 14 And death
and Hades were cast into the lake of fire. This is the second death, *even* the

---

names on God's record, or to have them rubbed out because of our sins, will be fatal to us. That is the important thing to remember.

and the dead were judged out of the things which were written in the books, according to their works.—This is a plain statement of what is already implied in the text. The "dead" is an unlimited term that means all the dead, unless the context or language limits it to some special class of the dead. The language here has no such limitation, but on the other hand the implied contrast between the saved and lost runs through the entire paragraph. Why say "according to their works" if only the wicked dead were in view? In that case it would have been necessary only to say that the dead were raised to be punished.

13 **And the sea gave up the dead that were in it; and death and Hades gave up the dead that were in them:**—The Bible definitely shows that it is the body that dies, in the common use of the word die; death can be affirmed of the soul or spirit only in a moral or figurative sense. That leaves the soul alive in the natural sense of the term "live." James says "the body apart from the spirit is dead" (James 2: 26), but no inspired writer anywhere says the spirit apart from the body is dead. Luke 16: 22-25 and Acts 2: 27 are final proofs that the souls in the Hadean world are not dead in the sense that the body is dead. Since the judgment is the door through which the final state is entered, of course a resurrection must precede. Hence, Hades must give up all souls, and the tombs be opened for the resurrection of bodies. But as the sea has claimed a large share of dead bodies, it must give up those in it. The resurrection must be complete and final. The language here forces the word "sea" to have its literal meaning; the word "earth" is implied in the resurrection of those buried in tombs.

and they were judged every man according to their works.—Once more the universal nature of the resurrection is indicated by the expression "every man." Doubtless repeated for emphasis.

14 **And death and Hades were cast into the lake of fire. This is the second death, even the lake of fire.**—The language

lake of fire. 15 And if any was not found written in the book of life, he was cast into the lake of fire.

---

means that both death and Hades will cease to exist at the judgment. The abolishment of death will render it impossible to have dead bodies for tombs in either earth or sea. If there will be no bodies for the tombs, there will be no disembodied spirits for Hades. No longer needed, naturally they will cease to exist. Personified, as if human beings, their final end is represented as in the lake of fire, called the second death. This is a forceful way of saying they are eternally banished, and the saved will no longer have reason to fear what does not exist.

15 **And if any was not found written in the book of life, he was cast into the lake of fire.**—Returning to the destiny of men, John says anyone not written in God's book will be cast into the lake of fire. While this is the last act in the career of the wicked, the implication is evident that those whose names are in the book of life will escape the second death. This event, of course, is still future, yet John said "was" cast into the lake of fire. As John was permitted to see the judgment in a pictorial representation, the whole matter appeared done; hence, symbolically it was finished, but in reality was then, and yet is, future. This judgment scene pictures what Jesus revealed would take place when he comes again. (Matt. 25: 31-46.)

At this point the curtain drops upon the earthly drama in which mankind has played its several parts. The acts will not be repeated; the stage and all furnishings will give place to that which will be suitable to the eternal nature of man in his final abode. The curtain will never rise again upon the lost; their doom is left to our imagination from the pictures already drawn. Not so with the redeemed; for with the most entrancing visions and the sweetest and most alluring promises John lays before his readers Revelation's last words concerning the mansions Jesus has gone to prepare for his own.

PART FIFTH

THE FINAL ABODE OF THE REDEEMED
21: 1 to 22: 21

SECTION ONE

THE NEW HEAVEN AND NEW EARTH
21: 1 to 22: 5

1. A VISION OF THE HOLY CITY
21: 1-4

1 And I saw a new heaven and a new earth: for the first heaven and the first earth are passed away; and the sea is no more. 2 And I saw [7]the holy city, new Jerusalem, coming down out of heaven from God, made

[7]Or, *the holy city Jerusalem coming down new out of heaven.*

(In this part brief quotations are made the basis for comments. For the complete text see the top of the pages.)

1 **And I saw a new heaven and a new earth: for the first heaven and the first earth are passed away; and the sea is no more.**—In this part of the book John presented to the seven churches, and through them to us, the strongest possible incentives to induce faithfulness to God regardless of any kind of opposition. The happiness of the saved is described in imagery beyond the power of human comprehension. In the vision of the judgment he saw the heaven and the earth flee away, because not suitable for the home of the redeemed; here he sees a new heaven and a new earth fitted for our bodies when "conformed to the body of his glory." (Phil. 3: 21.) That new heaven and earth will be a state, place, or condition "wherein dwelleth righteousness." (2 Pet. 3: 13.) This we must take by faith till we see the realities represented by these glorious emblems.

2 **the holy city, new Jerusalem.**—The scene changes and John's vision is limited to a city. That it should be called "holy" and named the "new Jerusalem" is most natural. That city had been the Jewish capital, spiritually the church had been described as the "city of the living God, the heavenly Jerusalem" (Heb. 12: 22), and most naturally the final state would be called "the city which hath the foundations, whose builder and maker is God"

ready as a bride adorned for her husband. 3 And I heard a great voice out of the throne saying, Behold, the tabernacle of God is with men, and he shall [1]dwell with them, and they shall be his peoples, and God himself shall be

[1]Gr. *tabernacle.*

(Heb. 11: 10). City carries the idea of place, but the symbols are so mingled that it is not always easy to distinguish between state and place. The false church is referred to as Babylon and a drunken harlot (17: 5, 6); the true church, as a holy city—Jerusalem—and a pure woman. The glorified church, under the same figure, is called the new Jerusalem and the "wife of the Lamb."

The descending of the city in such glorious form (a part of the vision appearing to John) is likened to a beautiful bride adorned to meet her husband. Clearly this indicates that the church at last will meet the Lord because attired in fine linen bright and pure which is "the righteous acts of the saints." (Rev. 19: 8.) The text does not say that the church will *become* the wife of Christ at that time, but only that her preparation for the Lord's coming will be made with the same care that a bride prepares for her husband-to-be. Spiritually the church is now married to Christ. (Rom. 7: 4; Eph. 5: 22-32.) A holy city and a beautifully adorned bride figuratively represent the beauty and holiness of the redeemed church. That is the only use here made of the comparisons; trying to get more out of the text is to misreprent the record. For other metaphysical uses of the word "marriage" see notes on 19: 7.

3 **Behold, the tabernacle of God is with men.**—As usual this announcement of the new state is made from heaven. God's dwelling with men is not a new idea, but doing so in his personal presence is. God's glory filled the tabernacle at Mount Sinai (Ex. 40: 34-38); Jesus in the flesh was Immanuel—God with us (Matt. 1: 23); in the eternal city the divine presence will be a glorious reality. The statement "they shall be his peoples" does not mean that they will become such at that time, for their entrance into the city depends upon their already being his. (22: 14; 7: 11.) It means that the relationship will become permanent with no chance for the saved to be lost. "Peoples"—plural—probably signifies nothing more than that the glorified church will be composed of those from all nations.

with them, [2]*and be* their God: 4 and he shall wipe away every tear from their eyes; and death shall be no more; neither shall there be mourning, nor crying, nor pain any more: the first things are passed away. 5 And he that

[2]Some ancient authorities omit, and be *their God.*

4 **wipe away every tear.**—In this verse are mentioned the most satisfying characteristics which make the heavenly state so appealing to people in the flesh. The most distressing and harrowing experiences known to human life are to disappear completely. The glorious body cannot be racked with pain; no incurable disease or death can make the heart cry out in anguish; all the innumerable and sad results attributable to sin will be banished forever, for the "first things are passed away." No appeal could be more tender or comforting than freedom from the ills and troubles of human existence.

2. THE INHERITANCE PROMISED
21 : 5-8

sitteth on the throne said, Behold, I make all things new. And he saith, [3]Write: for these words are faithful and true. 6 And he said unto me,

[3]Or, *Write, These words are faithful and true.*

5 **Write: for these words are faithful and true.**—The one sitting on the throne gave John the command to write. Whether Christ or God is not absolutely certain. Verse 6 favors Christ, but verse 7 the other view. The question is really unimportant since Christ and the Father are one; whatever Christ does the Father does through him. The words "Alpha and the Omega" refer to Christ in 1 : 18, which is presumptive evidence that they have the same reference here; but these words just as appropriately describe characteristics of God. "All things new" probably include not only the new heaven and earth, but the new method and manner of serving God. In that state the reign will be turned back to the Father. (1 Cor. 15 : 24.)

The command may be construed two ways: "Write these things, for they are faithful and true." That is, the speaker was assuring John that what he was to write was the exact truth. Or, write this sentence: "These words are faithful and true." That would be

They are come to pass. I am the Alpha and the Omega, the beginning and the end. I will give unto him that is athirst of the fountain of the water of life freely. 7 He that overcometh shall inherit these things; and I will be his God, and he shall be my son. 8 But for the fearful, and unbelieving, and abominable, and murderers, and fornicators, and sorcerers, and idolators, and all liars, their part *shall be* in the lake that burneth with fire and brimstone; which is the second death.

John's guarantee to the readers that he was delivering a true revelation of facts.

6 **They are come to pass.**—This does not mean that all had happened when John wrote, but all will have come to pass at the time indicated by the symbol. In this vision John was standing before the new Jerusalem, and was speaking from that point of view. All previous symbols had to appear as fulfilled at that time. To those who "hunger and thirst after righteousness" (Matt. 5: 6) there will be the privilege of drinking the "water of life freely."

7 **He that overcometh shall inherit these things;**—This is substantially the same promise made to the seven churches, with the same condition imposed—they must overcome. See chapters 2 and 3. "I will be his God" means I will continue to be.

8 **In the lake that burneth with fire and brimstone.**—Here we have another brief reference to the abominable characters whose part shall be in the lake of fire. This statement contains another feature of encouragement to him that overcometh; namely, he will never again be tormented by their ungodly conduct or brought under the spell of their temptations. He will never tremble in their presence nor be intimidated by their power. From the second death there is no relief.

3. THE HOLY CITY DESCRIBED
21: 9-27

9 And there came one of the seven angels who had the seven bowls, who were laden with the seven last plagues; and he spake with me, saying, Come

---

9 **and he spake with me.**—The speaker here was one of the seven angels that poured out the seven plagues. This final appearance of a plague angel indicates that the visions in 17: 1 to 22: 5 form a continuous revelation that comes under the period covered by the seven plagues. This, of course, puts the millennium before

hither, I will show thee the bride, the wife of the Lamb. 10 And he carried
me away in the Spirit to a mountain great and high, and showed me the holy
city Jerusalem, coming down out of heaven from God, 11 having the glory of
God: her [4]light was like unto a stone most precious, as it were a jasper
stone, clear as crystal: 12 having a wall great and high; having twelve
[5]gates, and at the [5]gates twelve angels; and names written thereon, which
are *the names* of the twelve tribes of the children of Israel: 13 on the east
were three [5]gates; and on the north three [5]gates; and on the south three

[4]Gr. *luminary*.
[5]Gr. *portals*.

Christ's personal coming, for the plagues bring us to the judgment. (16: 17-21.) In this paragraph we have a most graphic description of the final state under the emblem of a glorious city. The vision again mingles the figures—city and wife. See notes on verse 2 and 19: 7. Different figures are sometimes used in close connection to present different features of the same subject. For example, shepherd and door both refer to Christ. (John 10: 1-12.) The false church was called a harlot and Babylon (17: 5, 6); the true church is then appropriately represented as a holy city and a true wife.

10 **And he carried me away in the Spirit to a mountain great and high.**—In some kind of mental ecstasy John was transported to the mountain and saw the new Jerusalem appear to descend from heaven. This but repeats what is stated in verse 2. That may be a kind of brief introductory expression while verse 10 introduces a detailed description of that city.

11 **having the glory of God.**—In the descending city which John saw in the vision there was God's glory; its light was like a precious stone clear as crystal, dazzling bright. Truly an appropriate appearance for the dwelling place of God.

12 **having a wall great and high; having twelve gates.**—A great wall indicates that the eternal city of our God will be securely protected—no enemy can ever touch the redeemed again. Angels at the gates carries the same idea of protection or being safely guarded. Possibly there is here an allusion to the Cherubim and flaming sword that protected the tree of life in Eden. (Gen. 3: 24.) "Twelve tribes" taken literally and spiritually include God's people in different ages.

13 **on the east were three gates.**—If there is any spiritual sig-

[5]gates; and on the west three [5]gates. 14 And the wall of the city had twelve foundations, and on them twelve names of the twelve apostles of the Lamb. 15 And he that spake with me had for a measure a golden reed to measure the city, and the [5]gates thereof, and the wall thereof. 16 And the city lieth foursquare, and the length thereof is as great as the breadth; and he measured the city with the reed, twelve thousand furlongs: the length and the

---

nificance in placing three gates on each side, it probably indicates that entrance was open to those from all quarters.

14 **Twelve foundations.**—Expositors have offered different plans for the arrangement of the twelve foundations, but with nothing to support their views except supposition. It is not a question of enough importance to justify speculation. The simple statement is sufficient. The names of the apostles on the foundations agree with Paul's words in Eph. 2: 20 regarding the church. Occupying a position of authority in the church, it follows that those in the glorified church would be there because of their dependence upon the apostles; or heaven will be peopled with those who have obeyed the apostles, if old enough to be responsible.

15 **had for a measure a golden reed.**—He that talked with John was the angel. See verse 9. On the measuring reed see notes on 11: 1. A golden reed corresponds with the grandeur and value of the city. The object of measuring the temple, worship, and worshippers (11: 1, 2) was to enable those in the restoration work to reproduce congregations just as they existed in the apostolic days; here the measurement will show that the eternal city is according to divine plans and spacious enough for all the saved.

16 **And the city lieth foursquare.**—We should constantly remember that the description we are reading is what John saw in the vision; what it signifies is a different thing. The city which the apostle saw measured was not only foursquare, but was a cube—length, width, and height equal. Again we find commentators disagreed regarding the measurement. All agree that 12,000 furlongs equal 1,500 miles, but the difficulty comes in applying the figures. If the 12,000 furlongs applied to each side of the cube, then the city was 1,500 miles in every direction. But some view the 12,000 furlongs as the distance around the city. If that be correct, then each dimension was 375 miles. In either case, if the city be understood literally, it will be entirely too large to be in Palestine, for

breadth and the height thereof are equal. 17 And he measured the wall
thereof, a hundred and forty and four cubits, *according to* the measure of a
man, that is, of an angel. 18 And the building of the wall thereof was jasper: and the city was pure gold, like unto pure glass. The foundations of
the wall of the city were adorned with all manner of precious stones. The
first foundation was jasper; the second, [6]sapphire; the third, chalcedony; the
fourth, emerald; 20 the fifth, sardonyx; the sixth, sardius; the seventh,
chrysolite; the eighth, beryl; the ninth, topaz; the tenth, chrysoprase; the
eleventh, [7]jacinth; and twelfth, amethyst. 21 And the twelve [5]gates were
twelve pearls; each of the several [5]gates was of one pearl: and the street of

[6]Or, *lapis lazuli*
[7]Or, *sapphire*

the whole country is not that large. That this number should be taken symbolically seems to be unquestionably demanded. Such an enormous city, all beyond human imagination, if taken literally, indicates the ample provisions our God had made for the final home of his obedient children.

17 **And he measured the wall thereof.**—A wall was necessary to make the vision correspond with cities of that age. It also carries the idea of protection. That would be the significance here unless it is just a part of the symbolic imagery and used only to make the picture harmonious. The whole measurement is in multiples of twelve, which would indicate not only symmetry but perfection. According to the measure of a man evidently means that the reed used was the same length that man would use. Since the vision was for men, the standard measuring lengths had to be used.

18 **And the building of the wall thereof.**—The wall above the foundations was of jasper—at least, so it appeared to John; the edifices of the city appeared to be of pure gold, shining with the brilliancy of pure glass. Of course, this description need not be taken literally, but it does show the earth's richest jewels and most precious metals are but symbols of the richness of God's provisions for the saved in heaven. What more compelling inducement could be offered to earth's weary and heavy-laden?

19, 20 **The foundations of the wall of the city.**—Even the foundations of the wall were adorned with twelve manner of precious stones.

21 **The twelve gates were twelve pearls.**—Among ancients pearls were considered of the highest value among precious stone because their beauty was entirely natural and without effort of art.

the city was pure gold, [8]as it were transparent glass. 22 And I saw no [9]temple therein: for the Lord God the Almighty, and the Lamb are the [9]temple thereof. 23 And the city hath no need of the sun, neither of the moon, to shine upon it: for the glory of God did lighten it, [10]and the lamp thereof *is* the Lamb. 24 And the nations shall walk [11]amidst the light thereof: and the kings of the earth bring their glory into it. 25 And the [5]gates

[8]Or, *transparent as glass*
[9]Or, *sanctuary*
[10]Or, *and the Lamb, the lamp thereof*
[11]Or, *by*

Each gate appeared to be of one pearl, possibly because so adorned with them that it had the appearance of being one. The street of the city was pure gold. That literal metals could be meant is true, of course, when we remember the infinite power of God. But as the picture that John saw is clearly symbolical, there is no logical need for saying that what he saw were the real metals and stones. It is enough to meet all the demands of emblematic figures to say that they had the appearance of such objects.

22 **And I saw no temple therein.**—Under the Jewish system the most holy place of the temple was where God met the high priest, as representative of the people; in the Church—the true tabernacle—all are kings and priests and worship God; it is the place where he meets them spiritually. In the heavenly Jerusalem he will meet the saved personally; there will be no special place for a tabernacle, for the whole city will be the temple; or, in another view, God and the Lamb will be the temple. In 7: 15 it says that in the final state we will "serve him day and night in his temple." There is no conflict here, for the presence of God throughout the city makes a temple of it. The most holy place of the Jewish temple was a cube. The holy city being in the same form may suggest the idea that it is a temple. The presence of God and the Lamb is further justification for saying that the whole city will be a temple.

23 **And the city hath no need of the sun.**—Ordinary cities known to men must have lights both natural and artificial. Not so will it be in the new Jerusalem. The glory of God and the presence of the Christ will be all the light needed.

24 **And the nations shall walk amidst the light thereof.**—Evidently this means that the saved from all nations will be in that city. That is clear from the answer to the question as to who will be there. See 7: 13-15. The prophet said that all nations would

thereof shall in no wise be shut by day (for there shall be no night there): 26 and they shall bring the glory and the honor of the nations into it: 27 and there shall in no wise enter into it anything [12]unclean, or he that [13]maketh an abomination and a lie: but only they that are written in the Lamb's book of life.

[12]Gr. *common.*
[13]Or, *doeth*

flow into the mountain of the Lord's house. (Isa. 2: 2.) The redeemed will come from all nations, but in heaven will be spiritual beings with all national distinctions blotted out. To carry out the same figure kings—the rulers of nations—will bring their honor into it. They will not there be acting as kings, but rather will themselves become subjects to God and give him all the glory that once they received.

25 **And the gates thereof shall in no wise be shut.**—Ancient cities shut their gates by night and opened them by day. In God's eternal city there will be no night, for the glory of God and Christ will give it perpetual light. The open gate is another emblem of security. The closed gate with a guard indicates protection, but the gate open continually shows that nothing harmful will enter.

26 This verse is a repetition of the thought of verse 24.

27 **and there shall in no wise enter into it anything unclean.**—This verse is substantially the same in thought as verse 8 with the additional statement that none can enter except those written in the "lamb's book of life." This is both inclusive and exclusive—encouraging the faithful by the fact that no wicked can enter. Those who desire to enter must be righteous; in heaven they will be free from vexations due to the sins of men.

4. THE FINAL VISION
22: 1-5

1 And he showed me a river of water of life, bright as crystal, proceeding out of the throne of God and of [1]the Lamb, 2 in the midst of the street

[1]Or, *the Lamb. In the midst of the street thereof, and on either side of the river, was the tree of life &c.*

1 **And he showed me a river of water of life, bright as crystal, proceeding out of the throne of God and of the Lamb,**—This paragraph completes the vision of the new Jerusalem as the angel presented it to John. Attention was called to a river pro-

thereof. And on this side of the river and on that was [2]the tree of life, bearing twelve [3]*manner of* fruits, yielding its fruit every month: and the

[2]Or, *a tree*
[3]Or, *crops of fruit*

ceeding from the throne of God and Christ. Water is necessary to physical life; hence, the appearance of a river fits into a symbol that portrays life and happiness. Being bright as crystal and coming from the throne of God show that all genuinely pure blessings come from God. In harmony with his will heavenly mansions are being prepared by Jesus. (John 14: 2.) The throne in this glorious city is said to be "of God and of the Lamb." Paul tells us that in the final state even Christ shall be subject to the Father "that God may be all in all." (1 Cor. 15: 28.) This will be after Christ has turned the reigning power back to God. Notwithstanding that fact it is said that in heaven it will be the "throne of God and of the Lamb." This is said, doubtless, because God and Christ are one in providing the salvation. Question: If in the final state the throne (reign or rulership) can be called that of both God and Christ, though it strictly belongs to God, why cannot the kingdom in which Christ reigns now also be called God's? It can and is as the following passages show: (Luke 8: 1, 10; Mark 1: 15; John 3: 5; 18: 36; Col. 1: 13.) Paul speaks of the inheritance as being in the "kingdom of Christ and God." This use of the words "throne" and "kingdom" proves that Christ is now reigning, even though his throne is also the throne of God.

2 **in the midst of the street thereof.**—This completes the description of the river. Their reference to a river may be an allusion to Gen. 2: 10 which speaks of a river flowing from the original Paradise of God. In the restored Paradise there will be a river of divine blessing—here called the water of life.

And on this side of the river and on that was the tree of life.—Probably the most simple view here is that the word "tree" is not used to signify just one, but generically to mean that the "tree of life" is a class or kind of tree. This will allow for the streets and both sides of the river to be lined with this tree. Such a vision would indicate abundant life for all throughout the whole city. Twelve manner or twelve crops—one every month—would symbolically represent a perpetual abundance of spiritual bless-

leaves of the tree were for the healing of the nations. 3 And there shall be [4]no curse any more: and the throne of God and of the Lamb shall be therein: and his [5]servants shall serve him; 4 and they shall see his face; and his name *shall be* on their foreheads. 5 And there shall be night no more; and they need no light of lamp, neither light of sun; for the Lord God shall give them light: and they shall reign [6]for ever and ever.

[4]Or, *no more anything accursed*
[5]Gr. *bondservants.*
[6]Gr. *unto the ages of the ages.*

ings. Of course, months and years are inconceivable in a state where there is nothing but continuous light, but all unseen states must be presented through the medium of what is seen. Healing, of course, implies disease, but that happens to be one of the things that will be unknown in heaven. (21: 4.) The meaning is that the tree of life has supplied just the things that have healed people of all nations and will then protect them against disease. No tears or crying does not mean that there will be occasions for such things in heaven, and God will then wipe the tears away, but rather that nothing will come to produce them.

3 **And there shall be no curse any more.**—When man sinned in Eden he was driven out from the tree of life under a curse, including pain, sickness, sorrow, and death. In the final city of God, these curses can never come. The reason assigned is that the throne (reign of God and the Lamb) is there. A perpetual service by the saved will guarantee a perpetual freedom from all curses.

4 **and they shall see his face; and his name shall be on their foreheads.**—They will never be driven from his presence nor disowned, for his name will be upon them.

5 **And there shall be night no more.**—See notes on 21: 23-25.

and they shall reign for ever and ever.—There is absolutely nothing in this verse to indicate any special class as those who will reign over others. There will be no wicked in that heavenly place; the whole tenor of these two chapters is against that. The redeemed are represented as "his servants." (Verse 6.) So whatever the meaning given the word "reign," here it applies to all the saved in heaven. It cannot be understood literally as exercising authority over others for two reasons: (1) That prerogative, in whatever way it may be necessary, will belong primarily to God, and secondarily to Christ; and both will be present. (2) All the saved will be in the reigning and have no others but themselves to reign over. The language must be taken figuratively. It is not possible for one in the flesh to describe accurately a purely spiritual state. Nothing seems more reasonable than the thought that through the ceaseless age then to begin redeemed humanity will truly and completely submit to God's rule, and thus figuratively rule with him by a loving submission to his authority.

This completes the emblematic description of the new Jerusalem, and the ultimate blessings that await the faithful in God's spiritual family. It also brings to a close the symbolic part of the book of Revelation. The remainder of this chapter is a brief conclusion, in which the last warnings and promises of a loving Father are laid before a sinful race.

PART SIXTH

PRACTICAL WARNINGS, COMMANDS, AND PROMISES
22: 6-21

1. THE ANGEL'S ATTESTATION
22: 6, 7

6 And he said unto me, These words are faithful and true: and the Lord, the God of the spirits of the prophets, sent his angel to show unto his [5]servants the things which must shortly come to pass. 7 And behold, I come quickly. Blessed is he that keepeth the words of the prophecy of this book.

---

6 **These words are faithful and true.**—As the symbolic images are now completed the angel comes directly to John with the assurance that the words (visions and spoken words) are true, that there has been no deception and all things will come to pass just as disclosed. That an angel was the speaker is evident from verse 8 compared with 21: 9. John had already been commanded to write that the sayings were true. (21: 5.) He further assures John that the God who inspired the prophets of old had sent his angel to make these revelations; hence, the same proof that they were divine and properly classed as prophetic sayings.

the things which must shortly come to pass.—This is the same statement with which the book opens. See notes on 1: 1. It is appropriate, after the symbols had been finished, that John should again be assured that the revealed things would shortly come to pass. Of course, the natural meaning for this expression is that the things revealed would soon *begin* to transpire, not that all of them would soon begin. If these symbols contain a series of events, however few, then all of them could not begin at the same time. If the series is long, then some could be in distant centuries. Since the millennium and the judgment are a part of the imagery, it is unquestionably a fact that all did not begin soon; therefore, the beginning of the series must be the meaning.

7 **And behold, I come quickly. Blessed is he that keepeth the words of the prophecy of this book.**—Apparently the angel is here repeating the words of Jesus, or Jesus is speaking through the angel. The expression "I come quickly" evidently is intended to encourage saints to keep "the words of the prophecy of this book."

Of course, it cannot mean that he promised to come personally in a short time or soon from the time John received these revelations; for more than eighteen hundred years have passed and he has not come yet. If it means that he would come figuratively in blessings and punishments during the time covered by the symbols of the book, then he did come soon and the words are equivalent to "shortly come to pass" in the preceding verse. In a similar way he did come to those who faithfully suffered during the time signified; for each individual's death was a virtual coming of the Lord to him—it meant his sufferings would soon be over. If it refers to his actual coming at the judgment, then "quickly" must be understood as God views time, not as men do. In a practical sense the encouragement would apply to each individual with the assurance that his efforts would not be very long in comparison with the length of his reward. We have here the statement that the symbols of this book are a prophecy.

2. JOHN'S CONFIRMATION
22: 8-11

8 And I John am he that heard and saw these things. And when I heard and saw, I fell down to [7]worship before the feet of the angel that showed me these things. 9 And he saith unto me, See thou do it not: I am a fellow-servant with thee and with thy brethren the prophets, and with them that keep the words of this book: [7]worship God.

[7]See marginal note on ch. 3. 9.

8 **And I John am he that heard and saw these things.**—This is a plain declaration from John that he heard the revelations in the words and saw the symbols; he wrote what occurred or he misrepresented facts and that would destroy his veracity. When the angel had shown these things the apostle, after the ancient custom, fell at his feet thinking he should be worshiped.

9 **See thou do it not.**—The angel promptly forbade it and offered reasons for his refusal. He declared he was a "fellow-servant" with John and other prophets. Angels, prophets of old, and the apostles were all moved by the same Spirit, and were therefore "brethren" in prophetic labors. John should no more worship the angel than the angel worship John. Moreover, the angel was a fellow servant with those who "keep the words of this book"; he

10 And he saith unto me, Seal not up the words of the prophecy of this book; for the time is at hand. 11 He that is unrighteous, let him do unrighteousness [8]still: and he that is filthy, let him be made filthy [8]still: and he that is righteous, let him do righteousness [8]still: and he that is holy, let him

[8]Or, *yet more*

obeyed God in revealing the prophecies and they obey in keeping them.

10 **Seal not up the words of the prophecy of this book.**—The angel further instructed John not to seal up the words of this prophecy, the reason assigned being that "the time is at hand." That is, the time was near when the series of symbols would begin to be fulfilled, and the saints would need their instruction to aid them in successfully overcoming temptations. Regarding the seven thunders the opposite command was given, and John was told to seal them up. See notes on 9: 4. The explanation there of what is meant by sealing up is that he was not to write them. "Seal not up" would then mean that John was promptly to write them so the churches then in existence would have a knowledge of what they would receive for faithfulness amid trials.

11 **He that is unrighteous, let him do unrighteousness still.**—The same is mentioned for the filthy, and the opposite side for both characters is stated. This part of the book is not dealing with the inability of either saint or sinner to change his state after reaching the judgment, but with warnings and commands that can be heeded during the time covered by the symbols. In that period men can change, if they will; but will be lost, if they persist in sin. The only plausible application of these expressions seems to be this: with these prophecies and promises before him, if one cannot be influenced to serve God, then the truth will not reach him and he will have to continue wicked still and be lost; for, God offers to save none against his will. Do not "cast your pearls before swine" is just as appropriate now as when uttered. Those desirous of being righteous can continue to do so. The word "still" in the margin of the Revised Version is exchanged for *yet more*. Whatever either character determines to do, let him continue "yet more"—the only course that vindicates the justice of God and makes man responsible for his deeds.

3. THE TESTIMONY OF JESUS
22: 12-16

be made holy [8]still. 12 Behold, I come quickly; and my [9]reward is with me, to render to each man according as his work is. 13 I am the Alpha and the Omega, the first and the last, the beginning and the end. 14 Blessed are they that wash their robes, that they may have [10]the right *to come* to the tree of life, and may enter in by the [11]gates into the city. 15 Without are the dogs, and the sorcerers, and the fornicators, and the murderers, and the idolaters, and every one that loveth and [12]maketh a lie.

[9]Or, *wages*
[10]Or, *the authority over* Comp. ch. 6. 8.
[11]Gr. *portals.*
[12]Or, *doeth* Comp. ch. 21. 27.

12 **and my reward is with me.**—This verse is a repetition of verse 7 with assurance that each one will be rewarded according to his works. See notes on verse 7. On being judged according to works compare 2 Cor. 5: 10.

13 **I am the Alpha and the Omega.**—The text explains these words as first and last, beginning and end. Christ was with the Father in the creation (Col. 1: 15-17), has been in the plan of salvation, and will be at the judgment, and in the new Jerusalem. It is wonderfully encouraging to know we have one with such power to make us promises of rewards; he will make no mistakes.

14 **Blessed are they that wash their robes.**—The promise made to such is that they may have the right to the tree of life, and may enter through the gates into the city. Adam because of disobedience was denied this right; through Christ man by obedience may come to it. Washing robes means to be pardoned through the merits of Jesus' blood. Other texts show that the blessings of the eternal city depend upon faithfulness unto death. (2: 11.)

15 **Without are the dogs.**—This verse contains substantially the same thought as 21: 8. To the Jews the dog was an unclean animal and was a fit emblem of the abominable characters here named. "Without" means that such persons will not be allowed admittance to the heavenly city.

16 **I Jesus have sent mine angel.**—In these words Jesus directly confirms the testimony of the angel as being his own. His words were sent to churches then existing—the seven named—but are intended for all others in like conditions or subject to the same sins.

16 I Jesus have sent mine angel to testify unto you these things [13]for the churches. I am the root and the offspring of David, the bright, the morning star.

[13]Gr. *over.*

I am the root and the offspring of David.—Being a descendant of David, he was what the prophecies demanded he should be; without this lineage he could not have occupied the throne of authority. This fact was mentioned in the first chapter of the New Testament and confirmed by Jesus here in the last chapter. As the offspring of David, he now rules at the right hand of God; at the judgment he will be sitting on the same throne; in eternity he will still be in association with the Father. (Verse 2.)

4. AN INVITATION AND A WARNING
22: 17-19

17 [14]And the Spirit and the bride say, Come. And he that heareth, let him say, Come. And he that is athirst, let him come: he that will, let him take the water of life freely.
18 I testify unto every man that heareth the words of the prophecy of this book, If any man shall add [15]unto them, God shall add [15]unto him the

[14]Or, *Both*
[15]Gr. *upon.*

17 **And the Spirit and the bride say, Come.**—The invitation is to come to Christ, and is based upon his right to our devotion and service. This right rests upon his character as Creator and the legal Ruler in the "tabernacle of David." The Holy Spirit entreats us to come by the teachings of the apostles and prophets. These contain the motives of mercy and rewards, as found in this book and other parts of the sacred record. The church, which is the wife (21: 9), invites by preaching the word and proper Christian living. Those that hear (heed) are authorized to say, Come. Those who desire and are willing may take the water or life freely—that is, can have an abundant "entrance into the eternal kingdom of our Lord and Saviour Jesus Christ." (2 Pet. 1: 11.) With such invitations no earnest and honest soul need be lost.

18 **If any man shall add unto them, God shall add unto him the plagues which are written in this book.**—This is probably the language of John himself. He warns of the disasters that will come upon those who tamper with the divine record of this book.

plagues which are written in this book: 19 and if any man shall take away from the words of the book of this prophecy, God shall take away his part from the tree of life, and out of the holy city, [16]which are written in this book.

[16]Or, even from *the things which are written*

The same principle applies to all God's laws at whatever time they are in force. (Deut. 4:2; Gal. 1:6-9.) John, however, is here speaking of Revelation; the expression *this* book is sufficient proof. Being a prophetic book with the fulfillment of its symbols yet future when John wrote, there would be more temptations to change its words to fit supposed fulfillments. The desire to add other predictions would need to be curbed.

The opposite danger—leaving out what might seem to conflict with views already taken—would also be strong. Those rejecting any part of the book would lose their inheritance in the heavenly city. This will condemn not only actual mutilation of the book, but also its perversion through teaching to support a false theory. No book should be studied with more caution or care.

5. A FINAL PROMISE AND BENEDICTION
22:20, 21

20 He who testifieth these things saith, Yea: I come quickly. Amen: come, Lord Jesus.

20 **He who testifieth these things saith, Yea.**—Regardless of how or by whom these things were made known to John, Jesus was the real source of the revelation. He here places the stamp of approval upon them by saying "yea"—that is, they are true. On the promise "I come quickly" see note on verse 7. As already noted, Jesus could not have meant that he would come soon after talking to John, for centuries have passed since then and he has not come yet. To God it may be "quickly," but to us the point of importance is the element of certainty that the promise carries, regardless of its actual time. To these words John replied: "Come, Lord Jesus." The meaning is this: "Come, Lord, in your own time and for the purpose in view." Truly a pious wish that should fulfill every contrite heart.

21 The grace of the Lord Jesus[17] be [18]with the saints. Amen.

[17]Some ancient authorities add *Christ*.
[18]Two ancient authorities read *with all*.

21 The usual benediction closes this book, and with it ends God's written revelation to men.

This study of Revelation has been pursued with both pleasure and profit to the author. It is hoped that the results of his labors may prove helpful to the readers. With a prayer for the "grace of the Lord Jesus" to rest upon these comments upon the sublime symbols of man's duty and destiny, this book is submitted to the candid consideration of "honest and good hearts."

INDEX TO SUBJECTS